ACT

ADVANCED

The Staff of The Princeton Review

PrincetonReview.com

Penguin
Random
House

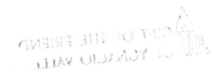

The Princeton Review
110 East 42nd St, 7th Floor
New York, NY 10017

Published in the United States by Penguin Random House,
LLC, New York, and in Canada by Random House of Canada,
division of Penguin Random House Ltd., Toronto.

Terms of Service: The Princeton Review Online Companion
Tools ("Student Tools") for retail books are available for only
the two most recent editions of that book. Student Tools may
be activated only once per eligible book purchased for a total
of 24 months of access. Activation of Student Tools more than
once per book is in direct violation of these Terms of Service
and may result in discontinuation of access to Student Tools
Services.

ACT is a registered trademark of ACT, Inc.

The Princeton Review is not affiliated with Princeton
University.

ISBN: 978-0-525-57169-8
eBook ISBN: 978-0-525-57183-4
ISSN: 2767-7222

Editor: Chris Chimera
Production Editors: Liz Dacey, Kathy Carter
Production Artist: Deborah Weber

Printed in the United States of America.

10   9   8   7   6   5   4   3   2   1

Editorial
Rob Franek, Editor-in-Chief
David Soto, Director of Content Development
Stephen Koch, Student Survey Manager
Deborah Weber, Director of Production
Jason Ullmeyer, Production Design Manager
Selena Coppock, Director of Editorial
Aaron Riccio, Senior Editor
Meave Shelton, Senior Editor
Anna Goodlett, Editor
Chris Chimera, Editor
Eleanor Green, Editor
Orion McBean, Editor
Patricia Murphy, Editorial Assistant

Penguin Random House Publishing Team
Tom Russell, VP, Publisher
Alison Stoltzfus, Publishing Director
Brett Wright, Senior Editor
Amanda Yee, Associate Managing Editor
Ellen Reed, Production Manager
Suzanne Lee, Designer
Eugenia Lo, Publishing Assistant

For customer service, please contact
editorialsupport@review.com,
and be sure to include:

- full title of the book

- ISBN

- page number

Acknowledgments

Very special thanks to Cat Healey, Sara Kuperstein, and Cynthia Ward for their hard work and dedication to the creation of this book.

Special thanks to Aleksei Alferiev, Chris Benson, Gabby Budzon, Elizabeth Evangelista, Brad Kelly, Dave MacKenzie, and Jess Thomas for their invaluable contributions to this book.

Thanks to Brian Becker, Jonathan Edwards, Melissa Hendrix, Bobby Hood, Elizabeth Owens, and Alice Swan for their contributions to previous editions of this book.

—Amy Minster
Content Director of High School Programs

Contents

Get More (**Free**) Content
at **PrincetonReview.com/prep**

As easy as **1·2·3**

1 Go to PrincetonReview.com/prep or scan the **QR code** and enter the following ISBN for your book: **9780525571698**

2 Answer a few simple questions to set up an exclusive Princeton Review account. *(If you already have one, you can just log in.)*

3 Enjoy access to your **FREE** content!

Once you've registered, you can...

- Get valuable advice about the college application process, including tips for applying for financial aid

- Use our searchable rankings of *The Best 387 Colleges* to find out more information about your dream school

- Download End of Chapter Drills

- Download our chapter on mastering the Writing Test

- Check to see if there have been any corrections or updates to this edition

Need to report a potential **content** issue?

Contact **EditorialSupport@review.com** and include:

- full title of the book
- ISBN
- page number

Need to report a **technical** issue?

Contact **TPRStudentTech@review.com** and provide:

- your full name
- email address used to register the book
- full book title and ISBN
- Operating system (Mac/PC) and browser (Firefox, Safari, etc.)

Part I
Orientation

Chapter 1
Introduction to the ACT

The pursuit of a perfect or near-perfect ACT score is an impressive goal. Achieving that goal requires a thorough command of the material and strategies specific to the ACT. To begin your quest, know everything you can about the test. This chapter presents an overview of the ACT, advice about when to take it, and how to report your scores.

WELCOME

So you think you can dance, ahem, score a 34 or better? We're all for it. The Princeton Review supports all students who want to do their best. We've written this book specifically for students who are in a position to score at the very highest levels. We believe that to achieve a perfect or near-perfect score, you have to know as much as possible about the test itself. Even more, however, you need to know about yourself as a test-taker.

You may already be familiar with many of the basic facts about the ACT, but even if you think you are, we encourage you to read through the following to be sure you know every single thing you can about the test you're going to conquer.

FUN FACTS ABOUT THE ACT

All of the content review and strategies we teach in the following chapters are based on the specific structure and format of the ACT. Before you can beat this test, you have to know how it's built.

Structure

The ACT consists of four multiple-choice, timed tests: English, Math, Reading, and Science, always given in that order. The ACT Plus Writing also includes an essay, with the Writing Test given after the Science Test. (ACT calls them tests, but we may also use the term "sections" in this book to avoid confusion.)

English	Math	Reading	Science	Writing
45 minutes	60 minutes	35 minutes	35 minutes	40 minutes
75 questions	60 questions	40 questions	40 questions	1 essay

Scoring

You'll earn one ACT score (1 to 36) on each test (English, Math, Reading, Science) and a composite ACT score, which is an average of these four tests. Usually, when people ask about your score, they're referring to your composite ACT score. The composite score falls between 1 and 36. The national average is about 21.

If, for example, you scored 31 on the English, 30 on the Math, 29 on the Reading, and 30 on the Science, your composite ACT score would be 30.

Students receive subscores in English, Math, and Reading that range between 1 and 18. These scores provide you with more detail about your performance, but they are not actually used by colleges or universities.

The ACT includes an optional essay, known as the Writing Test. Visit ACT.org for detailed information about how your ACT Writing Test will be scored. The Writing Test is scored on a scale of 1–36, but this score won't be factored into your composite. This is not to say that the Writing Test is unimportant, but rather that the Writing Test is not quite as important as the other four sections in your dogged pursuit of a 36 composite.

It's All About the Composite

Whether you look at your score online or wait to get it in the mail, the biggest number on the page is always the composite. While admissions' offices will certainly see the individual scores of all five tests (and their subscores), schools will use the composite to evaluate your application, and that's why, in the end, it's the only one that matters.

The composite is an average. When you're shooting for a 34 or higher, you need the best performance from both your strengths and weaknesses. You can't neglect your strengths and focus all your time on your weaknesses. In Chapter 3, we'll discuss in more detail how to think about the scores on the four multiple-choice tests and how to set your goals for your score.

> Use your best subjects to lift the composite as high as possible.
> Don't let your weakest subjects pull the composite down.

The higher your strongest scores, the less pressure on your weaker scores. While you can't afford for your weaknesses to drag the composite too far down, it's easier to earn a perfect score on your best subjects than it is to earn a perfect score on your weakest subjects.

Thus, when you divide your time among the four subjects, focus as much time and effort on your strengths—if not more—as you spend on your weaknesses.

Content

At the beginning of each part of this book, we'll thoroughly review the content and strategies you need for each test. Here is an overview of each test.

English Test

The English Test consists of five passages, accompanied by 14–16 questions per passage and four answer choices per question. Some words or phrases are underlined in the passage, and the accompanying questions ask whether the underlined portion is correct as written or whether one of the three alternatives listed would be better. The questions test conventions of usage mechanics (grammar, punctuation, sentence structure) and rhetorical skills. Other questions are marked by a boxed number embedded in the passage and ask about overall organization and style.

> **Answer Choices**
> Odd-numbered questions come with answers that are A/B/C/D (A–E on Math), and even-numbered questions come with answers that are F/G/H/J (F–K on Math). ACT designed the letter choices to alternate to help students avoid making mistakes while bubbling in their answers.

Math Test

The Math Test features 60 questions with five answer choices per question. The easier questions *tend* to come in the first 20 questions, but the test-writers can mix in easy, medium, and difficult problems throughout. The bulk of the difficult questions are found in the last 15–20 questions. Content is drawn from pre-algebra, elementary algebra, intermediate algebra, plane geometry, coordinate geometry, and trigonometry.

Reading Test

The Reading Test consists of four passages, accompanied by 10 questions per passage and four answer choices per question. The passages always appear in the same order: literary narrative, social science, humanities, and natural science. Within the four categories, ACT selects excerpts from books and articles to create one long or two shorter passages.

Science Test

The Science Test consists of six or seven passages, a total of 40 questions, and four answer choices per question. The number of questions per passage will vary, but it is usually 5, 6, or 7 questions. The order of the passages varies from test to test. Most passages are accompanied by figures, such as charts, tables, and graphs. The content is drawn from biology, chemistry, physics, and the Earth/space sciences (astronomy, geology, and meteorology). As on the Reading Test, at least one of these passages will consist of two different passages and will require students to compare and contrast to a certain extent.

Writing Test

The Writing Test consists of one essay designed to measure your writing skills. The prompt defines an issue and presents three perspectives on that issue, and you must write an essay that offers your analysis of the three perspectives while generating your own. The Writing Test has four subscores and a single subject-level score, each ranging from 2–12. Two readers score each essay on the four subscore areas on a scale of 1 to 6, those subscores are added for each area for a result between 2 and 12, and then the four subscores are averaged and rounded for the final Writing Test score. The score from the Writing Test is not included in the ACT composite score, but it will be part of your ELA subscore (an average of your English, Reading, and Writing scores).

The Writing Test is optional. Not all schools require it, but some do. Check with the schools on your list to see if they require you to submit a Writing Test score, and if *any* of them do, take the Writing Test.

THE ACT SCHEDULE

In the United States, Canada, and U.S. Territories, the ACT is offered seven times a year: September, October, December, February, April, June, and July. The February and July tests are not offered in international locations or in New York. Some states offer an ACT as part of their state-mandated testing. For students who live in those states, the state-mandated test offers an additional testing opportunity, and you can use the score from the state test for college admissions.

Your Schedule

Take the ACT when your schedule best allows. Many high-scorers take their first ACT in the fall of their junior year. If you have more commitments in the fall from sports, plays, or clubs, then plan to take your first ACT in the winter or spring.

Many counselors advise waiting to take the ACT until spring because students may be unfamiliar with some advanced math concepts before then. Students in an honors track for math, however, will have covered all of the content by the end of sophomore year at the latest. Even if you aren't in honors-track math, there are likely only 3–4 questions that will be unfamiliar to you, and those questions won't pull your score down if you bank all the others.

Most students end up taking the ACT two or three times. We recommend that you find a 3–4 month window in your schedule that covers at least 2 ACT tests. Prep first, take a test, and then continue prepping as needed for a second or third test. This way, you can be finished with the ACT in a relatively short period of time.

REGISTERING FOR THE ACT

Go to ACTstudent.org and create your free ACT Web Account. You will start at this portal to view test dates, fees, and registration deadlines. You can research the requirements and processes to apply for extended time or other accommodations. You will also start at ACTstudent.org to access your account to register, view your scores, and order score reports.

You must register yourself for any national test date. For state-mandated ACT administrations, most schools register their students for that exam only.

The fastest way to register is online, through your ACT Web Account. You can also obtain a registration packet at your high-school guidance office.

Bookmark ACTstudent.org. Check the site for the latest information about fees. The ACT Plus Writing costs more than the ACT (No Writing), but ACT also offers a fee waiver service. While you can choose four schools to send a score report to at no charge, there are fees for score reports sent to additional schools.

Registration Tips

You have options about ACT's survey, score reports, and copies of your test. We have recommendations on each.

ACT Survey

The registration process includes ACT's survey on your grades and interests, but you are not required to answer these questions. To save time, you can provide only the required information, which is marked by an asterisk.

Score Reports

When you register, do not supply the codes for any schools on your application list. Wait until you are happy with your score and no longer plan to take the ACT before you choose the scores to send to your schools. Any extra fees are worth this flexibility.

Test Information Release

If you take your first—or second—ACT on a date that offers the Test Information Release, choose this option when you register. Six to eight weeks after the test, you'll receive a copy of the test and your answers. This service costs an additional fee and is available only on certain test dates. You can order the Test Information Release up to three months after the test date, but it's easier to order it at the time you register. It's a great tool to help you prepare for your next ACT, as you'll be able to review all of your answers, right and wrong.

Through the 2020–2021 school year, the Test Information Release program has been offered for the December, April, and June tests. ACT may offer this program for different test dates in the future. Check ACTstudent.org when you register.

How Many Times Should You Take the ACT?

We would be thrilled if you review the content in this book, take the ACT for the first time, and earn the 34 or better you seek. But if you don't hit your target score on your first ACT, take it again. In fact, we recommend that you enter the process planning to take the ACT two or three times. Nerves and anxiety can be unpredictable catalysts, and for many students, the first experience can seem harder than what you've seen in practice. Perception is reality, so we won't waste your time explaining that it only *seems* harder and different. That's why we recommend you take your first test after a solid prep period but with enough time after that to take another test or two should you need it.

If you have scored 34+ in practice but not on a real test after your third try, take it again. We don't recommend going into the process planning to take the test every time it's offered, but we do support a goal of trying to achieve on a real test what you've done in practice. By April of your senior year, you won't care how many times you took the ACT.

But before you take the test again, evaluate what has suppressed your composite. If your composite has stayed flat because some scores have improved while others have fallen, then take more full-length ACT practice tests in one sitting. Take the practice tests in an environment as similar to a proctored test as possible. Take it outside of your house, such as in a library or empty classroom (but not a noisy coffeeshop). Time yourself, including the break, exactly as a real proctor would.

If one or two scores are stuck and are bringing your composite down, consider what you will do differently before taking the test again. Dedicate yourself to trying new strategies that you first thought you didn't need.

> **Maximum ACT Administrations**
>
> For security reasons, ACT will not let you take the exam more than 12 times. But we certainly hope no one is dismayed by this restriction. There are certainly better things to do with your time on a Saturday morning, and we don't believe any college will consider "taking the ACT" an extracurricular activity.

Score Choice, Super Composite, and Deletion

Our goal for you is to have one ACT official score report with a 34 or better, but that is not the only way to apply. Know your options about score choice, the super composite, and deletion of a score.

Score Choice and the Super Composite

We recommended above that you do not send your scores until you have taken your last ACT and are ready to apply. Choose your best composite score to send to your schools. ACT will send only the score reports you choose, and they do not currently provide a "Super Composite," an average composed of your best performance on each test from multiple administrations. However, many schools—and the common application—do super score. The common app asks you to report your best score, and test date, for each individual test and then has you calculate your super composite. Submit all of your score reports that support the super composite.

If you have a super composite of 34 or better from two or three tests, we recommend sending all the score reports, even to schools that do not explicitly ask for a super composite. In the worst-case scenario, the school will take only your top score. If you have one score report with a composite better than all your rest, and super scoring will not yield a higher score, we recommend sending only your highest score.

Coming Soon(ish): More Scoring Options
In 2020, ACT announced that students would soon have an option to get an official "super-score" report or to take individual section retests after their first full-length exam. However, this was postponed due to COVID-19. Check act.org for the latest news.

Deletion and Full Disclosure

Some schools require you to submit every ACT score regardless of super scoring. We trust that if these schools ask for every score report, they are looking for *improvement* and will use only your best scores.

You do have an option to delete scores from a particular test date. You must request in writing that ACT delete the test date from your records. Send your requests to the following address:

ACT Institutional Services
P.O. Box 168
Iowa City, IA 52243-0168
USA

We recommend this option only if you take a test and score well below your scores *and* you know you're applying to schools that require that you release all scores. For all other schools, you can send only the score reports you want them to see.

Do Your Research
Use *The Princeton Review's Best 387 Schools* to find out which schools require a release of all scores.

HOW TO PREPARE FOR THE ACT

The following chapters cover the most advanced content and strategies for the English, Math, Reading, and Science Tests. Also, the advanced strategies for the Writing Test can be found online in your Student Tools. You can find the basic strategies and content in our title *ACT Prep* if you need those. For this book, review all the chapters, even in the subjects that you already believe are your strengths. We want to make sure you're thoroughly prepared, and we'll risk boring you a tad to cover content you may know. But we won't waste your time. All of the content and strategies we cover are necessary.

As we noted above, the easiest path to your best score is to maximize your strengths. Find every point that you can from your strengths even as you acquire new skills and strategies to improve your weaknesses.

Some chapters include skill-reinforcement drills, and every part is followed by additional drills in that subject. Take a practice test after you've completed all the chapters.

Practice, Practice, Practice

To achieve a perfect or near-perfect ACT score, you have to practice as much as possible. For additional materials, we recommend you practice with real ACT tests as much as possible and use Princeton Review practice tests to supplement.

ACT publishes *The Official ACT Prep Guide*, which we think is well worth the price for the five real tests it contains (make sure you buy the latest edition). There may also be additional tests that ACT makes available for purchase, even if some are offered only to schools. Check to see if your school offers these extra tests for practice. In addition, in the registration bulletin and at ACT.org/aap/pdf/Preparing-for-the-ACT.pdf, ACT publishes a free practice ACT.

For more practice materials, The Princeton Review publishes *1,523 ACT Practice Questions*, which includes six tests' worth of material. We also publish additional practice tests in *ACT Prep*. We also recommend contacting your local Princeton Review office to investigate free practice test dates and follow-up sessions. Visit PrincetonReview.com for more information.

TEST-TAKER, KNOW THYSELF

To earn a perfect or near-perfect score on the ACT, it's not enough to know everything about the test. You also need to know yourself. Identify your own strengths and weaknesses. Stop trying to make yourself something you're not. You do not need to be a master of English, Math, Reading, or Science to earn a top score on the ACT. You do need to be a master test-taker. Stop the part of your brain that wants to do the question the *right* way. All that matters is that you get it right. *How* you get the question right doesn't matter. So, don't waste time trying to make yourself into the math or reading genius you thought you needed to be.

Read more in the next chapter about the overall strategies, and read through all the chapters in the individual subjects that follow. Be willing to tweak what you already do well, and be willing to try entirely new approaches for what you don't do well.

Summary

o   The ACT is always given in the same order: English, Math, Reading, Science, Writing.

o   Sign up for the ACT Plus Writing Test.

o   Set aside a few months in your schedule to allow for consistent ACT prep until you get your goal score.

o   Order the Test Information Release if it's available for your test date.

o   Plan to take the ACT 2–3 times.

o   Take the ACT again if you do not achieve the best score you've hit in practice.

o   Know your options about score choice, super composite, and deleting a score.

o   Practice on real ACTs as much as possible.

o   Use Princeton Review practice materials to supplement your practice.

Chapter 2
Strategy

To earn a perfect or near-perfect ACT score, you need strategies specific to the ACT. In this chapter, we'll provide an overview of the universal strategies. Each test on the ACT demands a specific approach, and even the most universal strategies vary in their applications. In Parts II through V, we'll discuss these strategies in greater detail customized to English, Math, Reading, and Science. Part VI discusses the Writing section and can be found in your Student Tools.

THE BASIC APPROACH

The ACT is significantly different from the tests you take in school, and, therefore, you need to approach it differently. The Princeton Review's strategies are not arbitrary. They have been honed to perfection, based specifically on the ACT.

Enemy #1: Time

Consider the structure of the ACT as we outlined in Chapter 1. The Math Test consists of 60 questions to answer in 60 minutes. That's just one minute per question, and that's as good as it gets. The English, Reading, and Science Tests all leave you with less than a minute per question. How often do you take a test in school with a minute or less per question? If you do at all, it's maybe on a multiple-choice quiz but probably not on a major exam or final. Time is your enemy on the ACT, and you have to use it wisely and be aware of how that time pressure can bring out your worst instincts as a test-taker.

Enemy #2: Yourself

There is something particularly evil about tests like the ACT and SAT. The skills you've been rewarded for throughout your academic year can easily work against you on the ACT. You've been taught since birth to follow directions, go in order, and finish everything. But treating the ACT the same way you would a school test won't necessarily earn you a perfect or near-perfect score.

On the other hand, treating the ACT as a scary, alien beast can leave our brains blank and useless and can incite irrational, self-defeating behavior. When we pick up a #2 pencil, all of us tend to leave our common sense at the door. Test nerves and anxieties can make you misread a question, commit a careless error, see something that isn't there, blind you to what is there, talk you into a bad answer, and worst of all, convince you to waste time on a question that you should approach strategically.

Work Smarter, Not Harder

When you're already answering *almost* every question right, it can be difficult to change your approach. But to answer *every* question right, you have to do something different. You can't just work harder. Instead, you have to work smarter. Know what isn't working. Be open-minded about changing your approach. Know what to tweak and what to replace wholesale. Know when to abandon one approach and try another.

The following is an introduction to the general strategies to use on the ACT. In Parts II through V in the book and Part VI online, we'll discuss how these strategies are customized for each test on the ACT.

ACT STRATEGIES

Personal Order of Difficulty (POOD)

If time may run out before you finish a section, would you rather it run out on the hardest questions or the easiest? Of course, you want it to run out on the ones you are less likely to get right.

You can easily fall into the trap of spending too much time on the hardest problems and either never getting to or rushing through the easiest. You shouldn't work in the order ACT provides *just because* it's in that order. Instead, find your own Personal Order of Difficulty (POOD).

Make smart decisions quickly for good reasons as you move through each test.

Now

Does a question look fairly straightforward? Do you know how to do it? Do it *Now.*

Later

Will this question take a long time to work? Leave it and come back to it *Later.* Circle the question number for easy reference to return.

Never

If you're trying for a perfect or near-perfect score, there may be no questions that fall into the *Never* category for you. But even one random guess may not hurt your score, particularly if it saves you time to spend on Now and Later questions you can definitely answer correctly.

The Best Way to Bubble In

Work a page at a time, circling your answers right on the booklet. Transfer one page's worth of answers to the bubble sheet at one time. It's better to stay focused on working questions rather than disrupt your concentration to find where you left off on the bubble sheet. You'll be more accurate at both tasks. Do not wait to the end, however, to transfer all the answers of that test to your bubble sheet. Go a page at a time on English and Math, and a passage at a time on Reading and Science.

Pacing

The ACT may be designed for you to run out of time, but you can't rush through it as fast as possible. All you'll do is make careless errors on easy questions that you should get right and spend way too much time on difficult ones that you're unlikely to answer correctly. Let your Personal Order of Difficulty (POOD) help determine your pacing. Go slowly enough to answer all the Now questions correctly, but quickly enough to get to the number of Later questions that you need to reach your goal score.

In Chapter 3, we'll teach you how to identify the number of questions you need to reach your goal score. You'll practice your pacing in practice tests, going slowly enough to avoid careless errors and quickly enough to reach your goal scores.

Process of Elimination (POE)

Multiple-choice tests offer one great advantage: they provide the correct answer right there on the page. Of course, the correct answer is hidden amid three or four incorrect answers. However, it's often easier to spot the wrong answers than it is to identify the right ones, particularly when you apply a smart Process of Elimination (POE).

POE works differently on each test on the ACT, but it's a powerful strategy on all of them. For some question types, you'll always use POE rather than waste time trying to figure out the answer on your own. For other questions, you'll use POE when you're stuck. ACT hides the correct answer among wrong ones, but when you cross off just one or two wrong answers, the correct answer can become more obvious, sometimes jumping right off the page.

POOD, Pacing, and POE all work together to help you nail as many questions as possible.

BE RUTHLESS

The worst mistake a test-taker can make is to throw good time at "bad" questions. You read a question, don't understand it, so read it again. And again. If you stare at it really hard, you know you're going to just *see* it. And you can't move on, because really, after spending all that time it would be a waste not to keep at it, right?

Wrong. You can't let one tough question drag you down, and you can't let your worst instincts tempt you into self-defeating behavior. Instead, the surest way to earn a perfect or near-perfect ACT score is to follow our advice.

- Use the techniques and strategies in the chapters to work efficiently and accurately through all your Now and Later questions.
- Know when to move on. Use POE, and guess from what's left.
- If you have any Never questions, use your LOTD.

In Parts II through V, you'll learn how POOD, Now/Later/Never, and POE work on each test. In Chapter 3, we'll discuss in greater detail how to use your Pacing to hit your target scores.

ACT HIGH-SCORER MYTHS, BUSTED

At the Princeton Review, we've worked with thousands of students who are aiming for a top ACT score, so we've witnessed all the mistakes they've made in their prep. Let's look at how typical high-scoring students approach the quest for near perfect ACT scores.

These students go through the test quickly and in the order the questions are given. After all, it's pretty easy! They don't write much on the test, since most math problems can be done only on the calculator or using mental math, and for the rest of the test they can just look at the answers and choose the correct one, right? Then, they make a bunch of careless mistakes, but these students dismisses them because, after all, those questions should have been easy. They take a full practice test every day for a week, thinking that more time spent doing ACT problems will result in a higher score. However, they don't take the time to learn ACT-specific strategies (instead doing everything the way it is taught in school) or to review why they missed the questions that were incorrect. They might eventually see some progress, but probably not before running out of practice materials!

These students have a completely wrong idea about how to effectively and efficiently boost their scores. Let's bust some myths that this example illustrates:

MYTH: If I need to answer all or almost all the questions on the test to get my goal score, it doesn't matter if I make the effort to find and answer the easier questions first.

BUSTED: It is always worth the small amount of time it takes to find easier questions to answer first. Say you are working the Reading section and you often miss a couple of questions on the Literary Narrative passage but never on the Natural Science passage. By starting with the Natural Science passage, you will build up points and confidence right away. When you get to the Literary narrative passage later on (probably working it last), you will not only have a good sense of how you are doing, but you will also know exactly how much time you have left for the passage that is hardest for you. If you don't have much time left, you can be sure to work only the easiest questions on the final passage and use your LOTD on any you don't get to. If, however, you have plenty of time, you can really work that last passage, confident that you've already gotten all the other questions on the section completed.

MYTH: If I move quickly through a section, I can save a few minutes at the end to check my work.

POOD!

Using your Personal Order of Difficulty (POOD) means skipping questions that are harder or more time-consuming *for you*, at least initially. For more on this topic, see page 17.

BUSTED: This is not a smart strategy. If you hurry through the section, you are likely to make careless errors on some questions you know how to do. Also, once you get to the end, you've already chosen an answer for the questions, so it will be difficult to identify ones that you got wrong. It is much better to work through the section at a steady pace to avoid careless errors. If you do hit a question you aren't sure about, skip it initially and come back to it if there is time. You can take timed tests or test sections to determine a good pace at which to work through a section without making careless mistakes.

MYTH: If I am missing only a handful of questions, I should work to learn the content I am weak on and not worry about the mistakes I made on questions covering the content I know.

BUSTED: High-scoring students do well on these tests because they know the content. Yes, you may not be an ace on matrices or reordering sentences, but you still know most of what you need for this test. And the ACT (unlike school) doesn't give partial points for work—if you get the question wrong, regardless of why you got it wrong, you get no points at all. So if ANY of your incorrect answers on a practice test or drill came from being careless, that is something to work on immediately. Study your errors to determine where your mistake is occurring—is it misreading the question or passage, is it falling for trap answers, is it making sloppy calculations? Whatever the error is, do drills on that type of question until you stamp out that error. After that, you can worry about a topic like matrices, which does not even get tested on every ACT.

MYTH: I am smart and a good student, so I don't really need to write much down in my test booklet or on practice questions.

BUSTED: One way to avoid those careless errors we just talked about—writing stuff down! High-scoring students tend to think they can and should do a lot of work in their heads, be it keeping track of Reading answers or doing mental math. These are surefire ways of making a mistake, and you are less likely to notice it because you can't *see* the mistake written down. Use your pencil to underline key words, take notes, eliminate answers, and do calculations. Unless you are not making a single careless error, you are likely to benefit from taking the time to use your pencil as a key part of your test-taking process. In addition, having work on the page is crucial when you practice: it's difficult to know why you missed a question on a practice drill or test if you don't have any physical record of how you chose your answer. Finally, writing your work down on the page can ironically *save* you time—you won't have to redo work if you need to double-check something or if your concentration is broken by something, which will keep you continuously working toward more answers.

> **Pencils only!**
> You may be the sort of student that prefers to use pens and/or highlighters over pencils. However, the ACT doesn't allow those tools on the test. So practice with a pencil on all your ACT work. (And we recommend using a wooden number 2 pencil rather than mechanical—mechanical pencils are also disallowed!)

MYTH: Doing as much practice as I can is the best way to improve my ACT score.

BUSTED (KIND OF): Yes, practice is good, but *how* you practice is very important. Just doing drill after drill aiming to get all the questions right is not going to guarantee a perfect score on the real ACT. In fact, just practicing over and over without reflection will reinforce any bad test-taking habits you have. Instead, review your work after each drill. Don't just score it—read the explanations, even for the ones you got right. For the ones you missed, you should be tracking if you made any careless errors. Aside from carelessness, if you get any wrong that you thought were right, keep track of why you were drawn to that wrong answer. Again, try to identify patterns, so you can work on that issue. Also, review your work to see if there were any questions on which you could have used a better or faster approach, often indicated in the explanations we provide for the answers. The biggest improvements come from thoughtful review, not from simply doing practice sections. Lastly, note that it is fine to take practice tests and do drills multiple times. If you take the same practice test a second time and don't get 100% on it, then you didn't truly learn from the review you did, did you? Ideally, if you have reviewed a question with its explanation, when you see that exact same question in the future, you'll get it right—and your odds of getting a *similar* question right are greatly improved.

Summary

- Don't let your own worst instincts work against you on the ACT. Work Smarter, Not Harder.

- Identify your own Personal Order of Difficulty (POOD). Let time run out on the most difficult questions.

- Pace yourself. Don't rush through Now and Later questions only to make careless errors.

- Use Process of Elimination (POE) to save time, when you're stuck, or out of time.

- If time does run out, never leave any blanks on your bubble sheet. Use your Letter of the Day (LOTD).

- Be ruthless. If one strategy isn't working, switch immediately to another.

Chapter 3
Score Goals

To hit a perfect or near-perfect score, you have to know how many raw points you need. Your goals and pacing for English, Math, Reading, and Science will vary depending on the test and your own individual strengths.

SCORE GRIDS

On each test of the ACT, the number of correct answers is converted to a scaled score of 1–36. ACT works hard to adjust the scale of each test at each administration as necessary to make all scaled scores comparable, smoothing out any differences in level of difficulty across test dates. Thus, there is no truth to any one test date being "easier" than the others, but you can expect to see slight variations in the scale from test to test.

This is the score grid from the free test ACT made available on its website, act.org, for the 2020–2021 school year. We're going to use it to explain how to pick a target score and pace yourself.

Scale Score	Raw Scores				Scale Score
	Test 1 English	Test 2 Math	Test 3 Reading	Test 4 Science	
36	74–75	59–60	40	40	36
35	71–73	57–58	38–39	—	35
34	70	55–56	37	39	34
33	69	54	36	38	33
32	68	53	34–35	—	32
31	67	51–52	33	37	31
30	66	49–50	32	36	30
29	64–65	47–48	31	—	29
28	63	45–46	30	35	28
27	61–62	42–44	—	34	27
26	59–60	39–41	29	32–33	26
25	56–58	37–38	28	31	25
24	53–55	34–36	26–27	29–30	24
23	50–52	32–33	25	26–28	23
22	47–49	31	23–24	24–25	22
21	44–46	29–30	22	22–23	21
20	41–43	27–28	20–21	20–21	20
19	39–40	25–26	19	18–19	19
18	37–38	22–24	18	17	18
17	35–36	19–21	16–17	15–16	17
16	32–34	16–18	15	14	16
15	29–31	13–15	14	13	15
14	26–28	10–12	12–13	11–12	14
13	24–25	8–9	11	10	13
12	22–23	7	10	9	12
11	19–21	5–6	8–9	8	11

PACING STRATEGIES

Focus on the number of questions that you need to hit your goal scores.

It's All About the Composite

To score a 34 composite, you could score a 34 on each test.

$$
\begin{array}{r}
34 \\
34 \\
34 \\
+\ 34 \\
\hline
136
\end{array}
\qquad
136 \div 4 = 34
$$

You can see that, to score a 34, you need a total of 136 points, a sum that any combination of the four individual scores could achieve. In fact, you really only need a total of 134 total points, since a score of 33.5 rounds up to a 34.

How can you earn 134 points?

$$
\begin{array}{r}
36 \\
36 \\
32 \\
+\ 30 \\
\hline
134
\end{array}
\qquad
\begin{array}{r}
35 \\
35 \\
35 \\
+\ 29 \\
\hline
134
\end{array}
\qquad
\begin{array}{r}
36 \\
36 \\
36 \\
+\ 26 \\
\hline
134
\end{array}
$$

In all cases, your strengths relieve the pressure on your weaknesses.

Even a perfect score does not require perfection across the board. To earn a 36, you need a total of 142 points.

$$142 \div 4 = 35.5, \text{ and } 35.5 \text{ rounds up to a } 36.$$

$$
\begin{array}{r}
36 \\
36 \\
36 \\
+\ 34 \\
\hline
142
\end{array}
\qquad\qquad
\begin{array}{r}
36 \\
36 \\
35 \\
+\ 35 \\
\hline
142
\end{array}
$$

> Don't pressure yourself to be perfect on all four tests. The highest possible score on your strongest subjects leaves you some flexibility on your weakest subjects.

Raw Score

Use the score grid to identify exactly how many questions you need to answer correctly to hit your goal scores.

English

For English, there is no order of difficulty of the passages or their questions. The most important thing is to finish, finding all the Now questions you can throughout the whole test.

Math

Pace yourself on Math to make sure you nail every question you know how to answer. Missing one or two of the very hardest questions won't hurt your score, but making several careless errors on Now and Later questions definitely will.

Reading

When it comes to picking a pacing strategy for Reading, you have to practice extensively to figure out what works best for you.

You could spend more time on three out of the four passages and earn 30 raw points. As long as you leave enough time on the fourth passage to answer 5 questions correctly, you would have a total of 35 raw points and a scaled score of 32. Or you could leave 1–2 tough questions on every passage—using smart POE to increase your chances when you have to guess and move on—and you could still earn 35 raw points and have a scaled score of 32.

Which is better? There is no answer to that. True ACT score improvement will come with a willingness to experiment and analyze what works best for *you*.

Science

In the Science chapters, you'll learn how to identify your Now and Later passages. To earn at least a 30 scaled score, you have to work all of the passages.

Our advice is to be aggressive. Spend the time you need on the easiest passages first, but keep moving to get to your targeted raw score. Use POE heavily to increase your chances of guessing correctly when you do have to guess and move on. Identify Never questions on Now Passages and use your LOTD. Find the Now questions on even the toughest passage.

PACING

Improvement comes in stages. Revisit this page as you practice. Record your scores from the practice tests that are placed at the end of each subject's section. Set a goal of 1–2 points improvement in your scaled score for each subsequent practice test until you hit your goals. Identify the raw score (the number of correctly answered questions) needed in order to reach the desired scale score using the chart on page 24.

> **Practice Materials**
> For practice, use real ACT exams in *The Official ACT Prep Guide*, the free exam on ACT's website, and Princeton Review titles such as *1,523 ACT Practice Questions*.

English Pacing

Remember that in English, your pacing goal is to finish.

Prior Score (if applicable): _____

Practice Test 1 Goal: _____

# of Questions Needed: _____

Practice Test 1 Score: _____

Next Practice Test Goal: _____

# of Questions Needed: _____

Next Practice Test Score: _____

Math Pacing

If your prior score in Math is at least a 33, work all 60 questions. If you are running out of time, use smart POE on the hardest questions.

If your prior score is under 33, add 5 questions to your targeted raw score to identify the number of questions to work. This will give you a cushion to get a few wrong—nobody's perfect—and you're likely to pick up at least a few points from your LOTDs. Track your progress on practice tests to pinpoint your target score.

Prior Score (if applicable): _____   Next Practice Test Goal: _____

Practice Test 1 Goal: _____   # of Questions Needed: _____

# of Questions Needed: _____   Next Practice Test Score: _____

Practice Test 1 Score: _____

Reading Pacing

Experiment with Reading, using different pacing strategies to find the one that is most likely to earn you the most points. Identify first how many questions you need.

Prior Score (if applicable): _____   Next Practice Test Goal: _____

Practice Test 1 Goal: _____   # of Questions Needed: _____

# of Questions Needed: _____   Next Practice Test Score: _____

Practice Test 1 Score: _____

Science Pacing

Be aggressive on Science. Get to every Now question you can on all of the passages.

Prior Score (if applicable): _____   Next Practice Test Goal: _____

Practice Test 1 Goal: _____   # of Questions Needed: _____

# of Questions Needed: _____   Next Practice Test Score: _____

Practice Test 1 Score: _____

Summary

○ The composite score is rounded up from .5.

○ Identify the number of raw points you need to hit your target score. A scaled score of 34 needs a total of 134 raw points. A scaled score of 35 needs a total of 138 raw points. A scaled score of 36 needs a total of 142 raw points.

○ Earn the best possible scores that you can in your strongest subjects to relieve pressure on your weaker subjects.

○ Use the score grid in this chapter to track your improvement from practice to practice.

○ Practice on real ACTs as much as possible.

○ Use Princeton Review practice materials to supplement your practice.

Part II
ACT English

Chapter 4
Introduction to the ACT English Test

To pursue a perfect or near-perfect score on the English Test, you have to apply a basic approach to correctly answer every question that tests an identifiable rule. But you must also be able to crack the trickiest questions. Even for the most difficult questions, you do not need to know every rule of English grammar that you either forgot or never learned. Review the rules that are tested most frequently and use appropriate strategies on the questions, and you can target a perfect score on the English Test. This chapter will teach you the 5-Step Basic Approach. Also, your online Student Tools include a Grammar Glossary that includes both the few terms you need to know and some additional terms we included just in case you were curious.

WHAT'S ON THE ENGLISH TEST

The English Test tests your editing skills: your ability to fix errors in grammar and punctuation and to improve the organization and style of five different passages. In this chapter, you'll learn the 5-Step Basic Approach to use on the questions.

On the English Test, there are five prose passages on topics ranging from historical essays to personal narratives. Each passage is typically accompanied by 15 questions for a total of 75 questions to answer in 45 minutes. Portions of each passage are underlined, and you must decide whether these are correct as written, or whether one of the other answers would fix or improve the selection. Other questions will ask you to add, cut, and reorder text, while still others will ask you to evaluate the passage as a whole.

HOW TO CRACK THE ENGLISH TEST

The Passages

As always on the ACT, time is your enemy. With only 45 minutes to review five passages and answer 75 questions, you can't read a passage in its entirety and then go back to do the questions. For each passage, work the questions as you make your way through the passage. Read from the beginning until you get to an underlined selection, work that question, and then resume reading until the next underlined portion and the next question. The exception is a question that requires you to read further: if you come across a question that references the main idea of the passage or of the following paragraph, circle the question, keep reading, and come back to the question once you have read enough to answer it.

The Questions

Not all questions are created equal. In fact, ACT divides the questions on the English Test into two categories: Usage and Mechanics and Rhetorical Skills. These designations will mean very little to you when you're taking the test. All questions are worth the same, and you'll crack most of the questions the same way, regardless of what ACT calls them. Many of the rhetorical skills questions, however, are those on organization and style and will come with actual questions. We'll teach you how to crack those in Chapter 6.

For all the questions accompanied only by four answer choices and with no actual question, use our 5-Step Basic Approach.

Step 1. Identify the Topic

When you reach an underlined portion, read to the end of the sentence and then look at the answers. The answers are your clues to identify what the question is testing. Read through the following example.

Canadian <u>author Alice Munro, has won wide</u> acclaim for her collections of short stories.
₁

1. **A.** NO CHANGE
   B. author, Alice Munro
   C. author Alice Munro
   D. author, Alice Munro,

Do any of the words change? No. What is the only thing that changes? Commas. So what must be the topic of the question? Commas.

Always identify the topic of the question first. Pay attention to what changes versus what stays the same in the answers.

Step 2. Use POE

You may have already identified the correct answer for Question 1, but hold that thought. To earn the highest possible English score, you have to use Process of Elimination (POE). If you fix a question in your head and then look for an answer that matches your fix, you will likely miss something, such as a new comma added or a comma taken away. Instead, once you've identified an error, always begin by eliminating the choices that do not fix it.

For Question 1, the comma is unnecessary and should be deleted. Cross off the choices that leave it, (A) and (D).

1. ~~**A.** NO CHANGE~~
   B. author, Alice Munro
   C. author Alice Munro
   ~~**D.** author, Alice Munro,~~

Now compare the two that remain, (B) and (C). Do you need the comma after *author*? No, you don't need any commas, so (C) is the correct answer. You could easily have missed the new comma and picked (B), however, if you had just been looking for an answer that did not have a comma at the end. POE on English isn't optional or a backup when you're stuck. Make it your habit to first eliminate wrong answers and then compare the ones that are left.

> **Confused by commas?**
> Review the rules for commas in the next chapter.

Let's move on to the next step.

 **Step 3: Use the Context**

Don't skip the non-underlined text in between questions. You need the context to help you choose answers that are both clear and consistent with the rest of the passage. Take a look at this next question.

Munro received the 2009 Man Booker International Prize for her lifetime body of work. In 2013, she will win the Nobel Prize in Literature for her work as "master of the contemporary short story."

2. **F.** NO CHANGE
   G. won
   H. wins
   J. would win

Don't forget to apply the first two steps. First, look at the answer choices to see that the verb is changing, specifically verb tense. How do you know which tense to use? Use the non-underlined verb *received* to identify the need for the past tense. Then you can eliminate the answer choices that don't use past tense, (F) (future tense) and (H) (present tense).

2. ~~**F.** NO CHANGE~~
   G. won
   ~~**H.** wins~~
   J. would win

Vexed by verbs?
Review all the rules for verbs, including tenses, in the next chapter.

Next, compare the remaining answers to each other. Choice (J) uses the past tense of the helping verb *will*, but there are no clues in the non-underlined portion that would justify such a shift. Choice (G) is correct because it's consistent with the other past tense verb, *received*.

Don't skip from question to question. The non-underlined text provides context you need.

Let's move on to the next step.

Step 4: **Trust Your Ear, But Verify**

For the first two questions, you may have identified the correct answers right away because they sounded right. If you had that thought, it turned out you were right, but don't depend exclusively on your ear.

Your ear is a pretty reliable tool for raising the alarm for outright errors and clunky, awkward phrasing. You should, however, always verify what your ear tells you by going through Steps 1 and 2. Always use the answers to identify the topic and use POE heavily.

You also have to be on the lookout for errors your ear *won't* catch. Using the answers to identify the topic will save you there as well.

Let's try another question.

The Swedish Academy was unable to reach

Munro before announcing their choice for the 2013 award.

3. **A.** NO CHANGE
   B. it's
   C. they're
   D. its

Your ear likely found no problem with the sentence as written. Looking at the answers identifies the topic as pronouns, so you need to confirm or correct the pronoun used. *Their* is a plural possessive pronoun, but it refers to the singular *Swedish Academy* and is therefore incorrect. Cross off (A) and (C). Since you need a possessive pronoun, cross off (B) as well. Choice (D) is the correct answer.

Let's move on to the last step.

> **Perplexed by pronouns?**
> Review all the pronoun rules in the next chapter.

Step 5: **Don't Fix What Isn't Broken**

Read the following sentence.

A master of the short form, Munro

uses sparse prose to capture the boundless universal truths of the human condition.

4. **F.** NO CHANGE
   G. writes with few yet well-chosen words
   H. adapts a style
   J. makes a strong impression built on few words

Even if it sounds fine to your ear, go to Step 1 and identify the topic. In this case, the changes do not make the topic obvious because so much changes. You can't confirm what you can't identify, so leave "NO CHANGE" as an option and ask yourself the following questions:

Does one of the answers fix something you missed?

Does one of the answers make the sentence better by making it more concise?

If the answer to both questions is *No* for all three other answers, the answer is NO CHANGE, which is the correct answer here. Choices (G) and (J) express the same sentiment as *uses sparse prose* but (ironically) with many more words. Choice (H) is roughly the same length as (F), but it doesn't identify the specifics of the style.

NO CHANGE is a legitimate answer choice. Don't make the mistake of assuming that all questions have an error that you just can't spot. If you use the five steps of our Basic Approach, you'll catch errors your ear would miss, and you'll confidently choose NO CHANGE when it's the correct answer.

Summary

○ Identify what the question is testing by changes in the answer choices.

○ Use POE heavily.

○ Don't skip the non-underlined text: use it for context.

○ Trust your ear, but verify by the rules.

○ NO CHANGE is a legitimate answer choice.

Chapter 5
The 4 C's

The English Test is not a grammar test. It's also not a test of how well you write. In fact, it tests your editing skills: your ability to fix errors in grammar and punctuation and to improve the organization and style of five different passages.

The topics in this chapter represent the rules tested most frequently. Questions on these topics should be in your "correct" column every time. The changes in the answer choices make the topics tested easy to identify, and simple rules to master make the errors easy to fix. While your ear may get most of these most of the time, learning *why* will help you get all of them correct every time.

THE 4 C'S: COMPLETE, CONSISTENT, CLEAR, AND CONCISE

You'll never be asked to identify a particular rule by name on the ACT. While we'll use some specific grammar terms to explain the most common rules, we advocate adopting a common-sense approach to English: use the 4 C's.

Good writing should be in *complete* sentences; everything should be *consistent*; the meaning should be *clear*. The best answer, free of any errors, will be the most *concise*. All of the rules we'll review fall under one or more of the C's. But even when you can't identify what a question is testing, apply the 4 C's and you'll still get the most difficult questions right.

While the idea of English grammar makes many of us think of persnickety rules that are long since outdated, English is actually a dynamic, adaptive language. We add new vocabulary all the time, and we let common usage influence and change many rules. Pick up a handful of style books and you'll find very few rules that everyone agrees upon. This is actually good news for studying for the ACT: you're unlikely to see questions testing the most obscure or most disputed rules.

This is not an exhaustive review of English grammar. It is an overview of the most common rules tested on the English Test. We focus on the rules we know show up the most AND that we know you can easily identify. Your online Student Tools include a Grammar Glossary that defines the common grammar terms that we use in this chapter. If you're unsure of any terms, consult that glossary.

QUIZ I: COMPLETE

Work the brief passage and then read the rules that follow, even if you answer all of the questions correctly. You may have a nuanced ear that can identify the right answer, or you may have internalized these rules and know how to use them correctly without being able to articulate *why* your choices are correct. However, in the pursuit of a perfect or near-perfect score on the English Test, the more you know *why*, the more you can count on answering questions correctly every single time.

The Homer Laughlin China Company of Newell, West Virginia, introduced affordable, brightly colored dinnerware called Fiesta in 1936, and continues to manufacture the ceramic dishes today. Serious collectors and casual fans alike are

1. **A.** NO CHANGE
   B. Fiesta, in 1936,
   C. Fiesta in 1936
   D. Fiesta, in 1936

drawn to the simple shapes and colorful glazes, because it is sold as open stock, Fiesta allows buyers to assemble their collections by the piece instead of by sets. The ceramic dishes are also prized for their range of colors. Some of the original glazes were made with detectable amounts of uranium oxide, which created the brilliant color effects, until the government, redirected all commercial uses of uranium toward development of the atom bomb during World War II. The dishes began to decline in popularity after World War II, dropping out of favor entirely by the late 1960s. In 1973, the company discontinued the line. Almost immediately, collectors began buying pieces at garage sales and in secondhand shops. When Homer Laughlin China Company noticed the surge in interest for vintage Fiesta pieces. The company relaunched the line with new glazes in 1986, the company's 50th anniversary. The range of colors

2. **F.** NO CHANGE
   G. glazes, because it is sold as open stock
   H. glazes. Because it is sold as open stock
   J. glazes. Because it is sold as open stock,

3. **A.** NO CHANGE
   B. effects until the government,
   C. effects until the government
   D. effects, until the government

4. **F.** NO CHANGE
   G. pieces, the
   H. pieces; the
   J. pieces the

available today <u>includes: Scarlet, Peacock,</u>
<u>Tangerine, Sunflower, and Lemongrass.</u>
₅

5. A. NO CHANGE
  B. includes Scarlet, Peacock, Tangerine, Sunflower,
  C. includes Scarlet, Peacock, Tangerine, Sunflower
  D. includes: Scarlet, Peacock, Tangerine, Sunflower

<u>Some vintage</u> pieces are radioactive because of
₆
the glaze, other original colors command hefty
prices on online auction sites. Collectors will
even pay top dollar for some of the modern

6. F. NO CHANGE
  G. Some
  H. Because vintage
  J. Although some vintage

colors if the colors have been <u>retired:</u> Lilac pieces
₇
sell for

7. Which of the following alternatives to the underlined portion would NOT be acceptable?

  A. retired,
  B. retired;
  C. retired.
  D. retired—

hundreds of dollars. <u>Dismissing all Fiesta as too</u>
₈
expensive, but Homer Laughlin China has stayed
true to its roots with brand-new sets for sale in
department stores for modest prices.

8. F. NO CHANGE
  G. While many people think that all Fiesta is
  H. Many people think that all Fiesta is
  J. Having dismissed all Fiesta as

The answers are 1. (C), 2. (J), 3. (D), 4. (G), 5. (B), 6. (J), 7. (A), and 8. (H). Now read all about Complete and Incomplete Ideas to learn why, and learn how to crack questions on sentence structure and punctuation.

COMPLETE

Many questions on the English Test involve sentence structure and punctuation. The correct structure and punctuation all depend on whether the ideas are complete or incomplete.

A complete idea can stand on its own, whether it's the entire sentence or just one part. In grammatical terms, it's an independent clause, consisting of a subject and a verb.

Complete ideas can be statements (*I finished my paper*), commands (*Leave me alone!*), or questions (*Why are you bothering me?*). Each example contains a subject and a verb. In the first example, the subject is *I* and the verb is *finished*. In the second example, the understood subject is *you*, and the verb is *leave* (I'm telling *you* to leave me alone), and in the third, the subject is *you* and the verb is *are bothering*. (That being said, the ACT very rarely tests commands or questions, so ACT English ideas will generally be statements.)

Incomplete ideas can't stand on their own. They're missing something, either the subject and verb, the main idea, or the rest of the idea. In grammatical terms, an incomplete idea can be a phrase (*in the evening, to get a good grade*), a dependent clause (*although I finished the paper, when I study*), or a subject with a verb that needs an object (*I broke*). But you don't need to get into the grammar weeds with terms like *dependent clause* if you're not already well-versed in those terms. An incomplete idea is missing something. It's unfinished. It's . . . incomplete.

On the ACT, questions on both sentence structure and punctuation depend on identifying complete and incomplete ideas.

STOP!

Complete ideas have to be separated with the correct punctuation. If complete ideas are two large trucks meeting at an intersection, then they need a red light or stop sign in between to prevent an accident. Stop punctuation can be used *only* in between complete ideas.

STOP Punctuation

Period (.) Semicolon (;) Question mark (?) Exclamation point (!)
Comma + FANBOYS (**F**or, **A**nd, **N**or, **B**ut, **O**r, **Y**et, **S**o)

Vertical Line Test

Any time you see STOP punctuation in any of the answer choices, draw a vertical line immediately to the right of the STOP punctuation. The vertical line identifies an intersection. Determine whether the ideas lying on either side are complete or incomplete. If one idea is incomplete, eliminate the choices with STOP punctuation. If both ideas are complete, eliminate the choices without STOP punctuation.

For the record, semicolons can be used to separate items on a very complicated list, but ACT almost never tests this. Exclamation points and question marks show up only occasionally.

Here's How to Crack #2

Choices (H) and (J) use a period after *glazes*, identifying the topic as STOP punctuation. Draw the vertical line to the right of *glazes*.

> *Serious collectors and casual fans alike are drawn to the simple shapes and colorful glazes,* | *because it is sold as open stock, Fiesta allows buyers to assemble their collections by the piece instead of by sets.*

Read from the beginning of the sentence to the vertical line. The idea is complete. Read from the vertical line to the end of the sentence. The idea is complete. Eliminate (F) and (G) because two complete ideas must be linked with STOP punctuation. Compare the two choices that are left. Choice (J) is correct because it provides the comma (H) lacks. Why is the comma needed? Read on.

GO!

While STOP punctuation puts a traffic light or stop sign at an intersection to prevent the complete ideas from crashing together, GO punctuation links ideas that aren't both complete. You can think of GO punctuation as being either a blinking yellow light, slowing down the ideas a little, or no sign or signal at all, telling the ideas to just keep going.

GO Punctuation

No punctuation (nothing, nada, zilch) or Comma (,)

Let's go back to the traffic analogy. Imagine a road with a stop sign at every block. Those stop signs prevent accidents, but when rush hour hits, traffic backs up. Punctuation functions the same way. Use it to prevent accidents, but don't slow down ideas and make the sentence longer than necessary.

Here's How to Crack #1

Commas are changing at the end of the answers, and the underlined portion is followed by the word *and*. A comma + FANBOYS is STOP punctuation, so use the Vertical Line Test. Draw lines around the word *and*, as that conjunction connects the two ideas rather than being part of them. The complete idea *The Homer Laughlin China Company of Newell, West Virginia, introduced affordable, brightly colored dinnerware called Fiesta in 1936* links with the incomplete idea *continues to manufacture the ceramic dishes today.* (Notice the incomplete idea is missing a subject). Since the second part of the sentence is incomplete, a comma + FANBOYS cannot be used, as STOP punctuation links only complete ideas. GO punctuation is needed here, so eliminate (A) and (B). Between (C) and (D), is there a reason to slow down the ideas after *Fiesta*? No, so no comma is needed. Eliminate (D). Therefore, (C) is the correct answer.

> Use the 4 C's: Be *Concise.* Use punctuation only to avoid accidents.

Here's How to Crack #4

Choices (F) and (H) use STOP punctuation, so draw the vertical line right after *pieces.* The vertical line will always help identify intersections and make POE much faster.

> *When Homer Laughlin China Company noticed the surge in interest for vintage Fiesta pieces.* | *The company relaunched the line with new glazes in 1986, the company's 50th anniversary.*

From the beginning of the sentence to the vertical line, the idea is incomplete. From the vertical line to the end of the sentence, the idea is complete. Eliminate (F) and (H) since STOP punctuation can be used only between two complete ideas. Compare (G) and (J).

The incomplete idea introduces the complete idea, so a comma is needed. Therefore, (G) is the correct answer. The same construction of *incomplete, complete* in the second part of Question 2 also requires a comma. Use a comma only when necessary, and it's necessary when an incomplete idea introduces a complete idea.

Commas

Commas work like blinking yellow lights: They slow down but do not stop ideas. Since the goal is to be concise, use a comma only for a specific reason. On the ACT, there are only four reasons to use a comma.

STOP

A comma by itself can't come in between two complete ideas, but it can when it's paired with one of the FANBOYS: *for, and, nor, but, or, yet, so*. A comma plus any of these is the equivalent of STOP punctuation. These words also affect direction, which might influence the correct answer.

> *Many people think that all Fiesta is too expensive,* **but** *Homer Laughlin China has stayed true to its roots with brand-new sets for sale in department stores for modest prices.*

FANBOYS

For the record, FANBOYS are called coordinating conjunctions. All conjunctions link things, but FANBOYS specifically come in between two ideas and are never part of either idea.

GO

A comma can link an incomplete idea to a complete idea, in either order. You will not always need to decide whether a comma is needed with this combination on the ACT, but if you do have to, consider whether there is a shift in ideas. If the sentence shifts into a different idea, then most likely a comma is needed; if the parts of the sentence make up the same idea, then a comma most likely is not needed.

Comma versus No Comma

When in doubt, choose an answer with no comma.

> *Almost immediately, collectors began buying pieces at garage sales and in secondhand shops.*

> *The popularity of the dishes began to decline after World War II, dropping out of favor entirely by the late 1960s.*

Lists

Use a comma to separate items in a list.

affordable, brightly colored dinnerware

Affordable and *brightly colored* both describe *dinnerware*. If you could say *affordable and brightly colored,* then you can say *affordable, brightly colored.* In a list of two items, use either *and* or a comma between the two items.

When you have three or more items in a list, always use a comma before the *and* preceding the final item. This is a rule that not everyone agrees on, but if you apply the 4 C's, the extra comma makes your meaning *Clear.* On the ACT, always use the comma before the *and.*

The range of colors available today includes Scarlet, Peacock, Tangerine, Sunflower, and Lemongrass.

Here's How to Crack #5, Part I

Eliminate (C) and (D) because neither one uses a comma before the *and* at the end of the list.

Unnecessary Info

Use a pair of commas around unnecessary info.

If information is necessary to the sentence in either meaning or structure, don't use the commas. If the meaning would be exactly the same but less interesting, use a pair of commas—or a pair of dashes—around the information. (A pair of parentheses can work in a similar way.)

Here's How to Crack #3

Some of the original glazes were made with detectable amounts of uranium oxide, which created the brilliant color effects, until the government, redirected all commercial uses of uranium toward development of the atom bomb during World War II.

Note the comma in the non-underlined portion of the sentence, just before *which.* The first comma opens the detour to unnecessary info, so use the changes in the answer choices to identify when the detour ends. The entire idea *which created the brilliant color effects* could be removed without changing the meaning of the sentence. Eliminate (B) and (C) because they do not contain a comma after this unnecessary phrase; then compare (A) and (D). The extra comma after *the government* in (A) would make *until the government* unnecessary, but it is needed because *the government* is the subject of *redirected* in the non-underlined portion. Choice (D) is correct because commas are used only where they are needed. Too many commas in one sentence is like hitting the gas...then the brakes...then the gas...then the brakes again, which would ruin any drive—or sentence.

Colons and Single Dashes

Colons and single dashes are very specific pieces of punctuation, and they are very flexible. They can link a complete idea to either an incomplete idea or another complete idea. The complete idea must come first, and the second idea will be a definition, explanation, or list. Since colons and single dashes are always used with at least one complete idea, use the Vertical Line Test whenever they appear in the text or in the answer choices.

Here's How to Crack #5, Part II

Draw a vertical line after *includes*.

> *The range of colors available today includes:* | *Scarlet, Peacock, Tangerine, Sunflower, and Lemongrass.*

The idea from the beginning of the sentence to the vertical line is incomplete, so a colon can't be used. Therefore, (A) and (D) can be eliminated. But recall that (C) and (D) have already been eliminated because both lack a comma before the *and*. Applying POE with the rules for commas and colons leaves only (B), the correct answer.

Here's How to Crack #7

First, note that there is an actual question above the four answer choices, and the question directs you to choose the alternative that is NOT acceptable. For the negative questions (phrased with EXCEPT, LEAST, or NOT), the sentence is always correct as written, and you can use it as a standard of comparison. Because STOP punctuation appears in several answer choices, draw a vertical line after *retired*.

> *Collectors will even pay top dollar for some of the modern colors if the colors have been retired:* | *Lilac pieces sell for hundreds of dollars.*

The idea from the beginning of the sentence to the vertical line is complete, and the idea from the vertical line to the end of the sentence is complete. A colon or a single dash, as in (D), can go in between two complete ideas, as can the STOP punctuation in (B) and (C). A comma by itself is GO punctuation and can never be used between two complete ideas. Thus, (A) is NOT acceptable, and it is the correct answer.

Conjunctions

Punctuation isn't the only way to link ideas. In some of the more difficult questions, you have to change ideas by adding or deleting a conjunction.

Here are some of the more common conjunctions you may see.

> although, as, because, if, since, that, until, how, what, which, while, when, where, who, whom

Proper grammarians would object to calling *how, what, which, when, where, who, whom* conjunctions, but the technical terms aren't important. It's not as if ACT makes you name any part of speech, and all that matters is that those words, when they are used in a statement instead of a question, act just like conjunctions by making an idea incomplete. For an example, look at how we used *when* in the last sentence or *how* in this sentence.

> **Conjunctions**
> Add a conjunction to make an idea incomplete or take one out to make the idea complete.

Here's How to Crack #6

Look at the answer choices to identify the topic as conjunctions. Check the entire sentence to see whether the ideas in it are correctly joined. *Some vintage pieces are radioactive because of the glaze* is complete, and *other original colors command hefty prices on online auction sites* is also complete. The two complete ideas, however, are incorrectly linked by a comma (GO punctuation). Since you can't fix the non-underlined punctuation, fix the idea by making it incomplete and therefore correct with GO punctuation. A conjunction makes an idea incomplete. Eliminate (F) and (G). Compare (H) and (J). Both add a conjunction, but *although* and *because* indicate different directions (we'll discuss that in more detail later in this chapter). Since the two ideas in the sentence show a contrast—*some vintage pieces* and *other pieces*—(J) is correct.

Subjects and Verbs

The minimum requirements of a complete idea are a subject and verb. Just as some difficult questions fix the error by adding or deleting a conjunction, so too do some questions add or delete a subject and verb to fix.

Here's How to Crack #8

Only (G) uses a conjunction, which is your clue to read the sentence to determine whether all ideas are linked correctly. In the non-underlined portion, *but* immediately follows the underlined comma in each choice. Because a comma + *but* is STOP punctuation, the ideas on either side have to be complete. In the non-underlined portion, *Homer Laughlin China has stayed true to its roots with brand-new sets for sale in department stores for modest prices* is complete. In (F), *Dismissing all Fiesta as too expensive* is incomplete because it lacks a subject and a verb. Similarly, *Having dismissed all Fiesta as too expensive,* in (J), also lacks a subject and verb and is therefore incomplete. In (G), *While many people think that all Fiesta is too expensive,* there is a subject and a verb, but the presence of the conjunction *While* makes the idea incomplete. Choice (H) is correct because *Many people think that all Fiesta is too expensive* adds a subject and verb to make the idea complete.

QUIZ II: CONSISTENT, CLEAR, CONCISE

Work the brief passage and then read the rules that follow, even if you answer all of the questions correctly. You may have a nuanced ear that can identify the right answer, or you may have internalized these rules and know how to use them correctly without being able to articulate *why* your choices are correct. However, in the pursuit of a perfect or near-perfect score on the English Test, the more you know *why*, the more you can count on answering questions correctly every single time.

After years of <u>disastrous, cataclysmic</u>
₁
<u>experimental attempts at baking sweet things,</u> I
₁
decided it was time to learn in a formal setting. I
investigated a community college and a grocery

store and saw that <u>it</u> offered several classes, from
₂
the basics to the

most advanced concepts. Some of the <u>cities</u> best
₃
chefs taught

the classes. <u>Unfortunately,</u> the most established
₄
chefs taught classes in the mornings, which didn't

fit my schedule. Only one

of the basic classes <u>were</u> taught in the evening.
₅
The instructor

was a pastry chef <u>whom began</u> her career on a
₆
reality cooking competition show.

1. **A.** NO CHANGE
   B. disastrously experimental attempts at baking pies, cookies, and cakes,
   C. disastrous attempts at baking,
   D. disastrous attempts at baking many different desserts,

2. **F.** NO CHANGE
   G. the store
   H. this
   J. she

3. **A.** NO CHANGE
   B. cities'
   C. citys
   D. city's

4. Which of the following alternatives to the underlined portion would be LEAST acceptable?
   F. Moreover,
   G. However,
   H. Sadly,
   J. DELETE the underlined portion and capitalize "the."

5. **A.** NO CHANGE
   B. was
   C. are
   D. have been

6. **F.** NO CHANGE
   G. who began
   H. who begun
   J. who was beginning

The answers are 1. (C), 2. (G), 3. (D), 4. (F), 5. (B), and 6. (G). Now read all about Verbs, Pronouns, Apostrophes, Transitions, and Concise to learn why, and learn how to crack these questions every time on every test.

VERBS

A verb expresses an action, feeling, or state of being. The form of a verb depends on the number of the subject—singular or plural—the time of the event, and the presence of helping verbs. Whenever you spot the verb changing among the answers, use these three steps along with your Basic Approach.

1. **Identify the subject.** The verb must be consistent with its subject: singular subject with a singular verb, and plural subject with a plural verb.
2. **Check the tense.** The tense must be consistent with the setting and the participle. Use the context of the non-underlined portion to determine whether the verb should be past, present, or future.
3. **Be concise.** Pick the shortest answer free of any errors.

Subject-Verb Agreement

Verbs have to be consistent with their subjects. Singular subjects take singular forms of the verb, and plural subjects take plural forms of the verb.

Your ear can alert you to many, if not most, subject-verb agreement errors. As a general rule, singular verbs end with *s* and plural verbs do not.

If you struggle to identify the subject, flip the statement into a question.

The list of famous chefs impresses students.

Q: *What impresses students?*

A: *The list.*

Be particularly careful of prepositional phrases that separate the subject from the verb and can easily fool your ear into identifying the subject incorrectly. In the example above, the subject *list* is singular and is modified by the prepositional phrase *of famous chefs*. Notice that the singular subject *list* uses the

Prepositional Phrases

Prepositions are little words that show a relationship between nouns. Some examples include *at, between, by, on, of, to,* and *with*. A prepositional phrase is a phrase beginning with a preposition. Examples include **on** *the stove,* **of** *recipes,* **with** *a frying pan.*

singular form of the verb *impresses*, but the plural noun *chefs* in between could easily cause a careless error.

Here's How to Crack #5

The changes in the answers identify the topic as verbs.

> *Only one of the basic classes were taught in the evening.*

Identify the subject: *one*. The prepositional phrase *of the classes* is there to trick you into thinking that the subject is plural. Eliminate (A), (C), and (D) because they are all plural. Choice (B) is correct because the verb *was* is singular to match the singular subject.

Verb Tense and Irregular Verbs

The tense of the verb marks the time of the event in the past, present, or future. Tenses come in different forms. The simple, progressive, and perfect tenses provide information about the duration, completion, or frequency of the event.

The simple tense uses the verb by itself, with the helping verb "will" added for the future tense. Simple tenses identify the general timeframe of events, or they are used with specific mentions of time.

> *I **studied** yesterday. I **study** weekends. I **will study** tomorrow.*

The progressive tense uses a present participle paired with the helping verb "to be." The helping verbs "will" and "to be" are also used for the future progressive. Progressive tenses reflect ongoing events within one timeframe, or events that are "in progress." Specific mentions of time can also be used with the progressive tenses.

> *I **was studying** when you called. I **am studying** today. I **will be studying** at the library tomorrow.*

The perfect tense uses a past participle paired with the helping verb "to have." The helping verb "will" is also used for the future perfect. Perfect tenses are used to describe events that are ongoing from past to present, were completed at an indefinite time, happened in a specific sequence in the past, or will be completed at a definite later time before a second event occurs. Often the perfect tenses are used with words such as "already," "ever," "just," "never," "recently," and "yet."

> *I **had** never **studied** at Starbucks before you suggested it. I **have** already **studied** for the Latin final. I **will** not **have studied** yet by the time you arrive.*

The perfect progressive tense uses a present participle paired with the helping verbs "to have" and "to be." The helping verb "will" is also used for the future perfect progressive. Perfect progressive tenses describe the sequence of events when at least one of the events is ongoing.

> I **had been studying** for days before you rescued me. I **have been studying** all day. I **will have been studying** for a month by the time I take the final.

All verbs add the suffix *-ing* to form the present participle. Regular verbs add the suffix *-ed* for the simple past and for the past participle. Irregular verbs use idiosyncratic forms, and many use one form for the simple past and a different one for the past participle. Here is a short list of some of the most common irregular verbs.

Infinitive	Simple Past	Past Participle
become	became	become
begin	began	begun
break	broke	broken
come	came	come
drink	drank	drunk
drive	drove	driven
eat	ate	eaten
fall	fell	fallen
forget	forgot	forgotten
get	got	gotten
give	gave	given
go	went	gone
know	knew	known
lead	led	led
ring	rang	rung
run	ran	run
see	saw	seen
speak	spoke	spoken
take	took	taken
teach	taught	taught
write	wrote	written

On the ACT, most questions on tense test the need for past, or present, or future. The difference among tenses within the same timeframe is very nuanced, and it's rare for questions to require choosing the perfect or progressive over the simple.

More commonly, when the perfect and progressive tenses appear, the question usually requires choosing the past, present, or future tense of the helping verb, the correct subject-verb agreement of the helping verb, or the correct participle of the main verb.

Here's How to Crack #6, Part I

The changes in the answer choices indicate verb tense and pronouns as topics. Let's look at the verbs first; we'll discuss the pronouns in the next section of this chapter. *The instructor was a pastry chef who/whom began her career on a reality cooking competition show* is in past tense, as are the verbs in the rest of the answer choices. The past tense is consistent with the setting and the non-underlined verbs. The answer choices show different participles. *To begin* is an irregular verb. Without the helping verb *to have*, *begun* on its own is incorrect. That is, you could say "has begun" or "had begun," for example, but not "begun" by itself. Eliminate (H). *Began* is more concise than *was beginning*. Eliminate (J). To decide between *who* and *whom*, move on to pronouns.

PRONOUNS

Pronouns take the place of a noun and make your writing more concise. Whenever you spot pronouns changing among the answers, use these three steps with your Basic Approach.

1. **Find the original.** The pronoun has to be consistent in number and gender with the noun it replaces or with a pronoun already in use.
2. **Check the case.** Choose the correct pronoun based on its specific function in the sentence.
3. **Be clear.** Do not use a pronoun if it could possibly refer to more than one noun of the same number and gender.

Pronoun Agreement

Pronouns have to be consistent with the nouns they replace in number and in gender.

	Female	Male	Things
Singular	she, her, hers	he, him, his	it, its
Plural	they, them, their	they, them, their	they, them, their

Pronoun Case

Pronouns also need to be consistent with the function they perform in a sentence. There are three different cases of pronouns.

	1st person	2nd person	3rd person
Subject	I, we	you	she, he, it, they, who
Object	me, us	you	her, him, it, them, whom
Possessive	my, mine, our, ours	your	her, hers, his, its, their, theirs, whose

Here's How to Crack #6, Part II

The instructor was a pastry chef whom began her career on a reality cooking competition show.

We've already eliminated (H) and (J). The difference between the remaining choices is in the pronouns *who* and *whom*. Follow the steps for pronouns, and identify the original, which in this case is *the pastry chef*. Both choices agree with the original, so next identify the case the pronoun performs in this part of the sentence, the incomplete idea. In the incomplete idea, the pronoun is the subject of the verb *began*. Choice (G) is the correct answer because it uses the subject pronoun *who* rather than the object pronoun *whom*.

Here's How to Crack #2

The changes in the answer choices indicate pronouns as the topic.

I investigated a community college and a grocery store and saw that it offered several classes, from the basics to the most advanced concepts.

It is singular, but it could refer to *community college* or *grocery store*, so eliminate (F). There is no reference to a woman in the sentence, so eliminate (J). *This* in (H) is ambiguous, leaving the meaning just as unclear as with the pronoun *it*. Choice (G) is correct because it makes the meaning clear by identifying the grocery store as the host of the cooking classes.

APOSTROPHES

Just as pronouns do, apostrophes make your writing more concise. They have two uses, possession and contraction.

Possession and Contractions

To show possession with singular nouns, add *'s*, and with plural nouns, add just the apostrophe. For tricky plurals that do not end in *s*, add *'s*. For personal pronouns, *never* use an apostrophe: use the proper pronoun.

A pronoun with an apostrophe is a contraction, which means the apostrophe takes the place of at least one letter. (*It's, you're,* and *you've* are all examples of contractions.)

Whenever you spot apostrophes changing among the answers, use these two steps with your Basic Approach.

1. **Confirm possession.** Look at the *next* word. Only nouns can be possessed. If the next word is a verb, preposition, conjunction, pronoun, or article, eliminate all choices with nouns and apostrophes or possessive pronouns.
2. **Check the number.** Determine whether the noun is singular or plural or whether the possessive pronoun replaces a singular or plural noun.

Here's How to Crack #3

The changes in the answer choices identify apostrophes as the topic.

> *Some of the cities best chefs taught the classes.*

The *best chefs* follow *cities*, and they belong to the city. The sentence could be rewritten as *the best chefs of the city*, proof that *the chefs* belong to *the city* and that an apostrophe is needed. Eliminate (A) and (C). There is no proof that there is more than one city, so choose the singular *city's* in (D).

TRANSITIONS

If good writing is like a pleasant drive, then transitions are road signs, preventing you from getting lost and helping you make important turns. Good transitions are consistent with the flow of ideas.

Many words can act as transitions. Some are specific to the context, in which only one word will fit the precise meaning. But others are just slight variations telling you to *turn around* or *keep going.* Here's a partial list.

Turn Around

although, but, despite, even though, however, nonetheless, nevertheless, yet

Keep Going

and, because, finally, furthermore, moreover, since, so, thus, therefore

---

Whenever you spot transitions changing among the answers, use these three steps with your Basic Approach.

1. **Be consistent.** Read the sentences on either side of the transition to determine the context to choose a transition with the correct direction.
2. **Be concise.** Use a transition only when necessary.
3. **Be complete.** Read the full sentence to confirm that the ideas are linked correctly.

Good transitions make the meaning clearer, but they are necessary only if they help connect the ideas correctly. FANBOYS, conjunctions, and adverbs can all be used as transitions. Adverbs provide only direction, but as we discussed in the Complete section above, FANBOYS and conjunctions do more than provide direction. A conjunction may be needed to make one of the ideas complete. With a comma, one of the FANBOYS may be needed to link two complete ideas.

Here's How to Crack #4

First, note that there is an actual question above the four answer choices. *Which of the following alternatives to the underlined portion would be LEAST acceptable?* For the negative questions (phrased with EXCEPT, LEAST, or NOT), the sentence as written is always correct and can be used as a standard of comparison.

> *Unfortunately, the most established chefs taught classes in the mornings, which didn't fit my schedule.*

Unfortunately works as a turn-around transition because the context shifts from something positive (famous chefs teach) to something negative (not on the narrator's schedule). Eliminate (G) and (H) because they are both turn-around transitions and therefore are acceptable. *Unfortunately* and the three other transitions in the answers are all adverbs, and there is no error in the way the ideas are linked. Therefore, the transition isn't necessary and could be deleted. Eliminate (J). *Moreover* is a keep-going transition and would be LEAST acceptable and is therefore the correct answer.

CONCISE

Good writing may be like a pleasant drive, but you're not on a joyride on the ACT. Get to your destination as fast as you can. Be Concise.

Eliminate the most concise choice *only* if it fails to correct an error or creates a new one. However, concise isn't just a strategy. The topic is frequently tested on the ACT. On concise questions, none of the answers are grammatically wrong, but three answers are unnecessarily wordy, featuring either redundant or irrelevant information.

Whenever you spot the use of the same word or phrase in all answer choices, use these two steps with your Basic Approach.

1. Eliminate answer choices that have unnecessary information.
2. Eliminate answer choices that are redundant.

Here's How to Crack #1
The sentence as written is wordy and redundant.

> *After years of disastrous, cataclysmic experimental attempts at baking sweet things, I decided it was time to learn in a formal setting.*

Eliminate (A) because it is redundant. Eliminate (B) and (D) because they also contain more words than are necessary. Choice (C) is concise and makes the meaning clear.

> Now try these strategies on your own. Go online to your Student Tools and answer the Chapter 5 Drills.

Summary

o   Shoot for perfection on questions that test punctuation, verbs, pronouns, apostrophes, transitions, and whether the sentence is concise. These topics are heavily tested, are easily identifiable from changes in the answer choices, and follow relatively few rules in their correct usage.

o   Good writing should be *complete, consistent, clear,* and *concise.*

o   STOP punctuation includes a period, a semicolon, an exclamation mark, a question mark, and a comma + a FANBOYS word. STOP punctuation can link only two complete ideas. Whenever you see STOP punctuation in the text or in the answers, use the Vertical Line Test.

o   GO punctuation includes no punctuation and a comma. GO punctuation can link anything except for two complete ideas. Use commas only when necessary.

o   Colons and single dashes must follow a complete idea but can precede a complete or incomplete idea.

o   Conjunctions make an idea incomplete. Transition words provide directions and connections between ideas.

o   Be consistent. Verbs have to be consistent in number with their subject and consistent in tense with the context of the sentence. Pronouns have to be consistent in number, gender, and case, and clear in which nouns they replace.

o   Singular nouns take *'s* to show possession. Plural nouns that end in *s* take an apostrophe after the *s* to show possession. Possessive personal pronouns show possession. Pronouns and verbs use apostrophes to form contractions.

o   Be concise.

Chapter 6
Rhetorical Skills

ACT categorizes the questions on the English Test as either Rhetorical Skills or Usage and Mechanics. For most questions, the basic approach used to crack them is the same, regardless of what ACT labels them. There are certain questions, however, that do require a different approach. In this chapter, we'll cover all the questions that come with an actual question and not just four answer choices. These are questions that many students find difficult and time-consuming, and they may be the main obstacle to getting a perfect or near-perfect score. We'll teach you how to crack questions that ask for wrong answers as well as questions on strategy and order.

EXCEPT/LEAST/NOT

You know a question is tricky when the right answer is wrong. That is, if the question asks you to identify the choice that does NOT work, you have to cross off three answers that work and choose the one that doesn't.

The EXCEPT/LEAST/NOT questions, or E/L/N for short, hide in plain sight and therefore pose a challenge to spot. Because most "questions" on the ACT English Test feature only four answer choices and no actual question, it is easy to miss the presence of a bona fide question. Moreover, many of the topics on E/L/N will look familiar: STOP/GO punctuation and transition questions are two topics heavily tested in this format, so the four answers look pretty much the same as they always do—except that the first choice won't be NO CHANGE. NO CHANGE is almost never an option on E/L/N questions. When it's not, then the sentence is correct as written.

ACT English Test Categories

Not all EXCEPT/LEAST/NOT questions are rhetorical skills questions by ACT standards. An E/L/N question on STOP/GO, for example, would be counted as Usage and Mechanics. But when most of the "questions" are just four answer choices, the presence of a true question demands a different approach. Thus, we're addressing the E/L/N questions in this chapter, regardless of how ACT may categorize them.

It's very easy to get confused with E/L/N questions. Use an organized strategy.

1. Cross out NOT.
2. Use the sentence as written as the standard of comparison to evaluate the answer choices.
3. Write "Y" (for Yes) next to each choice that IS acceptable and "N" (for No) next to the one choice that is NOT acceptable.

The correct answer is the one choice with an "N" next to it.

[1]

The golden age of live television in the late 1950s and early 1960s witnessed the

rise to prominence of a small band of actors,
———————————————————
                    1

writers, and directors who worked on revolutionary

shows such as *Playhouse 90.*

1. Which of the following alternatives to the underlined portion would be LEAST acceptable?
   A. increase in fame
   B. projection of fame
   C. rise to stardom
   D. rise to fame

Here's How to Crack #1

Cross out LEAST, and compare the answer choices to the sentence as written. The changes in the answer choices identify the topic as vocabulary and idioms, two of the most challenging topics ACT tests, either in regular or E/L/N format. Vocabulary requires selecting the precise word that fits with the context. An idiom is an expression whose form and meaning can be determined neither by grammatical rules nor by the usual definition of its elements.

Choices (C) and (D) use the same idiom (*rise to*), and *stardom* and *fame* mean in context the same as *prominence*, so write "Y" next to both of them. Choices (A) and (B) use different idioms, but only the idiom *increase in* means the same as *rise to,* so mark "Y" next to (A) and "N" next to (B). Choice (B) is the correct answer because it is the one choice that is LEAST acceptable.

> Look for changes in prepositions among the answer choices to identify idioms.

While the vocabulary and idioms that appear on the ACT tend to be fairly common words and expressions, they rarely repeat. Thus, there is no way to prepare for the particular ones that will show up on your ACT. You'll either know them or you won't. Use your ear, read for the context, and lean on POE heavily.

> Learn more about how to crack questions on vocabulary and idioms in Chapter 7.

STRATEGY QUESTIONS

Strategy questions come in many different forms, but they all revolve around the *purpose* of the text. Among the different types of strategy questions, expect to see questions asking you to add or replace text, determine whether text should be added or deleted, evaluate the impact on the passage if text is deleted, and judge the overall effect of the passage on the reader.

Add or Replace

Strategy questions that ask you to add or replace text always state a purpose for the proposed text. Identify the purpose and pick an answer that best fulfills it.

Let's see some examples.

———————————————⌣———————————————

Established stars and undiscovered talent alike

worked long hours <u>reading scripts.</u>
₂

2. Given that all the choices are true, which one most clearly indicates that the actors worked to improve their skills?
   F. NO CHANGE.
   G. honing their craft.
   H. constructing the set.
   J. skimming the want-ads.

Here's How to Crack #2

Identify the purpose stated in the question, and pick the choice that fulfills that purpose. In this case, the question asks for the choice that indicates that the actors worked to improve their skills. You don't even need to go back into the passage: find an answer choice that describes improving skills. Choices (F), (H), and (J) say nothing about acting skills. Only (G), the correct answer, does.

[2]

Because of this frantic pace, accidents happened frequently. David Niven once revealed that during an early show, <u>he accidentally locked his costume in his</u>
₃
<u>dressing room two minutes before air time.</u> As the
₃
announcer read the opening credits, the sound of axes splintering the door to Niven's dressing room could be heard in the background. ☐ ₄

3. Given that all choices are true, which one provides the most specific and relevant information?
   A. NO CHANGE
   B. a casting agent approached him about auditioning for the role of James Bond.
   C. cast members improvised changes in dialogue.
   D. the producers announced that the program had been renewed.

Here's How to Crack #3

Identify the purpose stated in the question, and pick the choice that fulfills that purpose. In this case, the question asks for the choice that *provides the most specific and relevant information*. Read through to the end of the paragraph and use the context to find an answer that *provides the most specific and relevant information*. The preceding sentence indicates that *accidents happened frequently,* and the succeeding sentence describes *axes splintering the door to the dressing room.* Choice (A) is the best introduction because it provides an example of a specific accident and makes sense of why the door was broken down.

Lose

Another type of strategy question asks you to identify what the passage would *lose* if a particular sentence or phrase were deleted.

Lean heavily on POE for these questions. Look for the choice that best describes the deleted portion.

---

[2]

Because of this frantic pace, accidents happened frequently. David Niven once revealed that during an early show, he accidentally locked his costume in his dressing room two minutes before air time. As the announcer read the opening credits, the sound of axes splintering the door to Niven's dressing room could be heard in the background. [4]

4. The writer is considering deleting the preceding sentence. If the writer were to make this deletion, the essay would primarily lose a statement that:
   F. explains the organization of the paragraph.
   G. adds a much needed touch of humor to the essay.
   H. explains how one accident was resolved.
   J. adds nothing since the information is provided elsewhere in the paragraph.

Here's How to Crack #4

Use POE heavily: the correct choice will accurately describe the sentence to be deleted. Choice (F) is incorrect because the sentence does not *explain the organization of the paragraph.* Choice (J) is incorrect because the information is NOT *provided elsewhere in the paragraph.* Choice (G) is possible, but (H) is better. The sentence relates how David Niven's costume was retrieved from behind a locked door. Choice (H) is correct because it provides the most specific description of the sentence.

Yes or No

Some strategy questions provide you with a choice to make. Should the author add something new to the passage? Two answers are *Yes,* and two answers are *No.* A variation can also ask whether some part of the passage should be kept or deleted. Two answers are *Kept,* and two answers are *Deleted.*

Even when you have a strong feeling of *Yes* or *No,* or *Keep* or *Delete,* always consider the reasons in the answer choices carefully. The correct answer has to provide a reason that accurately describes the proposed text and its role in the passage.

---

[4]

Despite the undeniable risks of live performance—or perhaps because of—the results rank among the greatest achievements in American entertainment. Many of *Playhouse 90*'s productions were later remade, both for television and film, including *Requiem for a Heavyweight, Judgment at Nuremberg,* and *Days of Wine and Roses.* ⬚5 Many critics maintain that none of the remakes could match the brilliance and electricity of the live performances displayed in *Playhouse 90.*

5. At this point, the writer is considering adding the following true statement:

> The theme song for *Days of Wine and Roses* was composed by Henry Mancini, who also wrote the theme song for *The Pink Panther.*

Should the writer add this sentence here?

A. Yes, because it explains how the film version of *Days of Wine and Roses* was different from the television version.

B. Yes, because it provides an important detail about one of the movies made from a *Playhouse 90* production.

C. No, because it doesn't clarify whether *The Pink Panther* was first performed on *Playhouse 90.*

D. No, because it distracts the reader from the main point of this paragraph.

Here's How to Crack #5

Evaluate the reasons in the answer choices carefully. The reason should correctly explain the purpose of the selected text. Choice (A) is incorrect because there is no information about how the movie was different. Choice (B) is incorrect because the composer of the theme song is not *an important detail.* Choice (C) is possible because the proposed text does not state whether *The Pink Panther* was performed on *Playhouse 90,* but (D) is better. Choice (D) is correct because the main point of the paragraph is on the quality of the productions that came out of *Playhouse 90,* and information on the composer of a score is irrelevant and a distraction.

ORDER

Just as strategy questions come in several different varieties, there are also several types of order questions. All order questions involve the correct placement of ideas. Some order questions will ask you to correctly place a modifier or a new sentence. Other questions will ask you to evaluate and possibly correct the order of sentences within a paragraph or the order of the paragraphs themselves.

To work order questions, use POE. Ideas should be consistent and the meaning should be clear, but that meaning can be difficult to understand until ideas are in their proper place.

Order of Modifiers

A modifier out of place will leave the meaning of the sentence at best vague and at worst incorrect. Try each placement given in the answer choices. When the modifier is placed in its proper position, it should make the meaning of the sentence clear.

Let's look at an example.

---

[3]

[1] For both the experienced and inexperienced

actors, the chance to perform attracted them

<u>on live television</u> to appear on *Playhouse 90.*
₆

6. The best placement for the underlined phrase would be:
   F. where it is now.
   G. after the word *actors.*
   H. after the word *perform.*
   J. after the word *attracted.*

Here's How to Crack #6

Use POE. Choices (F) and (J) are incorrect because placing *on live television* before *attracted* or after *them* makes it sound as if the performers were drawn to performing on *Playhouse 90* while they were already appearing on *live television*. Choice (G) is incorrect because placing *on live television* after *actors* makes it sound as if only actors who already were appearing on live TV were drawn to *Playhouse 90*. Choice (H) is correct because the placement of *on live television* after *perform* clarifies why the actors wanted to appear on *Playhouse 90*.

Order of Sentences

If there is a question on the order of the sentences in a paragraph, all of the sentences will be numbered. While NO CHANGE is a possible answer choice, it's also possible the sentences should be in a different order.

Just as you shouldn't try to fix a grammatical error in your head, don't waste time on an order question trying to put all the sentences in a paragraph into the perfect order. Look for one pair of sentences that need to go back-to-back, or one sentence that clearly begins or ends the paragraph, and use POE.

Certain clues can help determine the proper order. Transition words may be used to indicate an introduction or a conclusion. A pronoun may refer to a noun in a different sentence; in this case, the sentence that contains the pronoun should immediately follow the sentence that contains the original noun. In other cases, the context of the sentence may establish a chronology of events.

Try an example. Sentence 1 now shows the correct answer from Question 6.

[3]

[1] For both the experienced and inexperienced actors, the chance to perform on live television attracted them to appear on *Playhouse 90*. [2] Each week, a new "teleplay" was created from scratch—written, cast, rehearsed, and performed. [3] *Playhouse 90* was truly a remarkable training ground for the young talents. [4] Such future luminaries as Rod Serling, Sidney Lumet, Paddy Chayefsky, Marlon Brando, and Patricia Neal worked on various productions. [5] In some weeks, the censors would find something in it objectionable, and the network would intervene mere hours before airtime, leaving the cast and crew to scramble quickly to adapt. [7]

7. Which of the following orders of sentences makes the paragraph most logical?
   A. NO CHANGE
   B. 1, 3, 4, 2, 5
   C. 5, 4, 3, 2, 1
   D. 1, 4, 5, 3, 2,

Here's How to Crack It

Use the pronoun *it* in Sentence 5 to help determine the placement of that sentence. The pronoun has to refer to a noun in a sentence that immediately precedes Sentence 5. There is no singular noun in Sentence 4 that agrees with *it*, so eliminate (A) and (D). Sentence 5 can't begin the paragraph because the *it* has to replace a noun in a prior sentence, so eliminate (C). Choice (B) is correct because the *it* replaces the singular noun *teleplay* in Sentence 2. Moreover, the transition phrase *In some weeks* in Sentence 5 should follow the transition phrase *Each week* in Sentence 2.

AFTER THE PASSAGE

Questions 9 and 10 ask about the passage as
a whole.

Some order and strategy questions routinely appear at the end and are always preceded by
the announcement above.

Order of the Paragraphs

If there is a question on the order of the paragraphs in a passage, there will be a warning
at the beginning of the passage, alerting you that the passages may or may not be in the
correct order and identifying which question will ask about the order.

The following paragraphs may or may not be in the most logical order. Each
paragraph is numbered, and Question 8 will ask you to choose where Paragraph 2 should most logically be placed.

On a question that asks about ordering paragraphs, use a similar approach to that used
for order of sentences. Look specifically at the first and last sentence of the paragraph that
needs to be placed, and identify any transition words or pronouns that make the order of
events consistent and clear.

The passage in its entirety, with all corrected text, is reprinted and paired with an example of a question on the order of the paragraphs.

[1]

The golden age of live television in the late 1950s and early 1960s witnessed the rise to prominence of a small band of actors, writers, and directors who worked on revolutionary shows such as *Playhouse 90*. Established stars and undiscovered talent alike worked long hours honing their craft.

[2]

Because of this frantic pace, accidents happened frequently. David Niven once revealed that during an early show, he accidentally locked his costume in his dressing room two minutes before air time. As the announcer read the opening credits, the sound of axes splintering the door to Niven's dressing room could be heard in the background.

[3]

For both the experienced and inexperienced actors, the chance to perform on live television attracted them to appear on *Playhouse 90*. Each week, a new "teleplay" was created from scratch— written, cast, rehearsed, and performed. *Playhouse 90* was truly a remarkable training ground for the young talents. Such future luminaries as Rod Serling, Sidney Lumet, Paddy Chayefsky, Marlon Brando, and Patricia Neal worked on various productions. In some weeks, the censors would find something in it objectionable, and the network would intervene mere hours before airtime, leaving the cast and crew to scramble quickly to adapt.

[4]

Despite the undeniable risks of live performance—or perhaps because of—the results rank among the greatest achievements in American entertainment. Many of *Playhouse 90*'s productions were later remade, both for television and film, including *Requiem for a Heavyweight, Judgment at Nuremberg*, and *Days of Wine and Roses*. Many critics maintain that none of the remakes could match the brilliance and electricity of the live performances displayed on *Playhouse 90*.

8. For the sake of the logic and coherence of this essay, Paragraph 2 should be placed:
   F. where it is now.
   G. before Paragraph 1.
   H. after Paragraph 3.
   J. after Paragraph 4.

Here's How to Crack #8

Note that the pronoun in the phrase *this frantic pace* in Paragraph 2 means that the pace has already been described. Consider the placements for Paragraph 2 offered by the answer choices. Choice (F) is incorrect because *this frantic pace* has to be explained first, and because Paragraph 1 introduces the topic of *Playhouse 90*. For the same reason, Paragraph 2 can't come before Paragraph 1, so eliminate (G). Choice (J) is incorrect because the last sentence of Paragraph 4 doesn't mention the pace of the performances. Choice (H) is correct because the last sentence of Paragraph 3 describes the cast and crew scrambling *quickly*, and thus explains the *frantic pace*.

Grading the Passage

A question at the end that asks you to evaluate the passage as a whole is another type of strategy question. This type of question states the intended purpose of the passage and asks you to determine whether the author fulfills that purpose. Two answers are *Yes,* and two answers are *No.*

Even if you have a strong feeling toward *Yes* or *No*, consider the reasons in the answer choices carefully. The correct choice should offer a reason that both addresses the proposed purpose of the passage and describes the passage accurately.

Now that you've answered several questions on this passage, let's try a strategy question that asks you to grade the passage.

---

9. Suppose that one of the writer's goals has been to write a brief essay describing an influential program in television's history. Would this essay fulfill that goal?

   A. Yes, because it explains that many future stars underwent valuable training working on *Playhouse 90*.
   B. Yes, because it mentions that *Playhouse 90* had the greatest number of viewers in its time slot.
   C. No, because it fails to mention any future stars by name.
   D. No, because even though many future stars received their start on *Playhouse 90*, few ever returned to television.

Here's How to Crack #9

Identify *describing an influential program in television's history* as the purpose the writer was supposed to fulfill. The writer describes *Playhouse 90* as *revolutionary, a remarkable training ground,* and one of the *greatest achievements in American entertainment,* making a *Yes* likely. Review the reasons carefully. Choice (A) explains why the program was *influential* by pointing out the *future stars who underwent valuable training.* Choice (B) is incorrect because there is no information about viewership in the passage. Choice (C) is incorrect because several stars are mentioned by name. Choice (D) is incorrect because the passage never states that few stars *returned to television.* Choice (A) is correct because it agrees that, yes, the passage fulfilled the author's goal and provides a reason that describes the passage accurately.

> Don't be afraid to pick a "no" answer for these questions if the passage is not consistent with the goal stated in the question.

Now try these strategies on your own. Go online to your Student Tools and answer the Chapter 6 Drills.

Summary

○ Questions that come with actual questions—not just answer choices—need a different approach.

○ For EXCEPT/LEAST/NOT questions, cross off the E/L/N word and use POE. Mark each choice that is acceptable with a "Y" and the choice that is not acceptable with an "N." The "N" is the correct answer.

○ Strategy questions all involve a purpose. Pick an answer that fulfills the purpose stated in the question. On strategy questions that involve making a decision, pick an answer that provides a reason that describes the passage accurately.

○ Order questions involve the correct placement of words, sentences, and paragraphs. Try the placements provided in the answer choices and lean on POE.

Chapter 7
Advanced English

The pursuit of perfection, or near perfection, on the English Test requires banking every point you can on questions on which you can identify the topic and apply a basic approach to fix, just as we've shown in the last two chapters. But it also includes answering correctly the idiosyncratic English questions. In this chapter, we'll show you how to spot and crack the most challenging questions on the English Test.

VOCABULARY

Vocabulary isn't heavily tested on the ACT, but questions do appear on the English Test that require you to choose the best word for the context of a sentence. In some examples, the words offered are close enough in meaning that in some contexts, they could be synonyms. In other examples, the words sound alike but have different meanings.

HOMOPHONES

Homophones are words that sound similar but have different meanings and/or spelling. It is a little difficult to study for these, as there are many that could be tested. For a list of common homophones and their definitions, go to your Student Tools.

Strategy for Homophones on the ACT

The strategy for homophones depends on your familiarity with the pair or trio of words that is featured in the question. If you know both/all words well, you may be able to identify which is needed based on the meaning or the function.

- Use the context to identify the meaning of the word in the sentence. If the words are all the same parts of speech, substitute your own word and eliminate choices that don't match the meaning of your word.
- Use the context to identify the function of the word in the sentence. Eliminate choices that are the wrong part of speech. Eliminate choices that are verbs but that do not match the subject. Eliminate choices that are nouns but that are the wrong number (singular versus plural).
- Use POE aggressively, guess, and move on. You may not be certain which word means what or what word is which part of speech. Eliminate what you are confident is wrong, guess from what's left, and move on.

Try an example.

The increase in extreme weather patterns effects₁ countries all over the world.

1. **A.** NO CHANGE
   B. effect
   C. affect
   D. affects

Here's How to Crack It

Affect and *effect* can be very confusing because they sound alike and have related definitions. Both words can be verbs or nouns, but the more common verb is *affect* (to act on or have an impact on, to produce an *effect*, change, or consequence) and the more common noun is *effect* (a result or consequence produced by an agency or cause). Even if you have trouble remembering which word is the verb, start by identifying the underlined word as the verb in the sentence; then identify the subject to check subject-verb agreement. The singular subject *increase* needs a singular verb, so eliminate (B) and (C). At this point you have a fifty-fifty chance of guessing the right answer if you don't know which one is correct. *Affect* is the verb that means *have an impact on*, so (D) is the correct answer.

SYNONYMS

Synonyms are words that are close enough in meaning that they can be substituted for each other in a sentence without changing the meaning. That makes vocabulary a great subject for EXCEPT/LEAST/NOT questions, which require you to identify the one word that does not work for the context.

Strategy for Synonyms on the ACT

The strategy for synonyms depends on your familiarity with the words. However, most words that appear are fairly common words.

- If the question uses the E/L/N format, apply the strategy you learned in Chapter 6. The sentence is correct as written, so you can use the original word as the point of comparison for the words in the answer choices. Write a "Y" next to each choice that could replace the original word and work with the context. Write an "N" next to the one choice that can't replace the original word. The "N" is the correct answer.
- If the question is in the regular format, use the context to identify the meaning of the word in the sentence. Substitute your own word and eliminate choices that don't match the meaning of your word.
- Use POE aggressively, guess, and move on. You may not be certain of some words. Eliminate what you are confident is wrong, guess from what's left, and move on.

Try an example.

―――――――――――――――○――――――――――――――

Against the backdrop of an ink-black sky, the

constellations twinkled above us.
                    ‾‾‾‾‾‾‾‾
                       2

2. Which of the following alternatives to the underlined portion would NOT be acceptable?
   F. sparkled
   G. shimmered
   H. glittered
   J. glared

Here's How to Crack It

Cross out NOT. Use *twinkled* as the point of comparison for the words in the answers. Write a "Y" next to the choices that could replace *twinkled* and work in the context of the sentence. *Twinkled, sparkled, shimmered, glittered,* and *glared* all mean to give off light. Choices (F), (G), and (H) could all replace *twinkled* because each provides the same meaning of giving off a pleasant, intermittent light that *twinkled* does. Write "Y" next to each choice. Choice (J) is the correct answer because *glared* can't replace *twinkled. Glare* is used to describe a light that is strong, harsh, and constant in quality.

―――――――――――――――○――――――――――――――

IDIOMS

Idiomatic phrases are expressions whose form and meaning can be determined by neither grammatical rules nor the usual definitions of their elements. Therefore, you either know these phrases or you don't: they don't follow any rules.

Common Idioms

While the idioms that appear on the ACT rarely repeat, below is a list of some of the more common idioms. Even if you memorize every one of these, you are likely to encounter a question on the ACT that tests an idiom not on the list.

Allow to: I cannot *allow* you *to* leave the house without a jacket on.

Assert over: The oldest sister *asserted* her power *over* her siblings.

Associate with:	No one wants to be *associated with* cheats and frauds.
Benefit from:	Everyone can *benefit from* rest and relaxation.
Bring about:	A bipartisan effort can *bring about* real reform in the legislature.
Capable of:	You had no idea that I was *capable of* such an act.
Choose to:	I *choose to* ignore that criticism.
Complain about:	Don't *complain about* the food in front of the chef.
Create from:	The sculpture was *created from* discarded metal and rubber.
Decide to:	The guests *decided to* leave when the food ran out.
Demonstrated by:	The doctor *demonstrated* her concern *by* staying with the patient overnight.
Determined by:	The winner is *determined by* a simple majority.
Different from:	Apples are *different from* oranges.
Emerge from:	Diplomats *emerged from* the peace discussions feeling hopeful.
Exposure to:	*Exposure to* ultraviolet rays can be dangerous to your health.
Focus on:	Conservation efforts have *focused on* restoring the beachfront to its former glory.
Forbid to:	Invited guests were *forbidden to* reveal the location of the party.
Modeled on:	The new headquarters were *modeled on* the Parthenon.
Persuade to:	Nobody could *persuade* her *to* give up the search.
Problem with:	Many experts had *problems with* the theory.
Prohibit from:	Students are *prohibited from* wearing midriff-baring tops.
Refreshed in:	I left the spa *refreshed in* body and mind.

Regard as:	The members of the society are *regarded as* heroes in preservation circles.
Responsible for:	You are *responsible for* the outcome.
Responsibility to:	I have a *responsibility to* my fans.
Sit across from:	I *sat across from* a crying baby on the long bus ride.
Try to:	She *tries to* make everyone happy.
Typical of:	He is *typical of* most athletes.
Worry about:	I will never stop *worrying about* my grades.

Strategy for Idioms on the ACT

Your ear is your best tool for idioms. Many idioms use a preposition, and your ear can identify the wrong prepositions, if not the right one.

- Focus on the preposition, evaluating its use with the word in the idiom as well as the context of the sentence.
- Shut your eyes or look away from the example as you repeat each idiom in your head. Your eyes and brain will get in the way of your ear.
- Your ear may not identify the correct idiom, but it may identify the wrong ones.
- If the question uses the E/L/N format, cross off the NOT and use the sentence as written to compare the idioms in the answer choices. Write a "Y" next to each choice that could replace the original idiom and work with the context. Write an "N" next to the one choice that can't replace the original idiom. The "N" is the correct answer.
- Use POE aggressively, guess, and move on. You may not be familiar with the idiom. Eliminate what you are confident is wrong, guess from what's left, and move on.

Try an example.

---○---

Parents all over the world have

benefited by Marion Donovan's invention
₃
of disposable diapers.

3. **A.** NO CHANGE
   B. from
   C. in
   D. on

Here's How to Crack It

Use your ear as you work through the different choices, focusing on the prepositions. Your ear may more easily identify the wrong prepositions than the right one. *Benefited in* in (C) and *benefited on* in (D) may sound more wrong than either *benefited by* or *benefited from*, allowing you to eliminate (C) and (D). You have a fifty-fifty chance of picking the right answer, so guess and move on. Choice (B) is correct because the idiom is *benefited from*.

> Look for changes in prepositions among the answer choices to identify idioms.

---○---

COUNTABLE AND UNCOUNTABLE NOUNS

Certain words can describe items that can be counted in individual units, and other words are used to describe items that can't be counted. Some examples of countable nouns are *dog, child, problem,* and *idea*. Some examples of uncountable nouns are *integrity, nutrition,* and *wisdom*.

Countable

If a noun has both a singular and plural form, it's countable. You can also tell a noun is countable if it is preceded by the indefinite articles *a* or *an*. A singular countable noun can't stand alone and needs an article in front of it.

> A **child** gave me an idea. A **dog** was a **problem**. A **problem** gave me a **headache**.

> Another trick for identifying countable and uncountable nouns is saying "five" (or any number) before the noun. You can have five dollars, so "dollar" is countable. You can't have five money, so "money" is uncountable.

You can also tell a noun is countable if you can make it plural by adding an *s* or using the unique plural. Plural countable nouns can stand alone.

Children *played with* **dogs**. **Ideas** *can cause* **problems**.

Use the following adjectives with countable nouns.

Few: She had *few* complaints after the great lesson.

Fewer: He made *fewer* careless errors on the last practice test.

Many: *Many* children shouted out the answer.

Number: A *number* of students complained about the curve.

10 Items or Less

That sounds right to your ear, doesn't it? Walk into most grocery stores, and the express lane will likely be marked by such a sign. But according to the counting rules, *10* items can obviously be counted, and the sign should read "10 Items or Fewer" (as the sign reads in Whole Foods). "10 Items or Less" is so embedded in our culture (there was both a movie and unrelated TV series with that title) that it doesn't sound wrong to most people. English is a fluid language, and it's possible the rules about the distinction will fade. But for now, follow the rules about countable and uncountable nouns on the ACT.

Uncountable

Some nouns are uncountable. You can tell that a noun is uncountable when there is no plural form of the word. You can also tell that nouns are uncountable when you can't use the indefinite articles *a* and *an* in front of them.

I have **integrity**. *He showed* **wisdom**. *Good* **nutrition** *is important*.

Use the following adjectives with uncountable nouns.

Amount: A record-breaking *amount* of snow fell this winter.

Less: I have *less* patience for such pranks than you do.

Little: We have *little* time to waste.

Much: You spent too *much* money on me.

Strategy for Countable and Uncountable Nouns

- Look at the word that the adjective describes.
  - If the word is singular, say it in your head with *a* or *an* in front, or try to make it plural and say it in your head with an *s*. If the *a* or *an* works, it's countable. If the word can be made plural, it's countable.
  - If the word is already plural, it's countable.
- Eliminate choices that use the wrong adjective.
- Do not depend on your ear.

Try a few examples.

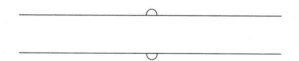

Compared to Mediterranean cuisines, Latin

American cooking uses <u>less lemons.</u>
₄

4. **F.** NO CHANGE
   G. the least
   H. fewer
   J. lesser

Here's How to Crack It

If a noun is in plural form, it's countable. The only countable adjective is *fewer* in (H). Choices (F), (G), and (J) all use a form of *less,* which is an adjective used for uncountable nouns.

Experienced chefs recommend that beginners use

<u>few creativity and more fidelity</u> when it comes to
₅
following the steps of the recipe.

5. **A.** NO CHANGE
   B. least creativity and more
   C. lesser creativity and much
   D. less creativity and more

Here's How to Crack It

Try *a creativity* or *creativities*. Neither works, which confirms that *creativity* is uncountable. Eliminate (F) because *few* is a countable adjective. Compare the remaining choices. *Creativity* should be consistent with *fidelity*. Choice (B) is incorrect because *least* is a superlative, but *more* is a comparative word. Choice (C) is incorrect because *lesser* is a comparative word, but *much* is not a comparative word. Read more on superlatives and comparatives in the next section of this chapter. Choice (D) is correct because *less* is used for uncountable nouns and is consistent with *more*.

Advanced Counting

Certain situations make the difference between countable and uncountable nouns more difficult.

Switch-Hitters

Some adjectives/adjectival phrases can be used with both countable and uncountable nouns.

Any: Are there *any* men in the book club? Do you have *any* milk?

Enough: I've read *enough* articles. I have *enough* time to go shopping.

More: I want *more* cookies. I need *more* air.

Plenty of: He had *plenty of* excuses. He has *plenty of* money.

Some: We have *some* questions for you. You need *some* water.

Time and Rate

Consider the following example.

> *I'll be there in 20 minutes or* less.

Minutes can be counted, but the meaning of the sentence is more about the amount of time rather than the number of minutes.

On the ACT, the correct answer uses *less than* for constructions about time or rate, regardless of whether the noun is countable.

> On questions that involve rate or time, use *less than*.

The act was repealed <u>less then</u> a decade later.
₆

6. **F.** NO CHANGE
   G. less than
   H. fewer then
   J. fewer than

Here's How to Crack It

A decade indicates time, so the correct construction is *less than,* which is (G). If you struggle to remember this rule, you can also apply the homophone strategy to *than* versus *then* and eliminate two wrong answers at least. *Than* is a preposition used with comparisons. *Then* is an adverb that means *next.* A good mnemonic (memory device) is to relate *then* with *next,* two words with an *e.* Relate *as* with *than,* two words with an *a* and both used for comparisons. Eliminate (F) and (H), and you have a fifty-fifty shot of guessing the correct answer before you move on. To repeat, the correct answer is (G) because *less than* should be used with time or rate.

HOT MESS

Some of the most challenging questions on the English Test underline most, if not all, of the sentence. It can be difficult to spot what the question is testing when *so much* is underlined, is changing, and sounds awful. Here's an example to clarify what Hot Mess questions look like.

> *Having been promoted brevet, or honorary, Brigadier General during the Civil War, George Armstrong Custer, Seventh Cavalry leader to the catastrophe at the Little Big Horn River, actually was a Colonel at the time of his death.*

These questions usually involve picking the correct form of the modifiers and placing them in the correct location. Review the rules of modifiers and apply a strategy for tackling these, and Hot Mess questions aren't so bad.

First up, more information on modifiers.

Modifiers

A modifier is a word, phrase, or clause that describes something.

Adjectives modify nouns.

> *I gave a* meticulous *response.*

Adverbs modify verbs and adjectives, and some adverbs can modify other adverbs.

> *I* responded thoroughly. *The teacher appreciated my* thoroughly *meticulous response.* *She* almost always *likes meticulous responses.*

Placement of Modifiers

Adjectives should immediately precede the noun they describe. When two adjectives modify a noun, use *and* or a comma in between them.

> *I gave a* meticulous *and* thorough *response. I gave a* meticulous, thorough *response.*

When an adjective modifies a compound noun, do not use either *and* or a comma in between the adjective and the compound noun.

> *The teacher gave a difficult final exam.*

When adverbs modify verbs, they can be placed before or after the verb, *and* can even be separated from the verb by other elements of the sentence.

> *The teacher* quickly *graded the exams. The teacher graded the exams* quickly.

Misplaced Modifiers

A modifier in the wrong place describes the wrong item and creates ambiguity and confusion.

> **Staring in panic at the final exam**, *my knees started to shake.*

Knees can't panic, stare, or take a final. A modifying phrase set off by a comma at the beginning or end of a sentence should be consistent with the subject of the sentence.

> **Staring in panic at the final exam**, *I felt my knees start to shake.* That makes a lot more sense.

When adjectives are misplaced, they create a situation that is either wrong or makes no sense.

> The **unfinished** student's exam earned an F. Huh?

> The student's **unfinished** exam earned an F. That makes a lot more sense.

Adverbs have more flexibility in where they can be placed, but changing their placement can affect the meaning of a sentence.

> She **almost** failed all of her exams.

In other words, she got a D– on every exam.

> She failed **almost** all of her exams.

In other words, she got an F on most of her exams but earned a higher grade on at least one of them. Both sentences make sense, but the meaning changes depending on the placement of the adverb.

Strategy for Hot Mess Questions

1. Use the answer choices to compare the changes in the form and placement of modifiers.
2. Place modifiers as close as possible to the items they describe and apply comma rules correctly.
3. When a modifying phrase is offset by a comma at the beginning or end of a sentence, identify the subject and confirm the modifying phrase is consistent with the subject.
4. Use the 4 C's: look for a *concise* choice that makes a *complete* sentence, is *consistent* with the rest of the passage, and makes the meaning most *clear*.

Use the strategy on an example.

Bill Gates, <u>a committed deeply vocal global</u>
₇
<u>philanthropist,</u> made his fortune as the founder of
₇
Microsoft.

7. **F.** NO CHANGE.
   G. deep global philanthropist committed and vocal,
   H. committed global vocal deep philanthropist,
   J. vocal, deeply committed global philanthropist,

Here's How to Crack It

Consider each choice in comparison to the others, noting the form and placement of the modifiers. The adverb *deeply* in (F) and (J) changes to the adjective *deep* in (G) and (H), and the adjectives *committed, vocal,* and *global* move all around. The modifiers in (G) and (H) are all adjectives, but there are no commas separating them. Eliminate (G) and (H) because they do not follow comma rules. Compare (F) and (J). Choice (F) has no commas, but (J) uses a comma to separate *vocal* from *deeply committed* (adverb modifying an adjective), both of which describe *global philanthropist* (which is a compound noun) and is the correct answer.

Try another.

<u>Brought by me to my favorite restaurants,</u>
₈
<u>all in Greektown, I started being taught by Beatrice</u>
₈
<u>how to cook the most popular Greek dishes.</u>
₈

8. **A.** NO CHANGE
   B. Bringing Beatrice to my favorite restaurants, all in Greektown, she started teaching me how to cook the most popular Greek dishes.
   C. Teaching me how to cook the most popular Greek dishes, Beatrice was brought by me to my favorite restaurants, all in Greektown.
   D. I brought Beatrice to my favorite restaurants, all in Greektown, and she taught me how to cook the most popular Greek dishes.

Here's How to Crack It

The sentence begins with an introductory modifying phrase in (A), (B), and (C). Choices (A) and (B) both use a modifying phrase that is not consistent with the subjects of their sentences, so eliminate both (A) and (B). The modifying phrase in (C) is consistent with the subject of the sentence. Compare (C) and (D). Choice (C) uses the passive voice (*Beatrice was brought by me*); (D) uses the active voice (*I brought Beatrice*). Choice (D) is correct because it is more concise.

Now try these strategies on your own. Go online to your Student Tools and answer the Chapter 7 Drills.

Summary

o   Questions on vocabulary feature synonyms, closely related words, or homophones. Context determines the correct choice.

o   Questions on idioms require choosing the correct preposition for the idiom. Studying the list of common idioms can help.

o   Questions on countable and uncountable nouns follow rules regarding which adjectives work with which type of noun.

o   Questions that underline most or all of a sentence usually require choosing the correct form and placement of modifiers.

Chapter 8
English Drills

Drills 1 and 2 are made up of select questions from different passages to allow you to work on a variety of topics. These are not representational English passages, and the bars indicate where text has been removed.

You'll be able to test your skills on a full English passage in Drill 3.

DRILL 1

Though it may seem a feat of nearly superhuman strength, the International Association of Ultrarunners (IAU) 24-Hour Run has been gaining popularity since its first European race in 1994. In this race, participants run as far as they can within a 24-hour period, with some running over 160 miles within the span.

Mami Kudo, who is now known as one of the great "ultramarathoners," actually has a pretty normal life.[1] Kudo is a friendly bank teller by day, who, like many people, has a passion for running. Even with her day job, however, Kudo is frequently invited to ultramarathons, and her relatively advanced age of 49 has

misleaded much of her competitors into thinking[2] she is too old to win such races. Kudo may be older than many ultramarathoners, but her age didn't prevent her from winning the race in 2009 and setting a new record, an incredible distance of 158.6 miles. [3]

1. Given that all the choices are true, which one provides the best transition between the preceding paragraph and this paragraph?
   - **A.** NO CHANGE
   - **B.** who also competes in 48-hour races and runs marathons, is Japanese.
   - **C.** who has incredible stamina, was born and trains in Japan.
   - **D.** a minor celebrity in her home country of Japan, likes to keep fit.

2. **F.** NO CHANGE
   G. miss lead many
   H. misled many
   J. misled much

3. Given that all the following statements are true, which one, if added here, would most specifically elaborate how Kudo uses her age to her advantage?
   - **A.** Kudo's approach is actually very similar for the 24-hour and the 48-hour races.
   - **B.** Kudo is actually not alone: the American who won the men's race in 2013 was 45.
   - **C.** She knows that running is a mental sport above all, and much of her focus is on keeping a positive dialogue with herself.
   - **D.** While younger runners burn themselves out by going too quickly too early, Kudo has learned through experience how to maintain a steady pace and outrun all of them.

In 2014, <u>at a race to be held in Soochow,</u>
₄
Kudo was heavily favored to win again, further

cementing her position as one of the greatest

ultramarathoners of all time.

4. Given that all the choices are true, which one clearly suggests that it is particularly noteworthy that Kudo is still favored for the 2014 race?

- **F.** NO CHANGE
- **G.** alongside the American Jon Olsen in the men's race,
- **H.** though the Japanese team as a whole would likely win second place,
- **J.** despite the more competitive field that the sport's popularity had attracted,

---

Sometimes, <u>because the horse insists on the</u>
₅
presence of his "pet," the goat will follow him all

the way to the paddock. Kept calm before

the race, <u>they are carrying the jockey to victory.</u>
₆

5. A. NO CHANGE
- **B.** the horse insisted
- **C.** the horse insists
- **D.** the horse who insists

6. F. NO CHANGE
- **G.** the horse carries
- **H.** they are carried by
- **J.** the horse is carrying

The stable goat has a long lineage in horse

racing. Some suggest that the stable goat may

have been used to calm horses before classical

Greek chariot races. We don't really know. We

can be much more certain, however, about <u>it's</u>
₇
more recent history.

7. A. NO CHANGE
- **B.** its
- **C.** their
- **D.** our

Although the ploy has died out, the saying

persists, and any racehorse trainer will tell you

that taking a horse's goat <u>away before a race, can</u>
₈
have very bad consequences.

8. F. NO CHANGE
- **G.** away, before a race
- **H.** away before a race
- **J.** away, before a race,

Full of tenderness and affection, <u>good horse</u>
<u>psychologists noting these essential friendships</u>
and show us a side of that psychology that we
may not have even suspected was there.

9. A. NO CHANGE
   B. good horse psychologists are saying how essential these friendships are
   C. these friendships are being called essential to good horse psychology
   D. these friendships are essential to good horse psychology

DRILL 2

When my <u>aunt, was a research chemist,</u> gave
me my first chemistry set, I set to work right
away, hoping to get proficient enough that she'd
start taking me along with her to work.

1. A. NO CHANGE
   B. aunt,
   C. aunt was
   D. aunt who was

"We all struggle at first," she told me, as she sat
next to me in my <u>"laboratory" nearly defeated,</u>
I watched as she set up one of the simple
experiments.

2. F. NO CHANGE
   G. "laboratory," near defeat,
   H. "laboratory." Near defeat,
   J. "laboratory," nearly defeated

Once she had completed the experiment,
she held up a small test tube of the red food
dye that I had slaved for weeks to try to create.
<u>Nevertheless,</u> she held up a tube of blue dye that
she had made during the same experiment. The
two colors, right next to each other in this

3. A. NO CHANGE
   B. Then,
   C. Still,
   D. Notwithstanding,

<u>way complimented</u> each other beautifully.

4. F. NO CHANGE
   G. way complemented
   H. way, complemented
   J. way, complimented

I had been combining all the elements haphazardly, but she'd combined all the elements to form the base and then allowed the coloring agent to <u>intertwine</u> with that base. In other words, once she created the foundation, then came all
₅

5. A. NO CHANGE
  B. mingle
  C. experiment
  D. react

the little <u>tweaks, that</u> could begin to produce a world of many colors.
₆

6. F. NO CHANGE
  G. tweaks that
  H. tweaks, that,
  J. tweaks that,

Although rap and political office have not often met <u>before, hip-hop artist, Wyclef Jean</u> has made a career out of his close involvement with both.
₇

7. A. NO CHANGE
  B. before, hip-hop artist Wyclef Jean,
  C. before, hip-hop artist Wyclef Jean
  D. before hip-hop artists, Wyclef Jean,

<u>As</u> Jean's 2006 song "If I Was President"
₈
would foretell many of the platforms on which he would run in 2010, long before he had any idea that he would do so.

8. F. NO CHANGE
  G. When
  H. Although
  J. DELETE the underlined portion.

While Jean has always been politically active, his true awakening came after the massive earthquake in Haiti in 2010. His EP of the same year, *If I Were President: My Haitian Experience*, gave a stark portrayal of a nation that had been devastated by an earthquake, a devastation made worse for then President René Préval's weak <u>9</u> response to the crisis. Jean felt that Préval had not done nearly enough to help Haiti emerge from the rubble. As a result, Jean led fundraising efforts in the United States, contributing most notably to "We Are the World 25 for Haiti," <u>which one *Washington Post* critic called the worst song of all time.</u>

9. **A.** NO CHANGE
   B. by than
   C. by then
   D. for than

10. Given that all the choices are true, which one best concludes the paragraph and reaffirms Jean's commitment to Haitian improvement?

   F. NO CHANGE
   G. a song whose proceeds went to earthquake relief.
   H. which was sold digitally on iTunes.
   J. a remake of a song that had raised funds for Africa.

This belief in the power of an organization to support Haiti—both its infrastructure and its residents—<u>were the main motivations</u> for Jean's candidacy for the 2010 Haitian presidential election.

11. **A.** NO CHANGE
   B. was the main motivation
   C. were the main motivation
   D. having been the main motivation

DRILL 3

Now it is time to practice your skills on a full English passage.

Migrations by GPS

[1]

Every winter, the Egyptian vulture migrates from its summer home [1] to the warmer climes of southern Africa.

1. At this point, the writer is considering adding the following accurate information:

   > in Europe, West Africa, and Asia

   Should the writer make this addition here?

   A. Yes, because it completes the sentence naming both the summer and winter homes of the Egyptian vulture.
   B. Yes, because it shows how the Egyptian vulture's endangered status is linked to its widespread habitat.
   C. No, because it provides an unnecessary detail about the habitat that is already implied in the vulture's name.
   D. No, because it suggests that the Egyptian vulture is a healthy enough species to migrate.

Because the vulture is so large, it flies overly large bodies of water as rarely as possible. Although these birds come from three different continents and migrate to a relatively underdeveloped region, their face with extinction by the use of pesticides in all the regions through which they fly.

2. F. NO CHANGE
   G. over
   H. higher
   J. high

3. A. NO CHANGE
   B. then facing with
   C. the face for them of
   D. they are faced with

[2]

[1] Though the boom in agricultural pesticides has been good for farmers, it has indifferently caused significant harm to Egyptian vulture populations. [2] Estimates for the remaining number of vultures can be as low as 10,000. [3] The scientists placed GPS devices inside three vultures and have tracked

the patterns of migration by following them from

4. F. NO CHANGE
   G. indecisively
   H. industrially
   J. indirectly

5. A. NO CHANGE
   B. the birds' migration patterns
   C. them by means of a tracking device that gives positional coordinates
   D. the vultures as they were migrating with the devices on them

Turkey to southern Africa and having mapped the routes. [4] Since 2012,

6. F. NO CHANGE
   G. mapped
   H. mapping
   J. they would map

a group of researchers, from University of Utah's Department of Biology and its Sekercioglu Laboratory

7. A. NO CHANGE
   B. researchers from University of Utah's Department of Biology,
   C. researchers, from University of Utah's Department of Biology,
   D. researchers from University of Utah's Department of Biology

has been conducting a study that will help to better understand Egyptian vulture behavior and

8. F. NO CHANGE
   G. is conducting
   H. have been conducting
   J. been conducting

to save the species from extinction. [9]

[3]

The tracking devices download the vulture's positions at certain intervals, showing that the vultures have traveled through as many as seven countries in the Middle East. [A] The scientists were fascinated to see, however, that the three birds they captured took very different flight patterns. One bird, Igdir, was crossing from the Arabian Peninsula to the Horn of Africa within a month of observation. [B] Another, Aras, spent a much longer time around the area which he was
10

captured. As the birds complete their migrations to Africa, the University of Utah website
11
updates its maps and blogs to show the birds' movements. [C]

[4]

The researchers are interested in bringing public attention to the Egyptian vultures. [D] They believe that in doing so, they can bring attention to the risks of wide-scale pesticide use, which has reduced the population of Egyptian vultures to less than 15,000 worldwide. The
12
pesticides improve farms' produce, but the collateral damage may outweigh the benefit. Vultures and other animals are essential to a

9. For the sake of the logic and coherence of this paragraph, Sentence 3 should be placed:
   A. where it is now.
   B. before Sentence 1.
   C. before Sentence 2.
   D. after Sentence 4.

10. F. NO CHANGE
    G. that
    H. where
    J. staying

11. A. NO CHANGE
    B. Africa the University of Utah website,
    C. Africa the University of Utah website
    D. Africa, the University of Utah website,

12. F. NO CHANGE
    G. fewer as
    H. less then
    J. few than

thriving ecosystem, and the University of Utah scientists hope to <u>save some of these endangered</u> <u>species.</u>
13
13

13. **A.** NO CHANGE
    B. prevent this outcome.
    C. put an end to all of it.
    D. improve life on Earth.

Questions 14 and 15 ask about the preceding passage as a whole.

---

14. The writer is considering adding the following sentence to the essay:

    > These countries include Azerbaijan, Iran, Iraq, Syria, Jordan, Saudi Arabia, and Yemen.

    If the writer were to add this sentence, it would most logically be placed at:

    F. Point A in Paragraph 3.
    G. Point B in Paragraph 3.
    H. Point C in Paragraph 3.
    J. Point D in Paragraph 4.

15. Suppose the writer's primary goal had been to describe the role the Egyptian vulture plays in its ecosystem. Would this essay accomplish that goal?

    A. Yes, because it shows clearly how the Egyptian vulture improves the ecosystem of Yemen and Eastern Turkey.
    B. Yes, because it describes how the scientists' plans have succeeded in improving the ecosystem in Turkey.
    C. No, because it instead focuses on a plan to save the Egyptian vulture and does not detail the vulture's role within the ecosystem.
    D. No, because it instead concerns itself with the migratory patterns of the Egyptian vulture.

ENGLISH DRILL ANSWERS AND EXPLANATIONS

Drill 1

1. **A**   Identify the purpose of the correct choice as stated in the question, which asks for a choice that provides *the best transition between the preceding paragraph and this paragraph*. The next few sentences of the paragraph discuss Kudo's day job and her "normal" life, which makes (A) the best transition.

2. **H**   *Misleaded* is not a word, so (F) can be eliminated, and *miss lead* is a misspelling of the word *misled*, so (G) can be eliminated. *Many* is for things that can be counted, and *much* is for things that cannot. Since *competitors* can be counted, this sentence needs the word *many*, as in (H).

3. **D**   Identify the purpose of the correct choice as stated in the question, which asks for a choice that indicates *how Kudo uses her age to her advantage*. The only choice that addresses Kudo's age advantage at all is (D), which talks about *younger runners* and the *things* that Kudo's age and *experience* have allowed her to learn.

4. **J**   Identify the purpose of the correct choice as stated in the question, which asks for a choice that *suggests that it is particularly noteworthy that Kudo is still favored*. Choice (J) is the most effective: although the field has grown more competitive, Kudo is *still* one of the best in it.

5. **A**   The conjunction *because* is needed to make the first idea incomplete. Otherwise, two complete ideas are linked incorrectly by a comma. The correct answer is (A).

6. **G**   The modifying phrase *Kept calm before the race* refers to the horse, so *the horse* must be the first words after the comma. Choices (F) and (H) create a misplaced modifier, while (J) switches the tense.

7. **B**   Choice (B) is correct because it is a singular possessive pronoun that refers to *the stable goat*, a singular noun. Choice (A) is the contraction *it is*, which cannot be used in this context. Choice (C) is plural, and while (D) is a possessive pronoun, it's in the plural form, which doesn't match the singular goat.

8. **H**   If you can't cite a reason to use commas, don't use them. There's no need for commas in the underlined portion, so any choice with commas can be eliminated. Only (H) is left.

9. **D**   The modifying phrase *Full of tenderness and affection* has to refer correctly to the words after the comma. The context of the rest of the sentence makes clear that it refers to the *friendship*, which eliminates (A) and (B). Choice (D) is correct because it's more concise than (C).

Drill 2

1. **B** In this portion of the sentence, the subject is *my aunt* and the verb is *gave*, so there's no reason to introduce another verb as (A), (C), and (D) do. Choice (B) is correct because it removes the verb and adds the necessary first comma needed to offset the unnecessary *a research chemist*.

2. **H** Use the Vertical Line Test. The first idea, *"We all struggle at first," she told me, as she sat next to me in my "laboratory,"* is complete. Evaluate the second idea in (H), the only one with STOP punctuation. *Near defeat, I watched as she set up one of the simple experiments.* The period works in between the two complete ideas, so (H) is correct.

3. **B** Choose a transition that is consistent with the meaning of the sentence. Choices (A), (C), and (D) suggest a contrast, but there is none in the passage. Only (B), *then*, shows a simple continuation from one event to another, as the passage itself contains.

4. **H** The word *complement* means "to complete" or "to go with"; the word *compliment* means "to say something nice." Therefore, *complement* is the correct word in this sentence, thus eliminating (F) and (J). Choice (H) is correct because the portion of the sentence, *right next to each other in this way*, is unnecessary to the meaning of the sentence and should therefore be set off with commas.

5. **D** The correct word in this sentence is *react*, as it describes a chemical reaction between two different things. The words in the other choices are not consistent with the context. The correct answer is (D).

6. **G** Choice (G) is correct because there is no need for a comma. If you can't cite a reason to use commas, don't use them.

7. **C** Two rules are being tested in this question. An introductory idea has to be followed by a comma. In this case, the introductory idea ends at the word *before*, so (D) can be eliminated. The words *Wyclef Jean* are essential to the sentence (that is, the sentence would not be complete without them), so there should be no commas around the words, eliminating (A) and (B). Only (C) has appropriately placed commas.

8. **J** The sentence as written does not give a complete idea. The only way to make this idea complete is to remove the word at the beginning, as (J) indicates. Whenever you see DELETE as an option, find a reason NOT to pick it. It is often correct, so unless you have a very good reason not to, go with DELETE.

9. **C** The correct idiom is *made worse by* rather than *made worse for*, thus eliminating (A) and (D). The word *then* is used in this sentence to mean *at that time*, so *then* is correct, as (C) has it. The word *than* in (B) is used for comparisons.

10. **G** Identify the purpose of the correct choice as stated in the question, which asks for the choice that *reaffirms Jean's commitment to Haitian improvement*. The only choice that addresses anything relating to Haiti is (G), which refers to the Haitian earthquake. The other choices do not fulfill the purpose stated in the question.

11. **B** The subject of this sentence is *belief*, which requires the singular verb *was*, eliminating (A) and (C). Choice (D) creates an incomplete idea, so it too can be eliminated. Only (B) remains, correctly using the singular verb *was* and the singular noun *motivation*.

Drill 3

1. **A** The non-underlined portion identifies the location of the summer home as *the warmer climes of southern Africa*. The proposed addition would present a useful counterpoint in adding the vulture's points of origin, so the writer *should* make the addition here, eliminating (C) and (D). Choice (B) can also be eliminated because it does not describe the proposed addition accurately. Only (A) remains, as it correctly states that the addition should be made and gives a correct reason for this addition.

2. **G** The Egyptian vulture flies *over* bodies of water, making (G) the correct answer. The other words provide adjectives and adverbs that do not work in this particular context.

3. **D** The sentence needs a complete idea, and a complete idea must have a subject and verb. Only (D) provides a subject and verb.

4. **J** There is a contrast in this sentence between the good that pesticides have done for farmers and the unintended negative consequences that the pesticides have had on vultures. Given this contrast, the words *indifferently*, *indecisively*, and *industrially* do not work in this sentence because they do not refer to these consequences. Only (J), *indirectly*, can work with the words *caused significant harm*.

5. **B** The four answer choices say essentially the same thing, so choose the most concise one that is grammatically correct. The correct answer is (B).

6. **G** The earlier verb in this context is *have tracked*, so this verb should be consistent. *Mapped* in (G) works, with the helping verb *have* applying to both *tracked* and *mapped*.

7. **D** If you cannot cite a reason to use commas, don't use them. In this case, all the information is necessary to the meaning of the sentence, and there is no other reason to introduce a comma. The correct answer is (D).

8. **F** The subject is *group*, a collective noun and therefore singular. Thus, the verb must be singular, which eliminates (H). Choice (J) is missing the helping verb *has*, which leaves the sentence incomplete. The action described in this sentence began in 2012 and continues into the present, so the present perfect is needed over the present tense in (G).

9. **D** Sentence 3 discusses the details of the experiment described in Sentence 4; therefore, Sentence 3 will need to come after Sentence 4, or at the end of the paragraph. The correct answer is (D).

10. **H** The underlined pronoun refers back to *the area*, a place. Choose the pronoun *where*, (H), over the pronouns that refer to things, *which* and *that*. *Staying* in (J) doesn't link the two parts of the sentence together the way the pronoun, acting as a conjunction, does.

11. **A** This sentence contains an introductory idea, *As the birds complete their migrations to Africa*, that must be followed by a comma, thus eliminating (B) and (C). Eliminate (D) because there is no reason to put a comma after the word *website*. The answer is (A).

12. **F** *Less* is used for noncountable things, such as *the population. Fewer* is used for countable things, but the choice is moot in this question since there is no viable choice containing the word *fewer. Than* is used for comparisons, and *then* is used for time or progression. Choice (F) is therefore the only viable answer.

13. **A** Choice (A) is specific and makes the sentence the clearest. Choices (B) and (C) contain ambiguous pronouns (*this, it*) that damage the meaning of the sentence, and (D) changes the meaning of the sentence altogether.

14. **F** The first sentence of Paragraph 3 ends by mentioning *as many as seven countries in the Middle East*. The list of countries in the proposed sentence should therefore go after this mention of the *seven countries*, or at Point A. The correct answer is (A).

15. **C** While the passage as a whole is about the Egyptian vulture, it does not describe the vulture's role within its ecosystem in any detail, which eliminates (A) and (B). Choice (D) is incorrect because the passage does more than just describe migration patterns. Choice (C) is correct because the reason provided describes the content of the passage accurately.

Part III
ACT Math

Chapter 9
Introduction to the ACT Mathematics Test

The second section of the ACT will always be the Math test. To perform your best, you'll need to become familiar with the structure and strategy of the ACT Math test. In this chapter, we discuss the types of questions you can expect to see and how you can use organizational strategy, estimation, and elimination skills to improve your Math score.

The ACT Math Test is always the second section of the ACT.

If you're aiming for the highest scores on the ACT, you probably already have a broad range of math skills. In fact, you probably already know the math required to answer almost every question on the typical ACT Math Test. So why aren't you already scoring a 36 on Math?

A student with strong math skills is often accustomed to solving problems with what we might call "brute force brainpower": see a question, attack it, try methods to solve it until you find a solution, and then move on to the next question. While this approach can get you a pretty good score on the ACT Math Test, you'll need to refine this approach with a few strategies to get to the highest scores.

For instance, students sometimes underestimate the easy and medium questions, not taking them as seriously as the "hard" questions near the end. But to get the highest scores, you can't afford errors on *any* of the easy and medium questions. So, you'll need to watch out for traps on those questions that might lead you into careless errors. And, of course, you'll need good time-management strategies, so that you can move through questions efficiently and ensure you have the time to get to the correct answer on the longer, tougher questions.

The first step is to make sure you understand the structure of the ACT Math Test and some fundamental strategies that will increase your test savvy. This chapter will discuss the types of questions you should expect and the ways you can use organizational strategy, estimation, and elimination skills to improve your efficiency and accuracy, and to earn a higher Math score.

WHAT TO EXPECT ON THE MATH TEST

You will have 60 minutes to answer 60 multiple-choice questions based on "topics covered in typical high-school classes." For those of you who aren't sure if you went to a typical high school, these questions break down into rather precise areas of knowledge.

Preparing for Higher Math (34–36 questions)
- Number and Quantity (4–6 questions)
- Algebra (7–9 questions)
- Functions (7–9 questions)
- Geometry (7–9 questions)
- Statistics and Probability (5–7 questions)

Integrating Essential Skills (24–26 questions)—This is what the ACT calls the Math you learned before high school, including percentages, rates, proportions, and much of geometry.

Modeling (15+ questions)—These are what the ACT calls Word Problems—questions that require you to use math to solve hypothetical situations. These questions are also counted in the above.

WHAT NOT TO EXPECT ON THE MATH TEST

Unlike the SAT, the ACT does *not* provide any formulas at the beginning of the Math Test. This means you need to memorize those formulas so you can recall them quickly as needed throughout the ACT Math Test. Does this mean that the ACT Math Test is harder than the SAT Math section? Not necessarily: since the SAT includes those formulas at the beginning of each Math section, the SAT math questions need to be trickier than they might otherwise be. On the ACT, a question could simply test whether you know the formula, so the Math Test doesn't need to be quite as tricky.

A NOTE ON CALCULATORS

The ACT allows calculators on the Math section, but it prohibits, among others, the TI-89, TI-92, and TI-Nspire CAS models. Be sure to check which calculators are allowed before you take the test! Your calculator can definitely come in handy for complicated calculations; to be efficient on the test, you'll probably want to use a calculator occasionally. But be careful, especially on the early questions! Some of them are designed with "calculator traps" in mind—careless errors the test-writers know you might make when you just dive into a problem on your calculator. Let's look at an example.

27. Given the function $r(s) = 5s^2 - s - 7$, what is $r(-4)$?

    A.   −91
    B.   −83
    C.   69
    D.   77
    E.   397

How to Solve It

This problem can be solved manually or with the calculator—whichever you prefer! But if you use a calculator, be careful with that −4. What you punch into your calculator should look something like this:

$$5(-4)^2 - (-4) - 7$$

When working with negative numbers or fractions, make doubly sure that you use parentheses. If not, a lot of weird stuff can happen, and unfortunately all of the weird, wrong stuff that can happen is reflected in the wrong answer choices. If you ran this equation and found 77, (D), you got the right answer. If not, go back and figure out where you made your calculator mistake.

Types of Calculators

Throughout the rest of the Math chapters, we discuss ways to solve calculator-friendly questions in an accurate and manageable way. Because TI-89, TI-92, and TI-Nspire CAS model calculators are not allowed on the ACT, we will show you how to solve problems on the TI-83. If you don't plan to use a TI-83 on the test, we recommend you make sure your calculator is acceptable for use on the test and that it can do the following:

- handle positive, negative, and fractional exponents
- use parentheses
- graph simple functions
- convert fractions to decimals and vice versa
- change a linear equation into $y = mx + b$ form

> Use your calculator, but use it wisely. Be careful with negative numbers and fractions.

THE PRINCETON REVIEW APPROACH

Because the test is so predictable, the best way to prepare for ACT Math is with

- a thorough review of the very specific information and question types that come up repeatedly.
- an understanding of The Princeton Review's test-taking strategies and techniques.

In each Math chapter in this book, you'll find a mixture of review and technique, with a sprinkling of ACT-like problems. In addition to working through the problems in this book, we strongly suggest you practice our techniques on some real ACT practice tests.

Let's begin with some general strategies.

Order of Difficulty: Still Personal Even for High Scorers

Why should a high-scoring student care about the order of difficulty on the ACT Math Test? If you've got the math skills to do all—or almost all—of the questions on the ACT Math Test, you may think the best approach for you is to dive straight in and do the questions in order. That's not necessarily the best approach, though.

The Math Test is the only part of the ACT that is presented in Order of Difficulty (OOD). What this means is that the easier questions tend to be a bit earlier in the exam, and the harder questions tend to be later. None of the other tests have an OOD, so they are all about Personal Order of Difficulty (POOD).

The Math OOD is helpful for planning how you will attack this part of the ACT. Just because the earlier questions are generally easier does not mean they are safe to move through quickly. Not every question near the beginning will be easy, and questions that are easy for one student may be difficult for another. Regardless, if you're aiming for the highest scores, you need to take every question seriously. It would be a shame to get all those "hard" questions right, and miss the top score because you made careless errors rushing through the earlier questions.

So what makes a hard question hard? Is it hard because it's a long word problem, or because it tests an arcane concept that you haven't reviewed in years? Only the very hardest questions will be both. So even on the Math Test of the ACT, you still need to use your POOD to adjust your approach for different types of questions. Know what sort of questions tend to lead you into careless errors, and slow down on them. Work every step of the problem methodically, showing your work at every step.

Now, Later, Never

Hard questions generally take longer to work through than easy questions. That's obvious, but as we've seen, the definition of an "Easy" question is a tough one to pin down. That's why you'll want to be careful with ACT's Order of Difficulty on the Math Test. The no-brainer approach is to open the test booklet and work questions 1 through 60 in order, but you can help to lock in the higher scores by outsmarting the test. You'll have a lot easier time drawing your own road map for this test rather than letting ACT guide you.

Of course, a lot of the easy questions will be near the beginning, but they won't all be. So, when you arrive at each question, you'll want to first determine whether it is a Now, Later, or Never question. Do the Now questions immediately: they're the freebies, the ones you know how to do and can do quickly and accurately. Skip any questions you think might take you a bit longer, or that test unfamiliar concepts—save them for Later. Make sure you first get all the points you can on the problems you know you can do, no matter what the question number.

Once you've done all the Now questions, go back to all the ones you left for Later. But you should be careful on these as well. For both Now and Later questions, don't rush and make careless errors. On the other hand, if you find yourself spinning your wheels on a question, circle the question number and come back to it at the end if you have time. Don't get stuck on a particular problem. In a 60-minute exam, think of how much it can cost you to spend 5 minutes on a single problem!

Finally, there's no problem with leaving a question or two behind in the Never category. But wait, what's a Never question for a top scorer? Sometimes a question might be on a topic that you simply didn't cover; maybe you missed the week your teacher taught matrices, or logarithms, or the unit circle. Or for whatever reason, you have no idea how to approach a problem. In that case, your time is likely better spent on other questions (and it's still possible to get a 34 or better on the Math Test even if you miss a question or two).

Note, of course, that you should **never leave a question blank** on the ACT, since there is no penalty for guessing. If you skip any questions, fill them in with a Letter of the Day: choose one pair of letters and bubble in all blanks this way. For example, always bubble in (A) and (F) or (B) and (G). This will maximize your chance of getting some of the guesses right.

Chapter 10
Geometry Fundamentals

The ACT test writers tell us the breakdown of numbers of questions into broad categories like Preparing for Higher Math, Integrating Essential Skills, and Modeling. It's difficult to know where any one question may fall within these categories, but it is clear that many of the questions test concepts in Plane Geometry and Coordinate Geometry. Many of the concepts you know well can be tested in tricky ways on the ACT, so you need to focus on how ACT presents these topics. This chapter will review a cross section of those formulas and topics and give you a strategic approach to apply those rules on the ACT.

Questions on the ACT Math Test can be divided into two categories: word problems and Plug and Chug problems. Plug and Chug problems are questions that present you with math problems you can just manipulate and solve, while word problems require you to translate the words of the problem into math before you start solving.

Plug and Chug problems often test skills from the following areas:

- Math Fundamentals (vocabulary, number theory, prime numbers, factors, multiples, exponents, and roots)
- Plane Geometry
- Coordinate Geometry
- Trigonometry

If you are aiming for a high score on the ACT, you likely already know the key terms and definitions that make up Math Fundamentals. Therefore, this chapter reviews the material you need to know in the geometry areas above in order to earn the highest scores on the ACT Math Test. We will focus on some strategies you may not be using yet and some ways you may get tripped up when working Plane Geometry and Coordinate Geometry questions. If you need to review geometry facts and formulas, check out the list in your Student Tools.

PLANE GEOMETRY

The ACT Math Test includes about 14 questions covering plane geometry. While some of these questions will cover complex shapes or advanced formulas, it's helpful to realize that most of the questions will test the <u>same</u> basic shapes and rules. Harder geometry questions generally just combine simple rules and shapes in ways that make them hard to identify. *Noticing this pattern is the key to solving ACT geometry questions quickly and accurately.*

Attacking ACT Geometry Questions

High-scoring students have a tendency to start solving geometry problems in their head as they go. As soon as you see a geometric shape and some values, it's tempting to simply start calculating everything you can about the figure. As often happens on the ACT, though, *thinking* turns out to be a bad—or at least an inefficient—way to start off any given problem.

Instead, always attack geometry problems by using these simple steps, and you will be amazed at how much more directly—and simply—you will arrive at the solution.

Step 1: Know the Question

Read through the entire problem before you begin calculating. Underline the actual question. Leave the *thinking* until later.

Step 2: Let the Answers Help

Take a look at the answers. Sometimes the form of the answers provides a good clue about how to efficiently work the problem.

Step 3: Break the Problem into Bite-Sized Pieces

Start back at the beginning of the problem, and work through the problem piece by piece. Start by labeling all the information in the problem on the figure (or drawing the figure, if one isn't provided). Next, write down all the geometry formulas related to the problem, fill in the information you know, and let the formulas show you what to solve for next.

POE and Ballparking

Step 2 of the approach to geometry questions ("Let the Answers Help") is a key to POE and Ballparking on geometry questions. Ballparking's not just a tool to use if you aren't sure how to do a question—it's also a powerful way of getting through questions quickly and easily.

Why spend three minutes fighting through a question when it can be solved quickly and easily by simply looking at the answers and estimating from the figure? The time and brainpower you save on questions like this can be used to attack the hardest questions that you need some extra time to work through.

Scale Matters

Although the ACT says that geometry figures are "NOT necessarily drawn to scale," most of them usually are—at least enough to do some estimating. The exception is problems that are specifically testing rules about shapes: if a problem asks what *must be true* about the figure above, usually you can't trust the scale of the figure at all. For example, look at angle *NLM* below.

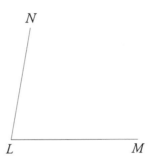

Obviously, you don't know exactly how big this angle is, but it would be easy to compare it with an angle whose measure you *do* know exactly, such as a 90-degree angle. Angle *NLM* is clearly a bit less than 90°. Now look at the following question, which asks about the same angle *NLM*.

1. In the figure below, *O*, *N*, and *M* are collinear. If the lengths of $\overline{ON}$ and $\overline{NL}$ are the same, and the measure of angle *LON* is 30° and angle *LMN* is 40°, what is the measure of angle *NLM* ?

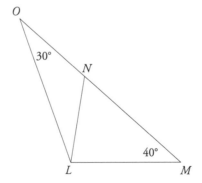

    A. 30°
    B. 80°
    C. 90°
    D. 110°
    E. 120°

Here's How to Crack It

Start with Step 1: Know the question. Underline "what is the measure of angle *NLM* ?" and even mark the angle on your figure. You don't want to answer for the wrong angle. Now move to Step 2 and focus on eliminating answer choices that don't make sense. We've already decided that ∠*NLM* is a little less than 90°, which means we can eliminate (C), (D), and (E). How much less than 90°? 30° is a third of 90. Could ∠*NLM* be that small? No way! The answer to this question must be (B).

In this case, it wasn't necessary to do any "real" geometry at all to get the question right, and it took about half the time. ACT has to give you credit for right answers no matter how you get them. Revenge is sweet. What's more, if you worked this problem the "real" way, you might have picked one of the other answers: as you can imagine, every answer choice gives some partial answer that you would've seen as you worked the problem.

Let's Do It Again

2. In the figure below, if $\overline{AB} = 27$, $\overline{CD} = 20$, and the area of triangle $ADC = 240$, what is the area of polygon $ABCD$?

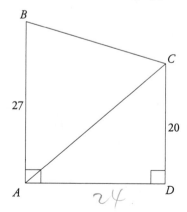

F. 420
G. 480
H. 540
J. 564
K. 1,128

Here's How to Crack It

Start with Step 1: Know the question. Underline "what is the area of polygon *ABCD*?" This polygon is not a conventional figure, but if we had to choose one figure that the polygon resembled, we might pick a rectangle. Try drawing a line at a right angle from the line segment $\overline{AB}$ so that it touches point *C*, thus creating a rectangle. It should look like this:

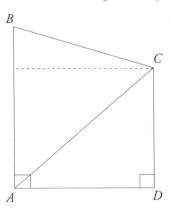

The area of polygon *ABCD* is equal to the area of the rectangle you've just formed, plus a little bit at the top. The problem tells you that the area of triangle *ADC* is 240. What is the area of the rectangle you just created? If you said 480, you are exactly right, whether you knew the geometric rules that applied or whether you just measured it with your eyes.

So the area of the rectangle is 480. Roughly speaking, then, what should the area of the polygon be? A little more. Let's look at the answer choices. Choices (F) and (G) are either less than or equal to 480; get rid of them. Choices (H) and (J) both seem possible; they are both a little more than 480; let's hold on to them. Choice (K) seems pretty crazy. We want more than 480, but 1,128 is ridiculous.

——————————————————————————

The answer to this question is (J). To get this final answer, you'll need to use a variety of area formulas, which we'll explore later in this chapter. For now, though, notice that your chances of guessing have increased from 20% to 50% with a little bit of quick thinking. Now what should you do? If you know how to do the problem, you do it. If you don't or if you are running out of time, you guess and move on.

However, even as we move in to the "real" geometry in the remainder of this chapter, don't forget:

> Always look for opportunities to ballpark on geometry problems even if you know how to do them the "real" way.

PLANE GEOMETRY REVIEW

Often on an ACT geometry question, several answer choices can be eliminated based solely on the diagram provided (or by drawing the diagram described by the problem, if a diagram is not given). Sometimes you can even completely solve the problem just from the diagram.

One important feature of ACT geometry questions is that the "hard" questions don't necessarily test "hard" concepts; rather, they often combine several basic concepts together and disguise them so that it's hard to determine where to start, and so that multiple steps are required to come to a solution. The first step, of course, is to ensure you have mastered all the basic geometry rules tested by the ACT. Work the following Plane Geometry questions and if you struggle at all, consider doing some more basic geometry review on your own or in our *ACT Prep* book. You will also find some geometry facts and formulas in your online Student Tools.

ANGLES AND LINES

Try the following problem.

1. In the figure below, line *L* is parallel to line *M*. Line *N* intersects both *L* and *M*, with angles *a*, *b*, *c*, *d*, *e*, *f*, *g*, and *h* as shown. Which of the following lists includes all the angles that are supplementary to ∠*a* ?

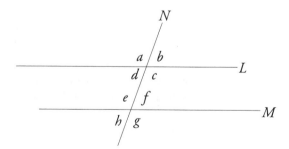

   A.   Angles *b*, *d*, *f*, and *h*
   B.   Angles *c*, *e*, and *g*
   C.   Angles *b*, *d*, and *c*
   D.   Angles *e*, *f*, *g*, and *h*
   E.   Angles *d*, *c*, *h*, and *g*

Here's How to Crack It

An angle is supplementary to another angle if the two angles together add up to 180°. Because $\angle a$ is one of the eight angles formed by the intersection of a line with two parallel lines, we know that there are really only two angles: a big one and a little one. $\angle a$ is a big one. Thus, only the small angles would be supplementary to it. Which angles are those? The correct answer is (A). By the way, in the following chapter, you will learn another way to deal with geometry questions like this that deal with variables or unknown quantities.

$$N$$

$a = 100°$ / $b = 80°$
$d = 80°$ / $c = 100°$ —— L

$e = 100°$ / $f = 80°$
$h = 80°$ / $g = 100°$ —— M

TRIANGLES

You likely know a lot about triangles, so let's look at some ways the ACT will test triangle concepts and some things to watch out for.

The ACT will test many concepts related to right triangles. The test-writers adore the 3-4-5 triangle and use it frequently, along with its multiples, such as the 6-8-10 triangle and the 9-12-15 triangle. Of course, you can always use the Pythagorean Theorem to figure out the third side of a right triangle, as long as you have the other two sides, but because ACT problems almost invariably use "triples" like the ones we've just mentioned, it makes sense just to memorize them.

The ACT has three commonly used right-triangle triples.

3-4-5 (and its multiples)

5-12-13 (and its multiples)

7-24-25 (not as common as the other two)

Don't Get Snared

- Is this a 3-4-5 triangle?

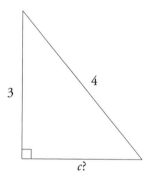

No, because the hypotenuse of a right triangle must be its *longest* side—the one opposite the 90° angle. In this case, we must use the Pythagorean Theorem to discover side c: $3^2 + c^2 = 16$. Therefore, $c = \sqrt{7}$.

- Is this a 5-12-13 triangle?

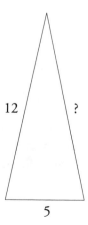

No, because the Pythagorean Theorem—and triples—apply only to *right* triangles. We can't determine definitively the third side of this triangle based on the angles.

Special Right Triangles

As fond as the ACT test-writers are of triples, they are even fonder of two other right triangles. The first is called the **isosceles right triangle**. The sides and angles of the isosceles right triangle are always in a particular proportion.

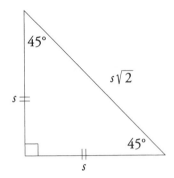

> ### Be on the Lookout…
> for problems in which the application of the Pythagorean Theorem is not obvious. For example, every rectangle contains two right triangles. That means that if you know the length and width of the rectangle, you also know the length of the diagonal, which is the hypotenuse of both triangles created by the diagonal.

The other right triangle tested frequently on the ACT is the **30-60-90 triangle**, which also always has the same proportions.

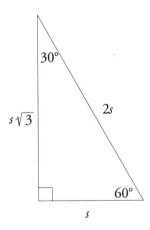

Because these triangles are tested so frequently, it makes sense to memorize the proportions, rather than waste time deriving them each time they appear.

Don't Get Snared

- In the isosceles right triangle below, are the sides equal to $3\sqrt{2}$?

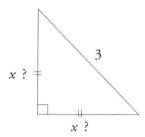

No. Remember, in an isosceles right triangle, in which x represents two of the triangle's sides, hypotenuse = the side $\sqrt{2}$. In this case, 3 = the side $\sqrt{2}$. If we solve for the side, we get $\dfrac{3}{\sqrt{2}}$ = the side.

For arcane mathematical reasons, we are not supposed to leave a radical in the denominator, but we can multiply top and bottom by $\sqrt{2}$ to get $\dfrac{3\sqrt{2}}{2}$.

- In the right triangle below, is x equal to $4\sqrt{3}$?

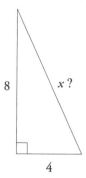

No. Even though it is one of ACT's favorites, you have to be careful not to see a 30-60-90 where none exists. In the triangle above, the short side is half of the *medium* side, not half of the hypotenuse. This is some sort of right triangle all right, but it is not a 30-60-90. The hypotenuse, in case you're curious, is really $4\sqrt{5}$.

Area

The **area** of a triangle can be found using the following formula:

$$\text{area} = \frac{\text{base} \times \text{height}}{2}$$

Height is measured as the perpendicular distance from the base of the triangle to its highest point.

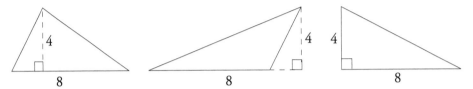

In all three of the above triangles, the area is

$$\frac{8 \times 4}{2} = 16$$

Don't Get Snared

- Sometimes the height of a triangle can be *outside* the triangle itself, as we just saw in the second example.
- In a right triangle, the height of the triangle can also be one of the sides of the triangle, as we just saw in the third example. However, be careful when finding the area of a *non-right* triangle. Simply because you know two sides of the triangle does not mean that you have the height of the triangle.

Similar Triangles

Two triangles are called *similar* if their angles have the same degree measures. This means their sides will be in proportion. For example, the two triangles below are similar.

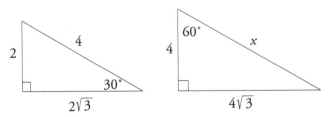

Because the sides of the two triangles are in the same proportion, you can find the missing side, x, by setting up a proportion equation.

$$\begin{array}{ccc} & \text{small triangle} & \text{big triangle} \\ \dfrac{\text{short leg}}{\text{hypotenuse}} & \dfrac{2}{4} = & \dfrac{4}{x} \end{array}$$

$$x = 8$$

Four-Sided Figures

The interior angles of any four-sided figure (also known as a quadrilateral) add up to 360°. The most common four-sided figures on the ACT are the rectangle and the square, with the parallelogram and the trapezoid coming in a far distant third and fourth.

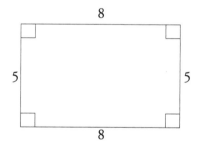

> **Your Friend the Triangle**
> Because a quadrilateral is really just two triangles, its interior angles must measure twice those of a triangle: 2(180) = 360.

Now that we've given you some of the basics on triangles and four-sided figures, it is time for you to try a question that combines these topics. Remember, "hard" plane geometry questions often just throw a bunch of basic concepts at you at the same time.

3. In the figure below, square *ABCD* is attached to △*ADE* as shown. If ∠*EAD* is equal to 30° and $\overline{AE}$ is equal to $4\sqrt{3}$, then what is the area of square *ABCD* ?

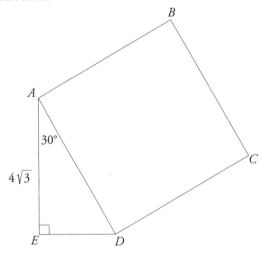

A. $8\sqrt{3}$
B. 16
C. 64
D. 72
E. $64\sqrt{2}$

Here's How to Crack It

Start with Step 1: Know the question. Underline "what is the area of square *ABCD*?" Move to Step 2 and look at the answers. We don't have any values for areas of other shapes within the figure, so there is nothing to ballpark. But note the presence of $\sqrt{2}$ and $\sqrt{3}$ in the answers: they're an additional clue, if you haven't absorbed the info given, that either 30-60-90 and/or 45-45-90 triangles are in play.

The triangle in the figure is in fact a 30-60-90. Now move to Step 3: Break the problem into bite-sized pieces. Because angle *A* is the smallest angle, the side opposite that angle is equal to 4 and the hypotenuse is equal to 8. Now move on to Step 3a: Mark your figure with these values. Now move to Step 3b: Write down any formulas you need. The area for a square is s^2. Because that hypotenuse is also the side of the square, the area of the square must be 8 times 8, or 64. This is (C). If you forgot the ratio of the sides of a 30-60-90 triangle, go back and review it. You'll need it.

POE Pointers

If you didn't remember the ratio of the sides of a 30-60-90 triangle, could you have eliminated some answers using POE? Of course. Let's see if we can use the diagram to eliminate some answer choices.

The diagram tells us that $\overline{AE}$ has length $4\sqrt{3}$. A good approximation for $\sqrt{3}$ is 1.7. So, $4\sqrt{3}$ is approximately 6.8. We can now use this to estimate the sides of square $ABCD$. Just using your eyes, would you say that $\overline{AD}$ is longer or shorter than $\overline{AE}$? Of course it's a bit longer; it's the hypotenuse of $\triangle ADE$. You decide and write down what you think it might be. To find the area of the square, simply square whatever value you decided the side equaled. This is your answer.

Now all you have to do is see which of the answer choices still makes sense. Could the answer be (A)? $8\sqrt{3}$ equals roughly 13.6. Is this close to your answer? No way. Could the answer be (B), which is 16? Still much too small. Could the answer be (C), which is 64? Quite possibly. Could the answer be 72? It might be. Could the correct answer be $64\sqrt{2}$? An approximation of $\sqrt{2}$ is 1.4, so $64\sqrt{2}$ equals 89.6. This seems rather large. Thus, on this problem, by using POE we could eliminate (A), (B), and (E).

CIRCLES

The key to circle problems on the ACT is to look for the word or phrase that tells you what to do. If you see the word *circumference*, immediately write down the formula for circumference, and plug in any numbers the problem has given you. By solving for whatever quantity is still unknown, you have probably already answered the problem. Another tip is to find the radius. The radius is the key to many circle problems.

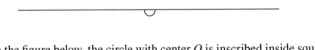

1. If the area of a circle is 16 meters, what is its radius in meters?

   A. $\dfrac{8}{\pi}$

   B. 12π

   C. $\dfrac{4\sqrt{\pi}}{\pi}$

   D. $\dfrac{16}{\pi}$

   E. $144\pi^2$

Here's How to Crack It

Step 1: Know the question. We need to solve for the radius.

Step 2: Let the answers help. We don't have a figure, so there's nothing to ballpark. But no figure? Draw your own.

Then write down any formulas you need and fill in the information you have. Set the formula for the area of a circle equal to 16, $\pi r^2 = 16$. The problem is asking for the radius, so you have to solve for r. If you divide both sides by π, you get $r^2 = \dfrac{16}{\pi}$. Take the square root of both sides to get $r = \sqrt{\dfrac{16}{\pi}} = \dfrac{4}{\sqrt{\pi}} = \dfrac{4\sqrt{\pi}}{\pi}$. The correct answer is (C).

2. In the figure below, the circle with center O is inscribed inside square *ABCD* as shown. If a side of the square measures 8 units, what is the area of the shaded region?

   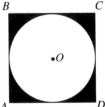

   F. $8 - 16\pi$
   G. 8π
   H. 16π
   J. $64 - 16\pi$
   K. 64π

Here's How to Crack It

Begin with Step 1 and underline "what is the area of the shaded region?" Step 2 brings us to the answers, and we see all of the answers have π in them. There is no obvious choice to ballpark just yet, so move to Step 3. Break the problem into bite-sized pieces, but don't get hung up on "inscribed." Yes, that's an important term to know, but since we have the figure, it's irrelevant. Move to Step 3a and 3b: Mark the side of the square "8" and write down the formulas for the area of a circle and square: πr^2 and s^2.

Is there a formula for the shape made by the shaded region? Nope. We just need the basic formulas for the basic shapes. $8^2 = 64$, so we at least know the shaded region is less than 64, the area of the square. But what's the link between the square and the circle? The side of the square equals the diameter. So if the diameter is 8, then the radius must be 4. Use that in the area formula, and $4^2\pi = 16\pi$. Subtract the area of the circle from the area of the square, and we get (J).

COORDINATE GEOMETRY

There are fewer coordinate geometry problems on the ACT Math Test than there are plane geometry questions. Most of the coordinate geometry questions are straight Plug and Chug questions. Just like in plane geometry, most questions will test the same few concepts over and over; the harder questions will just combine those same concepts in ways that are harder to identify.

Graphing in Two Dimensions

More complicated graphing questions concern equations with two variables, usually designated x and y. These equations can be graphed on a Cartesian grid, which looks like this.

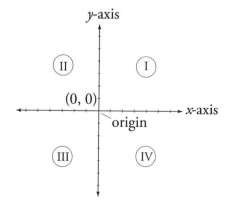

- In the first quadrant, x and y are both positive.
- In the second quadrant, x is negative but y is positive.
- In the third quadrant, x and y are both negative.
- In the fourth quadrant, x is positive but y is negative.

Note: This is when your graphing calculator (if you have one) will really get a chance to shine. Practice doing all the ACT coordinate geometry questions on your calculator now and you'll blow them away when you actually take the test.

Graphic Guesstimation

A few questions on the ACT might involve actual graphing, but it is more likely that you will be able to make use of graphing to *estimate* the answers to questions that the ACT test-writers think are more complicated.

1. Point B (4,3) is the midpoint of line segment AC. If point A has coordinates (0,1), then what are the coordinates of point C ?

    A. (−4,−1)
    B. (4, 1)
    C. (4, 4)
    D. (8, 5)
    E. (8, 9)

Here's How to Crack It

You may or may not remember the midpoint formula: ACT test-writers expect you to use it to solve this problem. We'll go over it in a moment, along with the other formulas you'll need to solve coordinate geometry questions. However, it is worth noting that by drawing a rough graph of this problem, you can get the correct answer without the formula.

On your TI-83, you can plot independent points to see what the graph should look like. To do this, hit [STAT] and select option [1: Edit]. Enter the x- and y-coordinate points in the first two columns; use [L1] for your x-coordinates and [L2] for the y-coordinates. After you enter the endpoints of the line, hit [2nd] [Y=] to access the [STAT PLOT] menu. Select option [1: Plot1]. Change the [OFF] status to [ON] and hit [GRAPH]. You should now see the two points you entered. Now you can ballpark the answers based on where they are in the coordinate plane. Keep in mind that you can also plot all the points in the answers as well. Just be sure you keep track of all the x- and y-values.

B is supposed to be the midpoint of a line segment *AC*. Draw a line through the two points you've just plotted and extend it upward until *B* is the midpoint of the line segment. It should look like this:

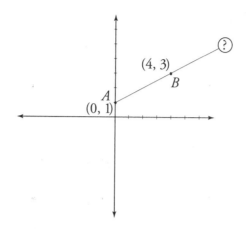

The place where you stopped drawing is the approximate location of point *C*. Now let's look at the answer choices to see if any of them are in the ballpark.

A.   (–4,–1): These coordinates are in the wrong quadrant.
B.   (4, 1): This point is way below where it should be.
C.   (4, 4): This point does not extend enough to the right.
D.   (8, 5): Definitely in the ballpark. Hold on to this answer choice.
E.   (8, 9): Possible, although the *y*-coordinate seems a little high.

Which answer choice do you want to pick? If you said (D), you are right.

THE IMPORTANT COORDINATE GEOMETRY FORMULAS

By memorizing a few formulas, you will be able to answer virtually all of the coordinate geometry questions on this test. Remember, too, that in coordinate geometry you almost *always* have a fallback—just graph it out.

And always keep your graphing calculator handy on these types of problems. Graphing calculators are great for solving line equations and giving you graphs you can use to ballpark. Be sure you know how to solve and graph an equation for a line on your calculator before you take the ACT.

The following formulas are listed in order of importance.

The Slope-Intercept Form

$$y = mx + b$$

A typical ACT $y = mx + b$ question might give you an equation in another form and ask you to find either the slope or the y-intercept. Simply put the equation into the form we've just shown you.

---

2. What is the slope of the line based on the equation $5x - y = 7x + 6$?

    F.   −6
    G.   −2
    H.   0
    J.   2
    K.   6

Here's How to Crack It

Isolate y on the left side of the equation. You can have your graphing calculator do this for you, or you can do it by hand by subtracting $5x$ from both sides.

$$
\begin{array}{rl}
5x - y = & 7x + 6 \\
-5x & -5x \\
\hline
-y = & 2x + 6
\end{array}
$$

We aren't quite done. The format we want is $y = mx + b$, not $-y = mx + b$. Let's multiply both sides by −1.

$$(-1)(-y) = (2x + 6)(-1)$$
$$y = -2x - 6$$

The slope of this line is −2, so the answer is (G).

The Slope Formula

You can find the slope of a line, even if all you have are two points on that line, by using the slope formula.

$$\text{slope} = \frac{\text{change in } y}{\text{change in } x} \quad \text{or} \quad \frac{y_2 - y_1}{x_2 - x_1}$$

The Slippery Slope
A line going from bottom left to upper right has a positive slope. A line going from top left to bottom right has a negative slope.

3. What is the slope of the straight line passing through the points (–2,5) and (6,4) ?

   A. $-\dfrac{1}{16}$

   B. $-\dfrac{1}{8}$

   C. $\dfrac{1}{5}$

   D. $\dfrac{2}{9}$

   E. $\dfrac{4}{9}$

Here's How to Crack It

Find the change in y and put it over the change in x. The change in y is the first y-coordinate minus the second y-coordinate. (It doesn't matter which point is first and which is second.) The change in x is the first x minus the second x.

$$\frac{y_2 - y_1}{x_2 - x_1} = \frac{5 - 4}{-2 - 6} = \frac{1}{-8}$$

The correct answer is (B).

Midpoint Formula

If you have the two endpoints of a line segment, you can find the midpoint of the segment by using the midpoint formula.

$$\left(x[m], y[m]\right) = \left(\frac{x_1 + x_2}{2}, \frac{y_1 + y_2}{2}\right)$$

Remember the first midpoint problem we did? Here it is again.

1. Point B (4,3) is the midpoint of line segment AC. If point A has coordinates (0,1), then what are the coordinates of point C ?

    A. (−4,−1)
    B. (4, 1)
    C. (4, 4)
    D. (8, 5)
    E. (8, 9)

Here's How to Crack It

You'll remember that it was perfectly possible to solve this problem just by drawing a quick graph of what it ought to look like. However, to find the correct answer using the midpoint formula, we first have to realize that, in this case, we already *have* the midpoint. We are asked to find one of the endpoints.

The midpoint is (4, 3). This represents the average of the two endpoints. The endpoint we know about is (0, 1). Let's do the x-coordinate first. The average of the x-coordinates of the two endpoints equals the x-coordinate of the midpoint. So $\frac{(0+?)}{2} = 4$. What is the missing x-coordinate? 8. Now let's do the y-coordinate. $\frac{(1+?)}{2} = 3$. What is the missing y-coordinate? 5. The answer is (D).

If you had trouble following that last explanation, just remember that you already understood this problem (and got the answer) using graphing. Never be intimidated by formulas on the ACT. There is usually another way to do the problem.

The Distance Formula

We hate the distance formula. If you need to know the distance between two points, you can always think of that distance as being the hypotenuse of a right triangle. Here's an example.

---

4. What is the distance between points *A* (2,2) and *B* (5,6) ?

   F. 3
   G. 4
   H. 5
   J. 6
   K. 7

Here's How to Crack It

Let's make a quick graph of what this ought to look like.

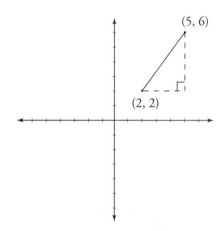

If we extend lines from the two points to form a right triangle under the line segment *AB*, we can use the Pythagorean Theorem to get the distance between the two points. What is the length of the base of the triangle? It's 3. What is the length of the height of the triangle? It's 4. So what is the length of the hypotenuse? It's 5. Of course, as usual, it is one of the triples of which ACT is so fond. The answer is (H). You could also have popped the points into your calculator and had it calculate the distance for you.

TRIGONOMETRY

The ACT Math Test usually includes only four trigonometry questions. And the good news is, those questions generally cover only a few basic topics in trigonometry.

SOHCAHTOA

If you've had trig before, you probably know this acronym like the back of your hand. If not, here's what it means:

$$\mathbf{S}ine = \frac{\mathbf{O}pposite}{\mathbf{H}ypotenuse} \quad \mathbf{C}osine = \frac{\mathbf{A}djacent}{\mathbf{H}ypotenuse} \quad \mathbf{T}angent = \frac{\mathbf{O}pposite}{\mathbf{A}djacent}$$

Sine, cosine, and tangent are often abbreviated as sin, cos, and tan, respectively.

The easier trig questions on this test involve the relationships between the sides of a right triangle. In the right triangle below, angle x can be expressed in terms of the ratios of different sides of the triangle.

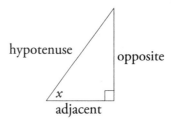

The **sine** of angle $x = \dfrac{\text{length of side opposite angle } x}{\text{length of hypotenuse}}$

The **cosine** of angle $x = \dfrac{\text{length of side adjacent angle } x}{\text{length of hypotenuse}}$

The **tangent** of angle $x = \dfrac{\text{length of side opposite angle } x}{\text{length of side adjacent angle } x}$

YOU'RE ALMOST DONE

There are three more relationships to memorize. They involve the reciprocals of the previous three.

$$\csc\theta = \frac{1}{\sin\theta} = \frac{hyp}{opp} \qquad \sec\theta = \frac{1}{\cos\theta} = \frac{hyp}{adj} \qquad \cot\theta = \frac{1}{\tan\theta} = \frac{adj}{opp}$$

One easy way to remember which reciprocal matches to which function is that the letters "co" appear exactly one time for each pair of reciprocals: sine and _co_secant; _co_sine and secant; and tangent and _co_tangent.

Let's try a few problems.

───────────○───────────

31. What is $\sin\theta$, if $\tan\theta = \frac{4}{3}$?

    A. $\dfrac{3}{4}$

    B. $\dfrac{4}{5}$

    C. $\dfrac{5}{4}$

    D. $\dfrac{5}{3}$

    E. $\dfrac{7}{3}$

Helpful Trig Identities

$$\sin^2\theta + \cos^2\theta = 1$$

$$\frac{\sin\theta}{\cos\theta} = \tan\theta$$

Here's How to Crack It

It helps to sketch out the right triangle and fill in the information we know.

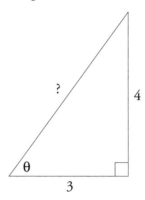

What kind of right triangle is this? That's right—a 3-4-5. Now, we need to know the sine

of angle θ: opposite over hypotenuse, or $\dfrac{4}{5}$, which is (B).

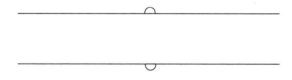

43. For all $\theta, \dfrac{\cos \theta}{\sin^2 \theta + \cos^2 \theta} = ?$

   A. $\sin \theta$
   B. $\csc \theta$
   C. $\cot \theta$
   D. $\cos \theta$
   E. $\tan \theta$

Here's How to Crack It

Remember that $\sin^2\theta + \cos^2\theta$ always equals 1. $\dfrac{\cos \theta}{1} = \cos \theta$. The answer is (D).

50. In a right triangle shown below, sec θ is $\dfrac{25}{7}$. What is sin θ ?

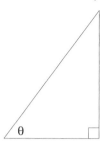

   F. $\dfrac{3}{25}$

   G. $\dfrac{5}{25}$

   H. $\dfrac{7}{25}$

   J. $\dfrac{24}{25}$

   K. $\dfrac{25}{7}$

Here's How to Crack It

The secant of any angle is the reciprocal of the cosine, which is just another way of saying that the cosine of angle θ is $\dfrac{7}{25}$.

Since sec $\theta = \dfrac{1}{\cos\theta}$, $\dfrac{1}{\cos\theta} = \dfrac{25}{7}$, which means that cos $\theta = \dfrac{7}{25}$. Are you done? No! Cross off (H) because you know it's not the answer.

Cosine means adjacent over hypotenuse. Let's sketch it.

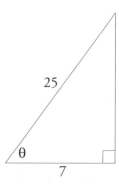

As you can see, we now have two sides of a right triangle. Can we find the third side? If you said this was one of the triples we told you about before, you are absolutely correct, although you also could have derived this by using the Pythagorean Theorem. The third side must be 24. The question asks for sin θ. Sine = opposite over hypotenuse, or $\frac{24}{25}$, which is (J).

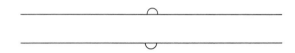

51. The expression $3\cos^2 x - 3\sin^2 x$ is equivalent to which of the following?

(Note: $\cos(x + y) = \cos x \cos y - \sin x \sin y$)

A. $3\sin(2x)$
B. $3\cos(2x)$
C. $3\cos(x^2)$
D. $6\sin(2x)$
E. $6\cos(2x)$

Here's How to Crack It

The question asks for an expression that is equivalent to the given trigonometric expression. The note that is given under the question says $\cos(x + y) = \cos x \cos y - \sin x \sin y$. This is a clue that solving this question requires rewriting the given expression in the form of the note. Expand the equation given in the question to get $3(\cos x)(\cos x) - 3(\sin x)(\sin x)$. If we substituted y for another x, it would look like $\cos(x + x) = \cos x \cos x - \sin x \sin x$, which is very similar to the expanded equation. The equation would be $3\cos(2x)$, so the correct answer is (B).

TRIGONOMETRY AND GRAPHING

When graphing a trig function, such as sine, there are two important **coefficients**, A and B: A{*sin* (B*θ*)}.

The two coefficients A and B govern the **amplitude** of the graph (how tall it is) and the **period** of the graph (how long it takes to get through a complete cycle), respectively. If there are no coefficients, then that means A = 1 and B = 1, and the graph is the same as what you'd get when you graph it on your calculator.

- Increases in A increase the amplitude of the graph. It's a direct relationship.

That means if A = 2, then the amplitude is doubled. If A = $\frac{1}{2}$, then the amplitude is cut in half.

- Increases in B decrease the period of the graph. It's an inverse relationship.

That means if B = 2, then the period is cut in half, which is to say the graph completes a full cycle faster than usual. If B = $\frac{1}{2}$, then the period is doubled.

You can add to or subtract from the function as a whole, and also to or from the variable, but neither of those actions changes the shape of the graph, only its position and starting place.

Here's the graph of sin *x*. What are the amplitude and period?

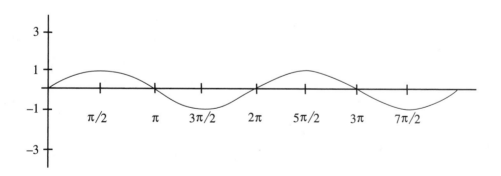

The simple function sin *θ* goes from –1 to 1 on the *y*-axis, so the amplitude is 1, while its period is 2π, which means that every 2π on the graph (as you go from side to side) it completes a full cycle. That's what you see in the graph above.

The graph below is also a sine function, but it's been changed. What is the function graphed here?

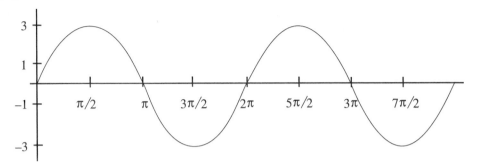

You have three things to check when looking at this graph: is it sin or cos, has the period changed, and has the amplitude changed?

- This is a sine graph because it has a value of 0 at 0. Cosine has a value of 1 at 0.
- It makes a complete cycle in 2π, so the period hasn't changed. In other words, B = 1.
- The amplitude is triple what it normally is, so A = 3. The function graphed, therefore, is 3 sin θ.

How about here?

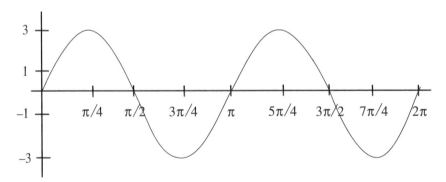

Once again, there are three things to check.

- This is a sine graph because it has a value of 0 at 0. Cosine has a value of 1 at 0.
- It makes a complete cycle in π, so the period has changed—it's half of what it usually is. B has an inverse effect, which means B = 2.
- The amplitude is triple what it normally is, so A = 3. The function graphed, therefore, is 3 sin 2θ.

Let's try some practice questions.

---

49. As compared with the graph of $y = \cos x$, which of the following has the same period and three times the amplitude?

  A. $y = \cos 3x$

  B. $y = \cos \dfrac{1}{2}(x + 3)$

  C. $y = 3 \cos \dfrac{1}{2}x$

  D. $y = 1 + 3 \cos x$

  E. $y = 3 + \cos x$

Here's How to Crack It

Recall that the coefficient on the outside of the function changes the amplitude, and the one on the inside changes the period. Because the question states that the period hasn't changed, you can eliminate (A), (B), and (C). The amplitude is three times greater, you're told; because there's a direct relationship between A and amplitude, you want to have a 3 multiplying the outside of the function. That leaves only (D) as a possibility.

---

52. Which of the following equations describes the equation graphed below?

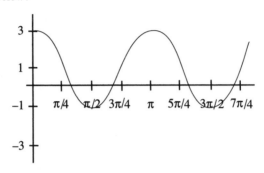

F. $2 \cos x$
G. $1 + 2 \cos x$
H. $\cos 2x$
J. $1 + \cos 2x$
K. $1 + 2 \cos 2x$

Here's How to Crack It

At first it looks like this graph has an amplitude of 3, but if you look closer, you'll see that though the top value is 3, the bottom value is –1, which means that the whole graph has been shifted up. Because (F) and (H) don't add anything to the function (which is how you move a graph up and down), they're out. The period of this graph is half of what it usually is, so B = 2, which eliminates (G). Because the amplitude has also changed, you can eliminate (J). The answer is (K).

Now try these strategies on your own. Go online to your Student Tools and answer the Chapter 10 Drills.

Chapter 11
Plugging In and PITA

Once you have a solid foundation in the ways that ACT tests geometry concepts, you are well-equipped to answer a wide variety of Math questions. Algebra makes up another main category of questions on the ACT Math test. This chapter will look at some of the questions that test concepts you may have seen in Algebra classes, but it will show how to work around some of the toughest algebra questions to improve your speed and accuracy. Remember, just because you are good at solving algebra problems doesn't mean that the "real way" is the best way!

Chapter 10 discussed various strategies for attacking tricky geometry questions. Once you master them, you will have the tools to attack a wide variety of ACT Math problems. This chapter will look at two more essential tools for the toughest algebra problems on the ACT: Plugging In and PITA (Plug In the Answers).

Always keep in mind that most of the ACT Math problems can be solved in multiple ways, and that the approach that seems the most familiar may not be the most efficient. Often, a strong test-taker will be tempted to apply a "brute-force" method to solving problems: just start doing algebra and work through the problem until a solution presents itself. But this could take minutes, could lead you down dead-end paths, and could lead you into trap answers that are based on mistakes the test-writers know you are likely to make!

In order to achieve the highest scores on the ACT, you can't afford to make any careless errors, waste any precious seconds, or fall into any traps. Plugging In and PITA will help ensure correct answers on the easy and medium questions, and can help you cut through distractions and solve difficult questions quickly and accurately, rather than wasting time taking an inefficient path. Recognize the opportunity to use Plugging In and PITA, and you'll ensure high accuracy and save lots of time—time you can use to work on solving other difficult questions!

WHEN ACCURACY COUNTS, ARITHMETIC BEATS ALGEBRA

Let's take a look at a challenging algebra problem:

59. If x and y are nonzero real numbers such that $3^{x-1} = 3y$, which of the following is equivalent to 3^{x+1} in terms of y ?

    A. $\dfrac{1}{27y^3}$

    B. $\dfrac{1}{27y}$

    C. $\dfrac{1}{9y}$

    D. $9y^3$

    E. $27y$

What's your first reaction to this problem? Most likely, your inclination is to apply "brute-force" algebraic manipulations and your knowledge of exponent rules until you understand the problem and can solve for the answer. If you have excellent algebra skills, you've got a good chance of getting it right—but also a good chance of making an algebra mistake and coming up with a trap answer, or of wasting time going down dead-end paths. That's what the test-writers want you to do. The problem is written in a way specifically intended to lead you into algebra errors, and the answer choices include traps for the various errors you might make. Before we attack this problem, let's talk about Plugging In.

PLUGGING IN

If you had 1 dollar and you bought 2 pieces of candy at 25 cents apiece, how much change would you have? 50 cents, of course. If you had d dollars and bought p pieces of candy at c cents apiece, how much change would you have? Your first inclination might be $d - pc$, right? But that's not the answer: it's actually $d - \dfrac{pc}{100}$, since you have to convert the cents to dollars. And the trap $(d - pc)$ will be right there waiting for you in the answers.

This helps explain why some top math students do well on the "hard" questions, but make careless errors on "easy" and "medium" questions. Why does this happen? Because your mind is much better at working with concrete numbers (doing arithmetic) than it is at working with abstractions such as variables (doing algebra).

> No matter how good you are at algebra, you've been doing arithmetic a lot longer.

Numbers are a lot easier to work with than variables. Therefore, when you see variables on the ACT, you can usually make things a lot easier on yourself by using numbers instead. Whenever there are variables in the answer choices or the problem, you can use Plugging In.

- Use Plugging In when there are variables in the answer choices.
- Plugging In works on both word problems and Plug and Chug questions.
- Plugging In works on questions of any difficulty level.

Let's take another look at Question 59:

59. If x and y are nonzero real numbers such that $3^{x-1} = 3y$, which of the following is equivalent to 3^{x+1} in terms of y ?

A. $\dfrac{1}{27y^3}$

B. $\dfrac{1}{27y}$

C. $\dfrac{1}{9y}$

D. $9y^3$

E. $27y$

WHAT TO DO WHEN YOU PLUG IN

1. **Identify the opportunity.** Can you use Plugging In on this question?
2. **Choose a good number.** Make the math easy on yourself.
3. **Find a target answer.** Solve the question using the number you plugged in; that gives you your target. Circle it.
4. **Test all the answer choices.** Plug the numbers you chose into the answer choices and look for the one that matches your target. If two of them work, try new numbers until only one answer is left.

Let's try it.

Step 1: Identify the opportunity.

Can you use Plugging In on this question? Yes: there are variables in the question and in the answer choices.

Step 2: Choose a good number.

We know that x and y are "nonzero real numbers" and that $3^{x-1} = 3y$. What number that meets these conditions might make the math more straightforward? Let's try $x = 4$. Replace x with 4 in the equation and see what happens:

$$3^{4-1} = 3y$$

$$3^3 = 3y$$

$$27 = 3y$$

$$y = 9$$

Ok, so if we plug in $x = 4$, we find that $y = 9$. But what is the question *asking for*? We are supposed to solve for 3^{x+1}.

Step 3: Find a target answer.

If $x = 4$, then $3^{x+1} = 3^{4+1} = 3^5 = 243$. So, when $x = 4$ and $y = 9$, the answer to the question is 243. Circle "243" on your paper—this is the target answer we need to match in the answer choices.

 **Step 4: Test all the answer choices.**

Since the answer choices all have y in them, replace y with 9 in each answer choice and calculate the result to find the one that matches 243.

A. $\dfrac{1}{27y^3} = \dfrac{1}{19{,}683}$ Not our target answer. Eliminate it. Note that calculating the actual amount is not necessary if you see that the answer will be less than 1.

B. $\dfrac{1}{27y} = \dfrac{1}{243}$ Not our target answer. Eliminate it. Note that calculating the actual amount is not necessary if you see that the answer will be less than 1.

C. $\dfrac{1}{9y} = \dfrac{1}{81}$ Not our target answer. Eliminate it. Note that calculating the actual amount is not necessary if you see that the answer will be less than 1.

D. $9y^3 = 6{,}561$ Not our target answer. Eliminate it.

E. $27y = 243$

Only (E) works, so it is the correct answer. How difficult was that? Not at all. How sure are we that we got the correct answer? Very sure. It's much less likely that you'll fall into an algebra trap answer when you solve the question without using any algebra!

Plugging In turns difficult problems into fairly straightforward arithmetic problems, while also greatly improving your accuracy. Could you have solved this question correctly using algebra? Sure. But more importantly, are you confident that you can solve *every* algebra question without falling into a trap and missing a couple? If you're aiming for the highest scores, you can't afford that risk. Plugging In will increase your accuracy while also saving you time that you can use to attack other difficult questions on the test.

Let's try another challenging algebra problem and see how the process works.

---

53. If x, y, and z are positive real numbers such that $\frac{1}{2}x = \frac{1}{3}y$ and $3y = 4z$, which of the following inequalities is true?

    A. $x < y < z$
    B. $x < z < y$
    C. $y < x < z$
    D. $y < z < x$
    E. $z < y < x$

Here's How to Crack It

Since the problem involves variables in the question and the answers, this looks like a great opportunity to use Plugging In. Try a number that looks like it will work well with the problem: since 12 is divisible by 2, 3, and 4, plug in $x = 12$ and see what happens: $\frac{1}{2}(12) = \frac{1}{3}y$, so $6 = \frac{1}{3}y$ and $y = 18$. Now plug in $y = 18$ to the second equation: $3(18) = 4z$, so $54 = 4z$ and $z = 13.5$. Therefore, since $x = 12$, $z = 13.5$, and $y = 18$, the correct inequality is $x < z < y$, which matches (B).

Compare Plugging In to the algebraic method for solving the same problem: eliminate the fractions from the first equation by multiplying each side by 6, resulting in $3x = 2y$. But then you need to combine the two equations, so multiply the first equation again by 3 on each side, resulting in $9x = 6y$. Multiply the right equation by 2 on each side, resulting in $6y = 8z$. Then, combine the equations: $9x = 6y = 8z$. Finally, find a number that has 9, 8, and 6 as factors, such as 72, and set the equation equal to it: $9x = 6y = 8z = 72$. Therefore, $x = 8$, $y = 12$, and $z = 9$, so $x < z < y$.

Which method is more likely to result in wasted time and the risk of careless errors? Plugging In reduces those chances dramatically and saves you lots of time on the test. Sometimes, it can feel like Plugging In takes longer at first—it's a new technique, after all! But if you're diligent in practicing it and allow it to become comfortable, you may even end up moving more quickly through the test.

PLUGGING IN THE ANSWERS

As we've seen, Plugging In is a great strategy when there are variables in the question or the answers. How about when there aren't? Can we use Plugging In on questions even when they don't have variables or equations? We can!

Take a look at this difficult word problem:

> **51.** Herman has written 75 pages of a novel, and his goal is to complete the 410-page novel over the next 12 months. He plans to write some pages next month, and then in each month thereafter, he plans to write exactly 2 more pages than he wrote in the previous month. If Herman follows this plan, what is the minimum number of pages he must write next month in order to reach his goal?
>
> **A.** 11
> **B.** 17
> **C.** 24
> **D.** 32
> **E.** 37

What's your initial reaction to this problem? First, it's time-consuming to read and it involves multiple steps. Second, it probably makes you feel like you should be writing down an algebra equation, even though it doesn't name any variables. When you get that feeling, check the answers. When you feel like writing an algebraic equation, and you see integers in the answer choices, this means you can Plug In the Answers (PITA) to solve the question.

Plug In the Answers (PITA) when:

- answer choices are numbers in ascending or descending order.
- the question asks for a specific amount. Questions will usually be "what?" or "how many?"
- you get the urge to do algebra even when there are no variables in the problem.

Okay, let's see how it works:

> **51.** Herman has written 75 pages of a novel, and his goal is to complete the 410-page novel over the next 12 months. He plans to write some pages next month, and then in each month thereafter, he plans to write exactly 2 more pages than he wrote in the previous month. If Herman follows this plan, what is the minimum number of pages he must write next month in order to reach his goal?
>
> **A.** 11
> **B.** 17
> **C.** 24
> **D.** 32
> **E.** 37

As soon as you identify the opportunity to use PITA, go right to the end of the question to find what the problem is asking for. Here, the question asks for the *minimum* number of pages Herman must write next month to reach his goal. Label the answers as the "first month minimum."

Since the answer choices are listed in ascending order, start in the middle with (C). That way, you can save time by moving to a smaller or larger answer choice if the first one doesn't work. So, if we start with the middle choice, Herman would write 24 pages in the first month.

Now, work through the problem step by step in bite-sized pieces. What's the first calculation we can make? Herman writes 24 pages in the first month, then adds 2 pages in each month thereafter for 12 months. How many pages does he write in total? Well, we know he would write that base amount (24 pages) in each of the 12 months, so that's 24×12 = 288 pages. Also, he would write additional pages each month, starting in month 2 up to month 12: $2 + 4 + 6 + 8 + 10 + 12 + 14 + 16 + 18 + 20 + 22 = 132$ additional pages. Plus, he started with 75 pages, so his total number of pages would be $288 + 132 + 75 = 495$ pages.

Here's how your work would look on the page:

Minimum First Month	12 Months	Additional Pages	Original Pages	Total > 410?
A. 11				
B. 17				
C. 24	288	132	75	495
D. 32				
E. 37				

Would he meet his goal of 410 pages? Yes, but the question asked for the *minimum* number of pages he must write in the first month, so let's try a smaller amount.

Try (B)—17 pages. The math is much easier once you've been through it the first time. If Herman writes 17 pages the first month, then over the 12 months he will write 17 × 12 = 204 pages. Also, he would write the same 2 additional pages each month, which would still add up to 132 additional pages, and he still starts with 75 pages, so his total number of pages would be 204 + 132 + 75 = 411 pages. This would be just enough to achieve his goal of writing 410 pages. Since (A), 11 pages, would be way too low to make 410 pages, (B) is the credited response. Now here's what your work would look like:

Minimum First Month	12 Months	Additional Pages	Original Pages	Total > 410?
A. 11				
B. 17	204	132	75	411 Yes! ✔
C. 24	288	132	75	495 Not min.
D. 32				
E. 37				

Since you're using PITA, once you find the correct answer, you're done—you don't need to check all five answers.

Let's look at another problem and see PITA in action:

> **43.** After playing games of skill at the county fair, Jenny has 168 prize tickets, all of which she uses to buy prizes for herself and 10 of her friends. Small prizes cost 12 tickets, and large prizes cost 21 tickets. How many small prizes does she buy?
>
> **A.** 3
> **B.** 4
> **C.** 6
> **D.** 7
> **E.** 8

Since this word problem asks "how many" at the end, has ascending numbers in the answer choices, and may give you the urge to do algebra, it is a great opportunity to Plug In the Answers.

Start at the end of the problem with what the question is asking for: since it's asking for the number of small prizes, label the answers "small prizes." Now start with the middle answer choice, (C), and work through the problem in bite-sized pieces.

If Jenny buys 6 small prizes, they would cost $12 \times 6 = 72$ tickets. How many large prizes would she buy? Since the prizes are for *herself* and 10 of her friends, she buys a total of 11 prizes, which means she would buy 5 large prizes, which would cost $21 \times 5 = 105$ tickets, for a total cost of $72 + 105 = 177$ tickets.

Here's how your work would look on the page:

Small Prizes	Tickets	Large Prizes	Tickets	Total	= 168?
A. 3					
B. 4					
C. 6	72	5	105	177	
D. 7					
E. 8					

Since the problem states that she uses 168 tickets, eliminate (C). Since Jenny needs to spend fewer tickets, you need a larger number of small prizes, so try (D).

If Jenny buys 7 small prizes, they would cost 12 × 7 = 84 tickets. She would also buy 4 large prizes, costing 21 × 4 = 84 tickets, for a total of 84 + 84 = 168 tickets. Since this matches the amount stated in the problem, choose (D). Now here's what your work would look like:

Small Prizes	Tickets	Large Prizes	Tickets	Total	= 168?
A. 3					
B. 4					
C. 6	72	5	105	177	Too high
D. 7	84	4	84	168	Yes! ✓
E. 8					

HIDDEN PLUG INS

As you saw with Plugging In the Answers, Plugging In isn't useful only on problems with variables in the questions and answer choices. You can also use Plugging In on problems that ask for ratios or percentages as answer choices.

Take a look at this challenging geometry problem:

60. The two diagonals of a square divide it into four isosceles triangles of equal size. What is the ratio of the perimeter of one of the four smaller triangles to the perimeter of the original square?

F. $\dfrac{1}{4}$

G. $\dfrac{\sqrt{2}}{4}$

H. $\dfrac{1+\sqrt{2}}{4}$

J. $\dfrac{2+\sqrt{2}}{4}$

K. $\dfrac{1}{2}$

When a problem asks for the relationship between amounts, but does not provide any values for variables, you can plug in any numbers you like, so long as you follow any rules the problem sets forth. In this case, you must follow the geometry rules for squares and triangles.

Start by drawing a square and drawing both diagonals from opposite corners. Note that this forms four 45-45-90 triangles, so you know that the hypotenuse of each triangle is equal to the sides multiplied by $\sqrt{2}$.

Pick a length for the sides of the square. Let's try 2. Therefore, each diagonal would have a length of $2\sqrt{2}$, and so each of the small triangles would have one side with a length of 2, and two smaller sides, each with a length of $\sqrt{2}$. So, the perimeter of each small triangle is $2 + \sqrt{2} + \sqrt{2} = 2 + 2\sqrt{2}$.

The perimeter of the original square is 4(s) = 4(2) = 8. Therefore, the ratio of the perimeter of one of the smaller triangles to the perimeter of the square is $\dfrac{2 + 2\sqrt{2}}{8} = \dfrac{2\left(1 + \sqrt{2}\right)}{8} = \dfrac{1 + \sqrt{2}}{4}$, which matches (H).

A NOTE ON PLUGGING IN AND PITA

Plugging In and PITA are not the only ways to solve these problems, and it may feel weird using these methods instead of trying to do these problems "the real way." You may have even found that you knew how to work with the variables in Plugging In problems or how to write the appropriate equations for the PITA problems. If you can do either of those things, you're already on your way to a great Math score.

But think about it this way. We've already said that ACT doesn't give any partial credit. So, do you think doing it "the real way" gets you any extra points? It doesn't: on the ACT, a right answer is a right answer, no matter how you get it. "The real way" is great, but unfortunately, it's often a lot more complex and offers a lot more opportunities to make careless errors.

The biggest problem with doing things the real way, though, is that it essentially requires that you invent a new approach for every problem. Instead, notice what we've given you here: two strategies that will work toward getting you the right answer on any number of questions. You may have heard the saying, "Give a man a fish and you've fed him for a day, but teach a man to fish and you've fed him for a lifetime." Now, don't worry, our delusions of grandeur are not quite so extreme, but Plugging In and PITA are useful in a similar way. Rather than giving you a detailed description of how to create formulas and use them on specific questions that won't ever appear exactly the same way on an ACT again, we're giving you a strategy that will help you work through any number of similar problems on future ACTs.

Now try these strategies on your own. Go online to your Student Tools and answer the Chapter 11 Drill.

Chapter 12
Hard Word Problems

We've covered most of what you'll need to get a great score on the ACT Math test. Now that you've refreshed some of the essential geometry and algebra concepts, we will see how those concepts can be made more difficult when tested in the context of Word Problems. In addition, we'll see some other Word Problems that test statistical concepts and give you strategies that will help you to complete these questions quickly and accurately.

Sometimes strong math students will achieve high accuracy on all the "hard" questions on the ACT Math Test—particularly the Plug and Chug problems—but lose points by missing tricky word problems, even those in the "easy" and "medium" sections. Word problems can often lead you into careless error traps with tricky wording. This chapter discusses ways to see those traps in word problems and avoid falling for them by using a careful, systematic approach.

First, let's review some overall strategies.

NOW, LATER, NEVER

Hard questions generally take longer to work through than do easier questions. That's obvious, but as we've seen, the definition of an "easy" question is a tough one to pin down. That's why you'll want to be careful with ACT's Order of Difficulty on the Math Test. As we've said before, the no-brainer approach is to open the test booklet and work questions 1 through 60 in order, but you can help to lock in the higher scores by out-smarting the test. You'll have a much more successful experience by drawing your own road map for this test rather than letting ACT guide you.

Of course, a lot of the easy questions will be near the beginning, but they won't all be. So, when you arrive at each question, you'll want to first determine whether it is a Now, Later, or Never question. Do the Now questions immediately: they're the freebies, the ones you know how to do and can do quickly and accurately. Skip any questions you think might take you a bit longer, or that test unfamiliar concepts—save them for Later. First, make sure you get all the points you can on the problems you know you can do, no matter what the question number.

Once you've done all the Now questions, go back to all the ones you left for Later. For both Now and Later questions, don't rush and make careless errors. On the other hand, if you find yourself spinning your wheels on a question, circle the question number and come back to it at the end if you have time. Don't get stuck on a particular problem. In a 60-minute exam, think of how much spending 5 minutes on a single problem can cost you!

Finally, there's no problem with leaving a question or two behind in the Never category. But wait, what's a Never question for a top scorer? Sometimes a question might be on a topic that you simply didn't cover yet in school; maybe you missed the week your teacher taught matrices, or logarithms, or the unit circle. Or for whatever reason, you have no idea how to approach a problem. In that case, your time is likely better spent on other questions (and it's still possible to get the highest score on the test even if you miss a question or two).

Note, of course, that you should never leave a question blank on the ACT, since there is no penalty for guessing. If you skip any questions, fill them in with your Letter of the Day: choose one pair of letters and bubble in all blanks this way. For example, always bubble in (A) and (F) or (B) and (G). This will maximize your chance of getting some of the guesses right.

USE PROCESS OF ELIMINATION (POE)

Remember the major technique we introduced in Chapter 2: Strategy, or the Process of Elimination (POE). ACT doesn't take away points for wrong answers, so you should always guess, and POE can help you improve your chance of guessing correctly. Don't make the mistake of thinking that POE is only for medium-scoring students—it's one of the keys to protecting yourself against careless errors that could cost you that top score! And POE is not a strategy just for English, Reading, and Science. Math has its own kind of POE, one facet of which we call Ballparking.

BALLPARKING ON WORD PROBLEMS

You can frequently get rid of several answer choices in an ACT Math problem (and protect yourself against careless errors) without doing any time-consuming math. Narrow down the choices by estimating your answer. We call this Ballparking. Let's look at an example:

17. Sarah pays $2.50 per 1,000 gallons of water used at her apartment each month for any usage up to 20,000 gallons. She pays 1.5 times that rate per 1,000 gallons used in excess of 20,000 gallons. If Sarah used 30,104 gallons of water last month, what was her approximate total water bill for the month?

    A. $50.00
    B. $75.00
    C. $90.00
    D. $100.00
    E. $110.00

Here's How to Crack It

Before we do any serious math on this problem, let's see if we can get rid of some answer choices by Ballparking.

First, do some rough calculations to see what the answer should look like. Sarah pays $2.50 per 1,000 gallons, so multiply by 10 to get a price of $25 for 10,000 gallons. So 20,000 gallons would cost $50, and if she kept paying the regular rate, 30,000 gallons would cost $75. But she paid a higher rate for the extra 10,000 gallons, so the answer has to be higher than $75; eliminate (A) and (B). How much did she pay for the extra 10,000 gallons? More than $25, but less than $50, because that would be double the original rate. So, her total amount should be greater than $75 but less than $100; only (C) makes any sense.

It may feel like we somehow cheated the system by doing the problem that way, but here's what ACT doesn't want you to know: the quick, easy way and the "real" way both get you the same number of raw points. Not all problems will be as easy to Ballpark, of course, but if you think before you start frantically figuring, you can usually eliminate at least an answer choice or two, and save yourself a lot of time (and brainpower) that you can use on tougher problems later in the test!

When dealing with word problems on the ACT Math Test:

1. **Know the question.** Read the whole problem before you calculate anything, and underline the actual question.
2. **Let the answers help.** Look for clues on how to solve and ways to use POE (Process of Elimination).
3. **Break the problem into bite-sized pieces.** When you read the problem a second time, stop at each step and make the necessary calculations before moving on. Write down your calculations, and watch out for tricky phrasing.

WORD PROBLEMS

The topics tested on the ACT Math Test aren't that difficult in themselves—you learned most, if not all, of this stuff by the end of middle school. So why do you miss questions? ACT knows that one way to make any problem more difficult is to simply phrase it as a word problem. Word problems can add confusing steps to mask the simple concepts tested by the problems. Trap answers, partial answers, and weird phrasing abound in word problems. Word problems (like pretty much everything else on the ACT) are often more about reading comprehension than about the underlying knowledge itself.

Word problems take a lot of different forms and test a variety of math concepts, but if you keep these three steps in mind, you should be able to solve most word problems pretty efficiently.

Let's try a problem:

---

14. Zachary is organizing his movie collection. $\frac{2}{5}$ of his movies are science-fiction films. Of his movies that are not science-fiction films, $\frac{3}{10}$ are comedies. Of his movies that are not science-fiction films or comedies, $\frac{1}{6}$ are foreign films. All of his remaining movies (those that are not science-fiction films, comedies, or foreign films) are dramas.

If Zachary has 300 movies, how many of them are dramas?

   F.   21
   G.   54
   H. 105
   J.   120
   K. 126

Here's How to Crack It

The following material explains how to use the steps of the Word Problem Approach to handle this question.

Step 1: Know the Question

There is actually a slightly tricky step on this one. First of all, the problem doesn't tell you until the very end that Zachary has 300 movies in total. Without this piece of information, the fractions don't mean much of anything. Second, the question is asking for the number of movies that are dramas, and we're going to have to figure out a bunch of other things before we figure that out.

Step 2: Let the Answers Help

There aren't any crazy answers in this one, though if you noticed we're taking less than half of the movies out each time, you're probably thinking that the answer won't be one of the smaller numbers.

Step 3: Break the Problem into Bite-Sized Pieces

The starting point of this word problem actually comes at the end: Zachary has 300 movies. Start with that information; then work the problem sentence by sentence, writing down the results as you go, and paying particular attention to the language of the problem.

$\frac{2}{5}$ of his movies are science-fiction films.

Zachary has 300 movies in total, and $\frac{2}{5}$ of 300 is 120, so Zachary has 120 science-fiction films.

Of his movies that are not science-fiction films, $\frac{3}{10}$ are comedies.

This looks just like the last piece, but there's a HUGE difference. This statement involves two separate calculations. The first step is to calculate the number of movies that are *not* science-fiction films. There are 300 total movies, and 120 of them are science-fiction films, so there are 180 movies that are not science-fiction films. The second step: $\frac{3}{10}$ of 180 is 54, so 54 of the movies are comedies.

Of his movies that are not science-fiction films or comedies, $\frac{1}{6}$ are foreign films.

Two steps again. First, we need to find the number of movies that are not science-fiction films or comedies. There were 180 movies left in the last step, but 54 of them are comedies, so now there are 126 movies that are not science-fiction films or comedies. The second step: $\frac{1}{6}$ of 126 is 21, so 21 of the movies are foreign films.

All of his remaining movies (those that are not science-fiction films, comedies, or foreign films) are dramas.

There were 126 movies left over in the last step, and 21 of them are foreign films, which means there are 105 movies left, and they are all dramas. Choice (H) is the correct answer. Look at those other answers; then look at the numbers you were dealing with in the problem: what a mess of partial answers!

—————————————◯—————————————

If it seems like this took a long time to do, don't worry—the strategy is actually much more efficient than it seems, and it will help you achieve that high accuracy you need to reach the top scores. The steps will come naturally after a while, and you'll have a solid base with which to begin any ACT Math problem in such a way that enables you to get to the answer as efficiently as possible.

ADVANCED STATISTICS

Word problems are often used to test concepts from statistics. You are probably comfortable with the basic statistic concepts like mean, median, and mode, so this chapter will focus on some advanced questions and concepts in statistics. If you need a refresher on any of the statistics terms, see the Statistics Glossary in your Student Tools.

THE FORMULAS

Rarely will you need to call on these formulas; most times, you should apply common sense and PITA skills to solve. But in case you just want to know...

- Average: $T = AN$, where T is the total, A is the average, and N is the number of things

- Arithmetic sequence: nth term = Original Term + $(n - 1)d$, where d is the constant difference between terms

- Direct Variation: $\dfrac{x_1}{x_2} = \dfrac{y_1}{y_2}$ or $y = kx$, where k is a constant

- Inverse Variation: $x_1 y_1 = x_2 y_2$ or $y = \dfrac{k}{x}$, where k is a constant

- Geometric sequence: nth term = Original Term $\times r^{(n-1)}$, where r is the constant ratio

- Group Formula: Total = Group 1 + Group 2 − Both + Neither

- Probability: $\dfrac{want}{total}$, where want is the number of outcomes that fit the requirements and total is the total number of possible outcomes

THE QUESTIONS

Some statistics questions are more complicated because they contain several vocabulary words or give information about unknown numbers. For these, use the tried and true strategies of Bite-Sized Pieces, Process of Elimination, and Plugging In.

---

54. Set *A* contains 12 distinct values. Set *B* contains 13 distinct values: the 12 values in Set *A* and a value that is lower than any value in Set *A*. Which of the following statements is true about the values of the mean and median for Set *B* as compared to those of Set *A* ?

   F. The mean and median of Set *B* will be equal to those of Set *A*.
   G. The mean and median of Set *B* will be less than those of Set *A*.
   H. The mean of Set *B* will be less than the mean of Set *A*; the medians of the two sets will be equal.
   J. The median of Set *B* will be less than the median of Set *A*; the means of the two sets will be equal.
   K. Using the given information, the means and medians of Set *B* and Set *A* cannot be compared.

Here's How to Crack It

The question asks for a true statement about the two sets of values. Because no actual values are given, plug in numbers for each set. Set *A* is to contain 12 distinct (different) values. Set *B* is to contain those same 12 distinct values and, in addition, a 13th value lower than any value in Set *A*. Make Set *A* {2, 3, 4, 5, 6, 7, 8, 9, 10, 11, 12, 13}. Make Set *B* {1, 2, 3, 4, 5, 6, 7, 8, 9, 10, 11, 12, 13}. The median is the middle value when a list of numbers is in order and it is usually easier to identify than the mean. Start by finding the median of each set. Because Set *A* has an even number of numbers, its median is the average of the two numbers in the middle. The two numbers in the middle of Set *A* are 7 and 8, so the median of Set A is $\dfrac{7+8}{2} = \dfrac{15}{2} = 7.5$. Because Set B has an odd number of numbers, its median is the number in the middle: 7. Since 7.5 > 7, the median of Set A is greater than the median of Set B. Eliminate the answer choices that do not reflect this. Choices (F) and (H) say that both medians are the same, which they are not. Eliminate (F) and (H). Choices (G) and (J) say that Set B's median is less than Set A's, so keep these answers. Also keep (K) because, even though a comparison can be made in this case, that doesn't necessarily mean that a comparison can always be made. Next, calculate the mean of each set using the formula for averages: *Total = Average × Number of things*. Set A has 12 numbers and their total (sum) is 90, so the mean of Set A is $\dfrac{90}{12} = 7.5$. Set B has 13 numbers and their sum is 91, so the mean of Set B is $\dfrac{91}{13} = 7$. Because 7.5 > 7, the mean of Set A is greater than the mean of Set B. Eliminate (J), which says that the means are equal. To eliminate (K), it is necessary to understand that the given comparisons will always hold true, no matter what the numbers are. Adding a value to a set of distinct numbers that is less than each of the other numbers in that set will always result in a decreased median and a decreased mean. The correct answer is (G).

Another way that the ACT may make statistics questions harder to solve is by presenting the data in an unusual way. Below is a stem-and-leaf plot. These figures show a series of numbers grouped by the lead digit(s) in each number, so the list below is 147, 150, 152, 157, 157, 159, etc. These figures will often come with a key, as shown below, but don't count on one. Once you know how to read the data, applying the basic statistics concepts to the data is not too tricky.

22. The heights, in centimeters, of students from a single section of a high school statistics class were recorded by the teacher. The stem-and-leaf plot below represents the heights of each of his students.

Stem	Leaf
14	7
15	0 2 7 7 9
16	0 0 1 3 3 3 7
17	0 2 5 5 5
18	3 5 8 9

Key: 17 | 5 = 175 centimeters

If one of the statistics students is selected at random, what is the probability that the student is shorter than 160 centimeters?

F. $\dfrac{6}{27}$

G. $\dfrac{7}{27}$

H. $\dfrac{6}{22}$

J. $\dfrac{7}{22}$

K. $\dfrac{8}{22}$

Here's How to Crack It

The question asks for a probability, which is defined as $\dfrac{want}{total}$. In this case, you want the number of students that are shorter than 160 centimeters out of the total number of students in the class. To count the students who are *shorter than 160 centimeters*, tally the number of values listed in the Leaf column for the stems 14 and 15. There is 1 value in the 14 row and 5 values in the 15 row for a sum of 1 + 5 = 6 students. This is the *want*, as no students who are 160 centimeters or taller should be counted. Now continue counting the remaining values in the Leaf column to get the total number of students in the class. There are 7 more in the 160 row, 5 more in the 170 row, and 4 more in the 180 row. This brings to total to 6 + 7 + 5 + 4 = 22. Therefore, the probability is $\frac{6}{22}$, so the correct answer is (H).

Now let's look at three more statistics concepts that may come up once on the ACT, if they appear at all.

Expected Value

Expected value is a statistical measure related to probability. The expected value in a situation is determined by both the values that are possible and the probability that those values will occur.

> To find expected value, multiply each possibility by the probability of its occurrence; then add all the products together.

---

56. Bill is playing a dice game in his gaming club. He will throw four fair, six-sided dice. Each face of each die displays a number between 1 and 6, inclusive, and no numbers are repeated. He will get two points for every die that displays a number less than three and no points for a number three or greater. If x is the number of points he will get on any toss of the dice, then what is the expected value of x ?

    F. $\dfrac{1}{2}$

    G. $\dfrac{2}{3}$

    H. 2

    J. $\dfrac{8}{3}$

    K. 8

Here's How to Crack It

The question asks for the expected value of x, the number of points Bill will get on any toss of the dice. There are four dice, so figure out the probability for each die separately. Then add up the probabilities to get the expected value. For the first die, there are 6 sides, only 2 of which have numbers *less than three*: a 1 or a 2. Bill will get points only if he rolls these numbers, so the probability of getting points on the first die is $\frac{want}{total} = \frac{2}{6} = \frac{1}{3}$. If Bill rolls one of these two numbers, he will get 2 points for doing so. Thus, for the first roll, the expected value is $\frac{1}{3}(2) = \frac{2}{3}$. The same will be true for each of the remaining three dice, so the overall expected value is the expected value of the first die times the number of dice: $\frac{2}{3}(4) = \frac{8}{3}$. The correct answer is (J).

Ordering

Most of the time, the ACT won't require you to use formulas for permutations and combinations. You will just need to write out the number of possibilities for each option and then multiply those numbers together. In a permutation, the order of the elements matters, like the number of ways 8 athletes can place in 1st, 2nd, and 3rd in a race. In combinations, the grouping of the elements matters, but the order does not, such as the number of ways a leadership team can be formed from a given number of candidates. To get rid of duplicates of the same group, the result of the permutation must be divided by a factorial of the number of options, so the team Amy and Beth is not counted as a different team than Beth and Amy.

20. A password for a website must have two letters in the first two positions, two single-digit numbers in the middle two positions, and in the last two positions, two special characters found above the digits 1 through 7 on a standard keyboard. The password is case-sensitive, so the letters may be upper or lower case. The special characters above the 8, 9, and 0 are not allowed. If all values can be reused, which of the following equations could be used to identify the total number of possible passwords?

F. 52(52)(10)(10)(7)(7)
G. 52(52)(9)(9)(7)(7)
H. 52(51)(10)(9)(7)(6)
J. 6(26)(10)(10)(7)(7)
K. 26(25)(10)(9)(7)(6)

Here's How to Crack It

The question asks for the number of possible passwords given the restrictions. It is very important to read carefully on these questions to get the right numbers for each option. After each option is determined, look for answers to eliminate. The password must have 6 characters, so draw 6 dashes and fill in the number of possibilities for each option. The first two options are letters of the alphabet, of which there are 26. These letters can be upper or lower case, so there are 26 + 26 = 52 possibilities. The question states that letters can be reused, so there is no need to subtract one that was already used in the first option to find the possibilities for the second option. The first two dashes will look like this:

$$\underline{52} \times \underline{52} \times \underline{} \times \underline{} \times \underline{} \times \underline{} \text{ -}$$

These values will be multiplied together, so eliminate (H), (J), and (K) which do not begin with 52(52). Now focus on the next two options, which must be single-digits numbers. There are 10 single-digit numbers, including 0, and there are no restrictions on using any of the 10 possibilities for options 3 and 4. Therefore, the next two dashes will have 10s on them.

$$\underline{52} \times \underline{52} \times \underline{10} \times \underline{10} \times \underline{} \times \underline{} \text{ -}$$

This means that (G) can be eliminated, since it has 9s in these places. The correct answer is (F).

37. A nonprofit company employs 3 project managers, 2 business analysts, and 8 programmers. For a new project, the company is creating a team consisting of one project manager, 1 business analyst, and 2 programmers. How many different teams are possible for this project?

   A.   48
   B.   96
   C.   168
   D.   336
   E.   672

Here's How to Crack It

The question asks for the number of possible teams for a project. Start with the same steps as with the previous question, making 4 dashes for the 4 options to be chosen. Then fill in each dash with the number of possibilities for that option. Only one project manager and one business analyst will be chosen, so those numbers are 3 and 2, respectively.

$$\underline{3} \ \times \ \underline{2} \ \times \ \underline{} \ \times \ \underline{}$$

$$\text{PM} \quad \text{BA} \quad \text{PR1} \quad \text{PR2}$$

For the first programmer slot, there are 8 to choose from, but for the second programmer slot, there are only 7 remaining after one has been assigned to the first slot. The options are as follows.

$$\underline{3} \ \times \ \underline{2} \ \times \ \underline{8} \ \times \ \underline{7}$$

$$\text{PM} \quad \text{BA} \quad \text{PR1} \quad \text{PR2}$$

Now, because these people are forming a team and not an arrangement or order, it is necessary to get rid of the duplicate teams. Because there is only one project manager and one business analyst, those groups don't need to be divided. However, it is necessary to divide the programmers to get rid of duplicates. Because there are two programmer slots, divide by 2 × 1. The result is $3 \times 2 \times \dfrac{8 \times 7}{2 \times 1} = 6 \times \dfrac{56}{2} = 168$. The correct answer is (C).

Standard Deviation

Though the ACT will ask about standard deviation on rare occasions, you will not be asked to calculate it. Here are a few things you will need to know to handle this topic if it comes up.

> Standard Deviation = Spread
>
> More spread out = greater Standard Deviation
>
> More closely grouped = lesser Standard Deviation
>
> For data that has a normal distribution, 68% of the data lies within one standard deviation of the mean.

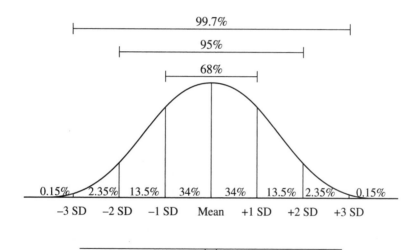

52. Which of the following sets has the greatest standard deviation?

    F. {10, 12, 14, 16, 18, 20, 22, 24}
    G. {10, 12, 16, 16, 16, 16, 18, 20}
    H. {10, 12, 16, 16, 17, 18, 21, 23}
    J. {10, 12, 16, 16, 21, 23, 23, 23}
    K. {10, 12, 16, 20, 48, 72, 124, 160}

Here's How to Crack It

The question asks for the list of numbers with the greatest standard deviation. Standard deviation is a measure of the spread of data, so look for the list with the biggest spread. For (F) through (J), all the values are two-digit numbers between 10 and 24. For (K), the numbers are much more spread out and random-seeming. Therefore, the list in (K) has the greatest standard deviation, making it the correct answer.

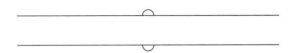

57. A normal probability distribution is sketched below with a mean of 0 and a standard deviation of 1. Which of the following represents the expected percent of data that falls within one standard deviation of the mean?

Normal Distribution

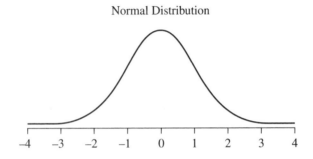

A. 50%
B. 68%
C. 95%
D. 98%
E. 99%

Here's How to Crack It

The question asks for the percent of the data that is within one standard deviation of the mean. According to the normal distribution graph above, the mean of the data is the line of symmetry of the curve. On this figure, that line is conveniently placed at 0. The data that is within one standard deviation of mean, or between 1 and –1 on the horizontal axis, accounts for 34% of the graph on either side of the mean line. This indicates that the data within one standard deviation accounts for a total of 34% + 34% = 68% of the data. The correct answer is (B).

Now try these strategies on your own. Go online to your Student Tools and answer the Chapter 12 Drill.

Chapter 13
Advanced Math

The ACT Math Test often includes questions based on a few advanced math topics, such as logarithms, matrices, series, ellipses, and advanced trigonometry. While these areas of math are complex to learn, the questions on the ACT that refer to these more advanced areas of math are usually fairly straightforward. Often, the key to these questions is simply a matter of knowing the basic rules in question.

SCIENTIFIC NOTATION

The ACT will sometimes test exponent questions using scientific notation. This notation is used to express numbers that are very large or very small. A number written in scientific notation is expressed in the form $m \times 10^n$, where the value of m is at least 1 but less than 10. The value of n is positive for large numbers, as it moves the decimal n places to the right. The value of n is negative for small numbers, moving the decimal n places to the left.

Let's try a couple of questions.

---

40. The approximate distance around the equator of the Earth, which is 2.5×10^4 miles, is about how many times the approximate distance from Detroit, MI, to Cleveland, OH, which is 9.4×10^1 miles?

    F. 2.4×10^6
    G. 4.2×10^4
    H. 2.7×10^4
    J. 4.2×10^2
    K. 2.7×10^2

Here's How to Crack It

The question asks for the number of times one distance is compared to another. The powers of 10 in this question are not very big, so transform the scientific notation into numbers that are easy to plug into your calculator. After moving the decimal 4 places to the right, the distance around the equator is 25,000 miles. After moving the decimal one place to the right, the distance from Detroit to Cleveland is 94 miles. Translate the question to get $25,000 = 94x$. Divide both sides by 94 to get $x \approx 266$ which is closest to (K).

---

37. A computer program can run through a simple program loop 1.4×10^6 times each second. Which of the following expresses the number of seconds it will take the program to complete 8.4×10^{12} passes through the loop, in scientific notation?

    A. 11.76×10^{18}
    B. 6.0×10^6
    C. 6.0×10^2
    D. 11.76×10^0
    E. 1.67×10^{-7}

Here's How to Crack It

The question asks for a calculation in scientific notation. Start by eliminating answers in the wrong form. Choices (A) and (D) do not start with a number less than 10, so eliminate them. To find the number of seconds it will take to run 8.4×10^{12} passes through the loop, divide this number by the number of passes run each second, which is 1.4×10^6. The powers of 10 are much larger here than in the previous question, so break the calculations into bite-sized pieces. This becomes $\frac{8.4 \times 10^{12}}{1.4 \times 10^6} = \frac{8.4}{1.4} \times \frac{10^{12}}{10^6}$.

The first fraction becomes 6.0, so eliminate (E). Use the MADSPM rules of exponents to find the value of the second fraction. The DS part means that when Dividing like bases, you Subtract the exponents. Therefore, the second fraction can be rewritten as $10^{(12-6)}$, which is 10^6. The correct answer is (B).

> When combining numbers with the same base and different exponents, follow these exponent rules:
>
> **M**ultiply
> **A**dd
> **D**ivide
> **S**ubtract
> **P**ower
> **M**ultiply

LOGARITHM RULES

A logarithm is just another way of expressing an exponent.

$$\log_b n = x \text{ means the same thing as } b^x = n$$

Your calculator can easily handle base-10 logs, written in the form $\log n$. Use your calculator when you can, as in the following question.

---

16. For which of the following values of a does $\log a = 5$?

F. 555
G. 1,000
H. 50,000
J. 100,000
K. 500,000

Here's How to Crack It

The question asks for a specific value and there are numbers in the answer choices, so plug in the answers! Label the answers as "*a*" and start in the middle with (H). If *a* = 50,000, you can find log *a* on your calculator by typing in "log 50,000." The result is about 4.699, which is close to 5 but not close enough. Eliminate (H). For (J), *a* = 100,000 and log 100,000 = 5. This works, so stop here. The correct answer is (J), and you needed absolutely no knowledge of how logs work to get it.

Of course, this won't always be the case. Knowing how to rewrite a log as a base with an exponent will be the key to solving more difficult log questions.

Since the logarithm itself represents an exponent, the MADSPM rules also apply to logarithms, but in a different way:

> When a logarithm doesn't have a base (the subscript next to "log"), the base is understood to be 10.

$$\log xy = (\log x) + (\log y)$$

$$\log\left(\frac{x}{y}\right) = \log x - \log y$$

$$\log x^y = y \log x$$

Let's see how this works on a couple of questions.

---

49. Which of the following ranges of consecutive integers contains the value of the expression $\log_4\left(4^{\frac{11}{4}}\right)$?

    A. 0 and 1
    B. 1 and 2
    C. 2 and 3
    D. 3 and 4
    E. 4 and 5

Here's How to Crack It

The question asks for the value of a logarithmic expression. Use the last log rule in the

box above to rewrite $\log_4\left(4^{\frac{11}{4}}\right)$ as $\frac{11}{4}(\log_4 4)$; then rewrite the part in parentheses as

$4^x = 4$. The value of x that makes this true is $x = 1$, so the expression becomes $\frac{11}{4}(1)$. This

is equal to 2.75, which is between 2 and 3. The correct answer is (C).

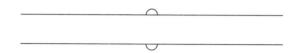

58. If $\log_5 36 = x$ and $\log_5 12 = y$, which of the following expressions
equals 6 ?

    F. $5^{x-y} + 3$

    G. 5^{x-y+3}

    H. 6^{x-y}

    J. $x - y + 3$

    K. $\dfrac{x}{y} + 3$

Here's How to Crack It

The question asks for the expression that equals 6 given two logarithmic equations. Since

these logs are of the same base, you can combine them using the log subtraction rule

above. The result is $\log_5\left(\dfrac{36}{12}\right) = x - y$, which simplifies to $\log_5 (3) = x - y$. Next, trans-

form the equation from a log into exponent form to get $5^{x-y} = 3$. Use this to determine

which of the answers is equal to 6. Choice (F) becomes $5^{x-y} + 3 = 3 + 3 = 6$. Keep (F), but

check the remaining answers. Choice (G) can be rewritten as $(5^{x-y})(5^3)$ using MADSPM

rules, so this becomes $(3)(125) = 375$. Eliminate (G). Solving for the exact value of $x - y$

is necessary to calculate the values of (H) and (J), but that sort of math is beyond what

the ACT test expects you to do. (For your information, $x - y \approx 0.68$. Because $x - y$ is the exponent that makes $5^{x-y} = 3$, so $x - y$ must be less than 1.) There is also no way to determine the exact values of x and y separately, so (K) cannot be calculated at all. The correct answer is (F).

———————————⌒———————————

MATRICES

Some (but not all) ACT Math Tests include a matrix problem. If you know the matrix rules, you should find these problems manageable. Also, if your calculator has matrix functions and you're familiar with their use, you may be able to solve matrix problems on a calculator.

On the ACT Math Test, matrix problems generally test data organization, multiplication of matrices, or matrix transformations.

Multiplication of Matrices

The size of a matrix is described as rows × columns; in order to multiply matrix A by matrix B, the number of *columns* of A must be the same as the number of *rows* of B. For instance, it would be possible to multiply a 3 × 2 matrix by a 2 × 5 matrix.

To find the product of matrix A and matrix B, each cell in the product is found by multiplying and adding the elements of the corresponding *row* of matrix A with the corresponding *column* of matrix B. For example:

$$\begin{bmatrix} a & b \\ c & d \end{bmatrix}\begin{bmatrix} w & x \\ y & z \end{bmatrix} = \begin{bmatrix} aw + by & ax + bz \\ cw + dy & cx + dz \end{bmatrix}$$

$$\begin{bmatrix} 1 & 2 \\ 3 & 4 \end{bmatrix}\begin{bmatrix} 5 & 6 \\ 7 & 8 \end{bmatrix} = \begin{bmatrix} 19 & 22 \\ 43 & 50 \end{bmatrix}$$

Matrix Transformations

The basic matrix transformation is the *identity matrix*; it is the equivalent of the number 1 for matrices. The identity matrix has 1's down the main diagonal from the top left to the bottom right, with 0 everywhere else:

$$\begin{bmatrix} 1 & 0 \\ 0 & 1 \end{bmatrix}$$

If you multiply a matrix by the identity matrix, the product is equal to the original matrix.

$$\begin{bmatrix} 1 & 2 \\ 3 & 4 \end{bmatrix}\begin{bmatrix} 1 & 0 \\ 0 & 1 \end{bmatrix} = \begin{bmatrix} 1 & 2 \\ 3 & 4 \end{bmatrix}$$

Changes to the identity matrix allow for other basic transformations:

$$\begin{bmatrix} 1 & 2 \\ 3 & 4 \end{bmatrix}\begin{bmatrix} -1 & 0 \\ 0 & -1 \end{bmatrix} = \begin{bmatrix} -1 & -2 \\ -3 & -4 \end{bmatrix}$$

Here are some matrix questions for you to try.

---

45. Matrices A, B, and C are defined as $A = \begin{bmatrix} 1 & 9 & 8 \\ 4 & 7 & 6 \\ 0 & 2 & 3 \end{bmatrix}$, $B = \begin{bmatrix} 5 & 6 \\ 9 & 2 \\ 3 & 8 \end{bmatrix}$, and $C = \begin{bmatrix} 7 & 1 & 3 \\ 9 & 6 & 5 \end{bmatrix}$. Which of the following matrix products is undefined?

   A. AB

   B. AC

   C. BC

   D. CA

   E. CB

Here's How to Crack It

The question asks for the matrix product that is undefined. Since the product of two matrices can be found only if the number of columns in the first matches the number of rows in the second, the matrix product will be undefined when this condition is not met. Look at the products in the answers and determine the dimensions of the matrices to be multiplied. Choice (A) multiplies A by B: A has 3 columns and B has 3 rows. That will work, so this product is not undefined. Eliminate (A). Choice (B) multiplies A by C: A has 3 columns, but C only has 2 rows. This product will be undefined, so the correct answer is (B).

Now that we've covered what requirements are needed to multiply matrices together, let's look at a question that requires us to do the actual multiplication.

---

59. Matrices X, Y, and Z are given below.

$$X = \begin{bmatrix} 4 & 1 & 0 \\ -2 & 6 & 3 \end{bmatrix} \qquad Y = \begin{bmatrix} 9 & -1 \\ 7 & 2 \end{bmatrix} \qquad Z = \begin{bmatrix} 8 & 1 & 2 \\ -3 & 9 & 3 \end{bmatrix}$$

If it is possible to calculate $X + YZ$, which of the following matrices is the result?

A. $\begin{bmatrix} 79 & 1 & 15 \\ 48 & 31 & 23 \end{bmatrix}$

B. $\begin{bmatrix} 75 & 0 & 15 \\ 50 & 25 & 20 \end{bmatrix}$

C. $\begin{bmatrix} 46 & 4 & -2 \\ 21 & 28 & 9 \end{bmatrix}$

D. $\begin{bmatrix} 33 & -4 \\ -3 & 69 \end{bmatrix}$

E. It is not possible to calculate $X + YZ$.

Here's How to Crack It

The question asks for the value of $X + YZ$ for matrices X, Y, and Z. Start with Process of Elimination. To determine if it is possible to calculate $X + YZ$, look at YZ first. This product is possible if the number of columns in Y matches the numbers of rows in Z. There are two columns in Y and two rows in Z, so the product is possible. Once YZ is found, it is possible to calculate $X + YZ$ by adding the value in each number position of X to the corresponding value in YZ if both matrices have the same dimensions. When multiplying matrices, the result will have the same number of rows as the first matrix and the same number of columns as the second matrix. When you calculate YZ, it will have two rows like Y and three columns like Z. Matrix X has two rows and three columns, and YZ will have two rows and three columns, so it will be possible to add the values in each position. Eliminate (E), which indicates that these calculations aren't possible. Next, (D) can be eliminated, as it doesn't have the correct dimensions. At this point, you may want to guess and go, but let's see if we can determine the correct answer with Bite-Sized Pieces and Process of Elimination. The three remaining answers all have different values in the upper left position, so focus on that. To find the value in the upper left of YZ, you need to find the dot product of the first row of Y and the first column of Z. This means to take the 9 and the 8 in the first positions, respectively, multiply them together, and then add the result to the product of the -1 and the -3 in the second positions, respectively. Therefore, the value in the upper left of YZ is $(9)(8) + (-1)(-3) = 72 + 3 = 75$. Now add the value in the upper left corner of X, which is 4, to get $75 + 4 = 79$ in the upper left of $X + YZ$. Only one answer has this value in this position. The correct answer is (A).

CIRCLES, ELLIPSES, AND PARABOLAS

Very few ACT Math questions will involve using the formulas for the circle, ellipse, and parabola. As long as you are familiar with these equations, you can figure out the answer to almost any of these questions by graphing.

The standard equation for a **circle** is shown below.

$$(x - h)^2 + (y - k)^2 = r^2 \qquad \text{Center of the circle: } (h, k) \qquad \text{Radius} = r$$

You need to memorize the circle formula and be able to apply it when it comes up in questions, because it will not be provided to you. For instance, a circle with the equation $(x - 2)^2 + (y + 3)^2 = 25$ is a circle with a radius of 5 and a center at $(2, -3)$.

An ellipse is a circle that has been squashed into an oval shape. The standard equation for an **ellipse** is shown below.

$$\frac{(x-h)^2}{a^2} + \frac{(y-k)^2}{b^2} = 1 \qquad \text{Center of the ellipse: } (h, k)$$

$$\text{Horizontal axis} = 2a$$

$$\text{Vertical axis} = 2b$$

Unlike the circle formula, you do *not* need to memorize the ellipse formula for the test. Whenever a question involves an ellipse, the ellipse formula will be provided for you, and you simply need to know how to work with it. For example, an ellipse with the equation $\frac{(x-4)^2}{9} + \frac{(y+3)^2}{25} = 1$ has the center (4, −3), a horizontal axis of 6, and a vertical axis of 10.

A parabola is a U-shaped curve. The standard equation for a **parabola** is shown below.

$$y = x^2$$

Here's the equation for a parabola in a more complicated form:

$$y = a(x-h)^2 + k \qquad \text{Vertex} = (h, k)$$

Parabolas with the above formula will open upward or downward. For a parabola that is "sideways" (opening to the left or the right), simply swap x and y in the equation, as shown below.

$$x = y^2 \qquad x = a\left(y - h\right)^2 + k \qquad \text{Vertex} = (h,\ k)$$

You need to know the parabola formula and recognize how to use it on the test, because it will not be provided to you. Any quadratic equation will form a parabola when graphed.

Let's try some questions:

42. A circle in the standard (x,y) coordinate plane has radius 8 coordinate units and center $(-4,3)$. Which of the following is an equation of the circle?

   F. $(x - 4)^2 - (y + 3)^2 = 8$
   G. $(x - 4)^2 - (y + 3)^2 = 64$
   H. $(x - 4)^2 + (y + 3)^2 = 64$
   J. $(x + 4)^2 + (y - 3)^2 = 8$
   K. $(x + 4)^2 + (y - 3)^2 = 64$

Here's How to Crack It

The question asks for the equation of a circle in the coordinate plane given its center and radius. Use the circle formula $(x - h)^2 + (y - k)^2 = r^2$ to plug in the information about the radius and the center of the circle. Just by looking at the standard form of a circle equation, (F) and (G) can be eliminated, as those feature subtraction between the x- and y-terms instead of addition. The radius is 8, so the r^2 part of the formula on the right side will be $8^2 = 64$. This eliminates (J), which is set equal to 8. Now plug the coordinates of the center, $(-4, 3)$, into the formula to get $(x - (-4))^2 + (y - 3)^2 = 8^2$. This becomes $(x + 4)^2 + (y - 3)^2 = 64$, so the correct answer is (K).

54. Shown below is quadrilateral *WXYZ* inscribed in an ellipse. The figure will be placed in a standard (x,y) coordinate plane, and the ellipse will be described by the equation $\dfrac{(x-2)^2}{25} + \dfrac{(y-1)^2}{9} = 1$. Given that $\overline{WY}$ is the major axis and $\overline{XZ}$ is the minor axis of the ellipse, what will be the coordinates of points *W* and *X* ?

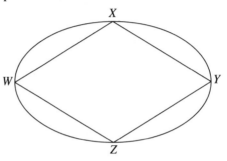

	point *W*	point *X*
F.	(−5,0)	(2,25)
G.	(−5,1)	(2, 1)
H.	(−3,0)	(2, 0)
J.	(−3,1)	(0, 9)
K.	(−3,1)	(2, 4)

Here's How to Crack It

The question asks for the coordinates of two points shared by a quadrilateral and an ellipse. Use the ellipse formula $\dfrac{(x-h)^2}{a^2} + \dfrac{(y-k)^2}{b^2} = 1$ to determine the center of the ellipse and the values of a and b. The center is (h, k), so this ellipse is centered at $(2, 1)$. The value of a^2 is 25, so $a = 5$, and the width of the ellipse is $2a = 10$. The value of b^2 is 9, so $b = 3$, and the height of the ellipse is $2b = 6$.

Use this information to sketch the coordinate plane on the figure of the ellipse.

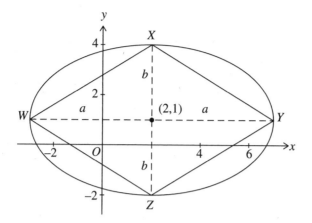

Point *W* is on the same horizontal line as the center, so it will have a *y*-coordinate of 1. Eliminate (F) and (H), which have 0 as the *y*-coordinate of point *W*. The *x*-coordinate of *W* will be *a* units to the left of the center. Since *a* = 5, the *x*-coordinate of *W* is at 2 − 5 = −3. Eliminate (G), which has −5 for the *x*-coordinate. Now compare the coordinates for point *X* in the remaining answers (J) and (K). Both the *x*- and *y*-coordinates of *X* are positive, so it must be at (2, 4). The correct answer is (K).

Domain and Asymptotes

Now let's look at two other ideas related to curves in the coordinate plane, starting with domain. It is rare to see the words *domain* and *range* in relation to functions on the ACT. The domain is the set of all *x*-values that can be put into a function, and the range is all the *y*-values that come out.

Let's look at a couple of examples that specifically ask for the domain of a function so you can get an idea of the notation that is used.

49. If $f(x) = \dfrac{7}{x^4 - 16}$, what is the domain of $f(x)$?

    A. $\{x | x \neq -2\}$
    B. $\{x | x \neq 2\}$
    C. $\{x | x \neq -2 \text{ and } x \neq 2\}$
    D. $\{x | x \neq -4, x \neq -2, \text{ and } x \neq 2\}$
    E. $\{x | x \neq 16\}$

Here's How to Crack It

The question asks for the domain of a function. In the notation in the answers, the x in front of the $|$ indicates "all values of x." Values after the $|$ indicate the values of x that are excluded. For (A), this notation would read "all values of x such that x is not equal to -2." The values of x that will not be allowed are ones that make the fraction undefined. In other words, if the value of x makes the denominator equal to 0, that value of x must be excluded. This is a great opportunity to plug in values from the answers. Pick a value that is in more than one answer, such as $x = -2$. The function becomes $f(-2) = \dfrac{7}{(-2)^4 - 16} = \dfrac{7}{16 - 16} = \dfrac{7}{0}$. This is undefined, so $x = -2$ must be excluded from the domain. Eliminate (B) and (E), as those do not exclude this value. Now try $x = 2$. The function becomes $f(2) = \dfrac{7}{(2)^4 - 16} = \dfrac{7}{16 - 16} = \dfrac{7}{0}$. This is also undefined, so $x = 2$ must be excluded from the domain. Eliminate (A). Finally, try $x = -4$. The function becomes $f(-4) = \dfrac{7}{(-4)^4 - 16} = \dfrac{7}{256 - 16} = \dfrac{7}{240}$. This is defined, so $x = -4$ does not need to be excluded from the domain. Eliminate (D). The correct answer is (C).

49. The graph of $g(x) = \dfrac{x+2}{x^2+5x+6}$ is shown below. The domain of $g(x)$ is the set of all real numbers EXCEPT:

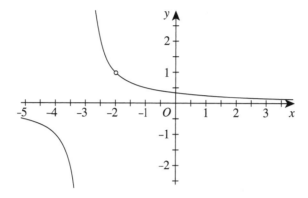

- **A.** −3
- **B.** −2
- **C.** 0
- **D.** −2 and −3
- **E.** 2 and 3

Here's How to Crack It

The question asks for the values of x that are excluded from a domain. This one is a lot like the last one, but with the added bonus of having a graph. The hole in the graph indicates a place where the function is undefined, so look up the x-value where that happens. It occurs at $x = -2$, so that must be one of the values not included in the domain. Eliminate (A), (C), and (E), as these don't include −2. To decide between (B) and (D), plug in $x = -3$ from (D). The function becomes $g(-3) = \dfrac{-3+2}{(-3)^2+5(-3)+6} = \dfrac{-1}{9-15+6} = \dfrac{-1}{0}$. The function is undefined, so $x = -3$ must be part of the correct answer, which is (D).

You may have also noticed that the graph approaches, but does not touch, $x = -3$. This feature brings us to the topic of asymptotes, which are lines that a curve approaches but generally does not cross. (There are exceptions where the curve does cross the asymptote, but those won't be tested on the ACT.) Vertical asymptotes arise at x-values that are excluded from the domain, so in the last question, there is a vertical asymptote at $x = -3$. As x approaches the excluded value from the left or the right, the curve goes toward infinity or negative infinity.

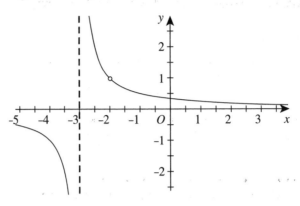

Some questions will specifically ask for the equation of an asymptote, as seen below.

---

37. What value of x represents the vertical asymptote of the graph of the equation $y = \dfrac{3x+2}{3x-24}$?

    A. -2

    B. $-\dfrac{2}{3}$

    C. 2

    D. 3

    E. 8

Here's How to Crack It

The question asks for the value of x that represents a vertical asymptote of a graph. To find the vertical asymptotes of a graph, find the values of x that are excluded from the domain. In this equation, the value of x that makes the denominator 0 is the only excluded value. Either plug in the answers as we did in the last two questions or solve this algebraically. Since we've already tried PITA on this type of question, let's look at how to solve it. Set the denominator equal to 0 to get $3x - 24 = 0$; then add 24 to both sides of the equation to get $3x = 24$. Divide both sides by 3 to get $x = 8$. The correct answer is (E).

For horizontal asymptotes, the curve approaches some constant value of y as the x-values go to infinity or negative infinity. Horizontal asymptotes occur in two situations. The first is with a rational equation for which the degree of the denominator is greater than the degree of the numerator. In these cases, the x-axis becomes the horizontal asymptote. This is very unlikely to appear on the ACT. The second situation is more likely to show up: a rational equation for which the degrees of the numerator and the denominator are the same. For these, the horizontal asymptote is found by dividing the lead coefficient in the numerator by the lead coefficient in the denominator. The lead coefficient is the number in front of the variable with the greatest exponent.

---

59. Which of the following linear equations gives the horizontal asymptote

for the graph of $f(x) = \dfrac{x^2 + 4x}{3x^2 - 12}$ in the standard (x,y) coordinate plane?

A. $x = -2$

B. $x = 2$

C. $y = 0$

D. $y = \dfrac{1}{3}$

E. $y = 3$

Here's How to Crack It

The question asks for the equation of a line that represents a horizontal asymptote of a graph. Start with Process of Elimination. The question asks for a *horizontal asymptote*, so the equation of that asymptote must be a constant value for y. Eliminate (A) and (B), as these represent possible *vertical asymptotes*. The degree of the numerator is 2, as is the degree of the denominator. Therefore, the horizontal asymptote is at the y-value that is the quotient of the coefficients: $y = \dfrac{1}{3}$. The correct answer is (D).

Don't forget that you've got that calculator sitting on your desk for the math section. If all else fails, you can graph the equations and ballpark the locations of the asymptotes. The graph of the equation in the question above looks like this:

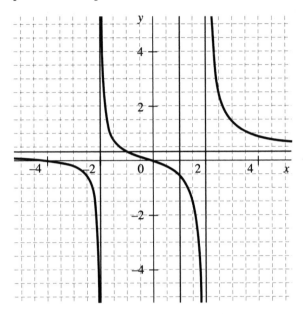

From this, you can see any asymptotes that exist, no calculations needed!

Vectors

Vectors are measures of displacement. They can be represented by arrows, often drawn in the coordinate plane. The length of the line shows the magnitude of the vector, and the arrow points in the direction of the vector. A vector can be broken up into component parts (which, on the ACT, will correspond to displacement in the x and y directions), and those parts can be added to the corresponding parts of another vector. The convention for vector notation is to have the name of the vector and the component parts **i** and **j** in bold text.

42. In unit vector notation, **u** = a**i** + 5**j**, **v** = 2**i** + b**j**, and **u** + **v** = 4**i** − 3**j**. What is the ordered pair (a,b) ?

    F. (−2,−5)

    G. (2,−8)

    H. (2, 5)

    J. (4,−8)

    K. (5, 2)

Here's How to Crack It

The question asks for the values of a and b in terms of vectors **u** and **v**. In unit vector notation, **i** represents the change in the x-value, and **j** represents the change in the y-value. To find the sum **u** + **v**, you need to add the **i** values and the **j** values: **u** + **v** = $(a + 2)$**i** + $(5 + b)$**j**. The question states that **u** + **v** = 4**i** − 3**j**, so set the two expressions equal to get $(a + 2)$**i** + $(5 + b)$**j** = 4**i** − 3**j**. When working with vectors on the ACT, the x-values and y-values should be dealt with separately. Look at the **i** terms first: $(a + 2)$**i** = 4**i**, so $(a + 2)$ = 4 and a = 2. Eliminate (F), (J), and (K), which do not have a 2 for a. Now, look at the **j** terms: $(5 + b)$**j** = −3**j**, so 5 + b = −3 and b = −8. The ordered pair (a, b) is (2, −8). The correct answer is (G).

---

52. The component forms of vectors **u** and **v** are given by **u** = $\langle -3,2 \rangle$ and **v** = $\langle 7,5 \rangle$. Given that 4**u** + (−2**v**) + **w** = 0, what is the component form of vector **w** ?

    F. $\langle -26,-2 \rangle$
    G. $\langle -10,-3 \rangle$
    H. $\langle -4,-7 \rangle$
    J. $\langle 10, 3 \rangle$
    K. $\langle 26, 2 \rangle$

Here's How to Crack It

The question asks for the component form of vector **w**. The component form of a vector describes the vector in terms of the changes in the x- and y-values. In other words, if **u** = $\langle -3,2 \rangle$, vector **u** changes x by −3 and y by 2. When adding or subtracting vectors in component form, add or subtract the x-values and the y-values. Start by plugging in the given values for **u** and **v** to get $4\langle -3,2 \rangle + [-2\langle 7,5 \rangle] + \mathbf{w} = 0$. Distribute and this becomes $\langle -12,8 \rangle + \langle -14,-10 \rangle + \mathbf{w} = 0$. Next, combine the vectors in component form by adding the x-values and adding the y-values to get $\langle -12+(-14),8+(-10) \rangle + \mathbf{w} = 0$, which is $\langle -26,-2 \rangle + \mathbf{w} = 0$. The sum of the resulting vector $\langle -26,-2 \rangle$ and **w** equals 0, which represents a vector with x- and y-components of 0. Therefore, add $\langle 26,2 \rangle$ to both sides to isolate **w** and get **w** = $\langle 26,2 \rangle$. The correct answer is (K).

Now let's look at a couple of questions about vectors in the coordinate plane.

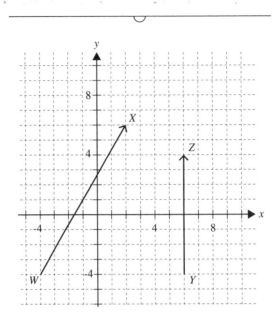

59. The vectors $\overrightarrow{WX}$ and $\overrightarrow{YZ}$ are shown in the xy-plane. Which of the following is the unit vector notation of vector $\overrightarrow{WX}$ + $\overrightarrow{YZ}$?

A. 2**i** – 8**j**
B. 2**i** + 6**i**
C. 6**i** + 6**j**
D. 6**i** + 18**j**
E. 10**i** – 8**j**

Here's How to Crack It

The question asks for the unit vector notation of the sum of two vectors in the coordinate plane. As before, in unit vector notation, **i** represents the change in the x-value, and **j** represents the change in the y-value. Vector $\overrightarrow{WX}$ starts at $(-4, -4)$ and ends at $(2, 6)$, so it increases the x-value by 6 and increases the y-value by 10. Therefore, the unit vector notation of $\overrightarrow{WX}$ is 6**i** + 10**j**. Vector $\overrightarrow{YZ}$ starts at $(6, -4)$ and ends at $(6, 4)$, so the unit vector notation of $\overrightarrow{YZ}$ is 0**i** + 8**j**. When adding two vectors in unit vector notation, add the coefficients on the **i** terms and the coefficients on the **j** terms. Therefore, the unit vector notation of $\overrightarrow{WX}$ + $\overrightarrow{YZ}$ is $(6 + 0)$**i** + $(10 + 8)$**j** = 6**i** + 18**j**. The correct answer is (D).

45. Vectors $\overrightarrow{AB}$ and $\overrightarrow{CD}$ are shown in the standard (x,y) coordinate plane below. What is the component form of vector $\overrightarrow{AB} + \overrightarrow{CD}$?

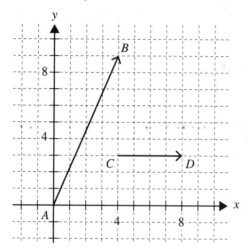

- **A.** $\langle 0,\ 4 \rangle$
- **B.** $\langle 4,\ 3 \rangle$
- **C.** $\langle 4,\ 9 \rangle$
- **D.** $\langle 8,\ 9 \rangle$
- **E.** $\langle 8,12 \rangle$

Here's How to Crack It

The question asks for the component form of the sum of two vectors in the coordinate plane. As we have already seen, the component form of a vector describes the vector in terms of the changes in the x- and y-values. Vector $\overrightarrow{AB}$ starts at $(0, 0)$ and ends at $(4, 9)$, so it increases the x-value by 4 and increases the y-value by 9. Therefore, the component form of vector $\overrightarrow{AB}$ is $\langle 4,9 \rangle$. Vector $\overrightarrow{CD}$ starts at $(4, 3)$ and ends at $(8, 3)$, so the component form is $\langle 8 - 4, 3 - 3 \rangle = \langle 4,0 \rangle$. When adding or subtracting vectors in component form, add or subtract the x-values and the y-values. $\overrightarrow{AB} + \overrightarrow{CD} = \langle 4 + 4, 9 + 0 \rangle = \langle 8,9 \rangle$. The correct answer is (D).

One final thing that may come up on a vector question is subtraction of vectors. To do that, simply reverse the direction of the one you are subtracting; then add them as normal. For the last question, if it had asked for the component vector form of $\overrightarrow{AB} - \overrightarrow{CD}$, you would change $\overrightarrow{CD}$ to start at (8, 3) and end at (4, 3), for a component form of $\langle -4, 0 \rangle$. Then adding this to $\overrightarrow{AB}$ would result in $\overrightarrow{AB} + \overrightarrow{CD} = \langle 4 - 4, 9 + 0 \rangle = \langle 0, 9 \rangle$.

ADVANCED TRIG

In the Geometry chapter, you reviewed the basic trig definitions and identities. Now we will look at two advanced trig concepts—laws and the unit circle.

The Laws of Sine and Cosine

Occasionally, the ACT will give you a question that requires you to use the Law of Sines and the Law of Cosines. As an added bonus, the ACT Math Test will actually give these formulas to you whenever they apply, so you only need to be familiar with their use.

Law of Sines: $\dfrac{\sin A}{a} = \dfrac{\sin B}{b} = \dfrac{\sin C}{c}$ Law of Cosines: $c^2 = a^2 + b^2 - 2ab \cos C$

Let's try a question.

53. In $\triangle XYZ$, the measure of $\angle X$ is 57°, the measure of $\angle Y$ is 72°, and the length of $\overline{XZ}$ is 12 inches. Which of the following is an expression for the length, in inches, of $\overline{YZ}$?

(Note: The Law of Sines states that for any triangle, the ratios of the lengths of the sides to the sines of the angles opposite those sides are equal.)

A. $\dfrac{\sin 57°}{12 \sin 72°}$

B. $\dfrac{\sin 72°}{12 \sin 57°}$

C. $\dfrac{12 \sin 72°}{\sin 57°}$

D. $\dfrac{12 \sin 57°}{\sin 72°}$

E. $\dfrac{(\sin 57°)(\sin 72°)}{12}$

Here's How to Crack It

The question asks for *the length, in inches, of $\overline{YZ}$*. The question also provides *The Law of Sines*, so that law is likely necessary to answer the question. Since no figure is provided, draw and label $\triangle XYZ$. Label $\angle X$ and $\angle Y$ as 57° and 72°, respectively. The third vertex must be Z, so label the side opposite $\angle Y$, $\overline{XZ}$, as 12. The Law of Sines states that *the ratios of the lengths of the sides to the sines of the angles opposite those sides are equal*, so this can be written as $\dfrac{XZ}{\sin Y} = \dfrac{YZ}{\sin X}$. Plugging in the given measures gives $\dfrac{12}{\sin 72°} = \dfrac{YZ}{\sin 57°}$. Cross-multiply to solve for YZ: $(YZ)\sin 72° = 12 \sin 57°$. Divide both sides by $\sin 72°$ to get $YZ = \dfrac{12 \sin 57°}{\sin 72°}$. The correct answer is (D).

Unit Circle

The *Unit Circle* is used to determine the values for trig functions.

Fill in the angle measurements in degrees and (*x*, *y*) coordinates for the circle below with a radius of 1.

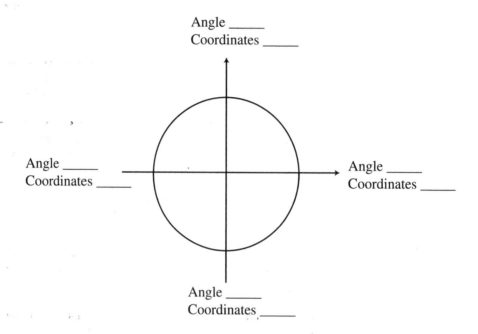

Angle _____
Coordinates _____

Angle _____
Coordinates _____

Angle _____
Coordinates _____

Angle _____
Coordinates _____

Now complete the table below, using your calculator. Make sure you are in "Degree" mode.

Angle	Sine	Cosine
90°		
180°		
270°		
0/360°		

Sine and cosine are another way of expressing *y* and *x* in the standard (*x*, *y*) coordinate plane.

Try this question.

56. If $\cos\theta = \dfrac{3}{4}$ and $0 < \theta < \dfrac{\pi}{2}$, which of the following is equal to $\sin\theta \tan\theta$?

F. $\dfrac{7}{12}$

G. $\dfrac{4}{3\sqrt{7}}$

H. $\dfrac{4}{3}$

J. $\dfrac{4\sqrt{7}}{3}$

K. $\dfrac{12}{7}$

Here's How to Crack It

The question asks for the value of $\sin\theta \tan\theta$ given $\cos\dfrac{3}{4}$ when $0 < \theta < \dfrac{\pi}{2}$. This question is dealing with a triangle in Quadrant I of the unit circle as indicated by $0 < \theta < \dfrac{\pi}{2}$. In that quadrant, all trig functions are positive, so deal with this as if it is a regular triangle outside of the coordinate plane. Use SOHCAHTOA and the geometry basic approach to draw and label a right triangle. Label one of the non-right angles as θ; label the side adjacent to θ as 3 and the hypotenuse as 4. It will look like this:

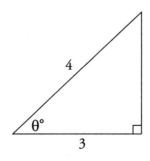

Pythagorean Triples do not work to solve for the remaining side in this question because 3 and 4 are not the legs of the triangle, so use the Pythagorean Theorem to find the remaining leg: $3^2 + b^2 = 4^2$. This becomes $9 + b^2 = 16$ or $b^2 = 7$. Take the square root of both sides to get $b = \sqrt{7}$. Label the missing length as $\sqrt{7}$. Use SOHCAHTOA to find that $\sin\ \theta = \dfrac{opposite}{hypotenuse} = \dfrac{\sqrt{7}}{4}$ and $\tan\ \theta = \dfrac{opposite}{adjacent} = \dfrac{\sqrt{7}}{3}$. Therefore, $\sin\ \theta\ \tan\ \theta = \dfrac{\sqrt{7}}{4} \times \dfrac{\sqrt{7}}{3} = \dfrac{7}{12}$. The correct answer is (F).

Now try these strategies on your own. Go online to your Student Tools and answer the Chapter 13 Drill.

Chapter 14
Math Drills

Now it is time to put all your math skills to the test. Drill 1 focuses on geometry concepts. Make sure to watch out for the snares ACT often sets for you on these questions. Drill 2 will give you a chance to practice your Plugging In skills. Remember, even if you know the "real way," it is not always the fastest or most accurate way, so try to plug in on these drill questions. It will help you get used to that strategy so you can use it easily when necessary. Finally, Drill 3 focuses on Word Problems and Advanced Math questions, which are likely the key to you getting those last few points. Practice all your new skills on these drills, then check the explanations that follow.

DRILL 1—GEOMETRY

28. Mario is standing on the ground and looking at the top of a flagpole. He knows that the flagpole is exactly 18 feet high and that $\sin \theta = \dfrac{5}{13}$, where θ is the angle indicated in the figure below. About how many feet long is the indicated distance from the top of the flagpole to where Mario is standing?

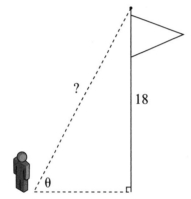

F. 46.8
G. 43.2
H. 19.5
J. 13.0
K. 6.9

37. Triangle *XYZ* below has an area of 72 square inches. Circle *O* is tangent to the triangle at *W*, and the height of the triangle is equal in length to the base. If the line *WY* is a diameter of circle *O*, what is the area, in square inches, of the circle?

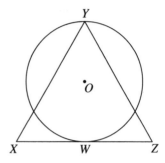

A. 6π
B. 12π
C. 24π
D. 36π
E. 144π

Use the following information to answer questions 39–40.

Shown below is a rectangular pool with a ramp leading up to one side. A water pump fills the pool at an average rate of 70 cubic yards per hour. The pool is a rectangular box with a length of 20 yards, a width of 10 yards, and a height of 3 yards. Also shown below is a ramp that leads to the top of the pool. The ramp is attached to the top of the pool and has an angle of elevation of 48°.

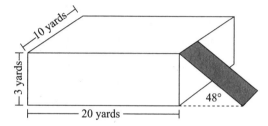

39. The water pump starts to fill a completely empty pool and continues until the pool is completely filled. To the nearest 0.1 hours, for how many hours does the pump fill the pool with water?

A.   8.5
B.   8.6
C.   14.3
D.   103.0
E.   114.3

40. Rosie wants to build a pool that is geometrically similar to the pool shown in the figure. The new pool will have a height of $4\frac{1}{2}$ yards. What will be the length, in yards, of the longest side of the new pool?

F.   10
G. $13\frac{1}{3}$
H.   15
J. $21\frac{1}{2}$
K.   30

41. Triangle *ABC* shown below is isosceles, and line segment *DE* is parallel to *AC*. What is the perimeter, in inches, of the quadrilateral *ADEC* ?

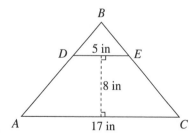

A.   20
B.   22
C.   30
D.   38
E.   42

> Use the following information to answer questions 44–45.

The points $P(-5,6)$, $Q(-3,4)$, $R(-3,12)$, and $S(4,4)$ are shown in the standard (x,y) coordinate plane below.

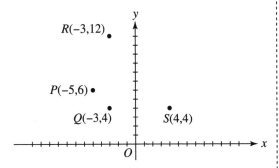

44. What is the slope of $\overrightarrow{PR}$?

  F.　3

  G.　$-\dfrac{2}{9}$

  H.　-1

  J.　$-\dfrac{9}{4}$

  K.　-4

45. What is the tangent of the smallest angle in right triangle QRS ?

  A.　$\dfrac{7}{15}$

  B.　$\dfrac{7}{\sqrt{105}}$

  C.　$\dfrac{8}{\sqrt{105}}$

  D.　$\dfrac{7}{8}$

  E.　$\dfrac{8}{7}$

48. Tommy lives on the edge of a lake and wants to travel by boat to his friend Sherrie's house. Tommy travels the 550 yards from his house to Sherrie's house along a straight line in a direction (shown below) that is 33° clockwise from due east. To the nearest yard, Sherrie's house is how many yards due south and how many yards due east from Tommy's house?

(Note: $\sin 33° \approx 0.545$, $\cos 33° \approx 0.839$)

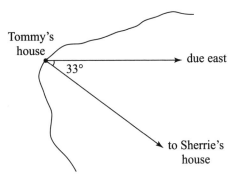

	Due south	Due east
F.	275	476
G.	300	461
H.	325	550
J.	389	389
K.	461	300

50. In the figure below, a table in the shape of an equilateral triangle is placed on top of 3 circular stands. The length of each side of the table is 20 inches. The stands are congruent, and each stand is tangent to the other 2 stands. Each vertex of the table lies on the center of a circle. The region that is interior to the table and exterior to all 3 stands is shaded. What is the area, to the nearest square inch, of the shaded region?

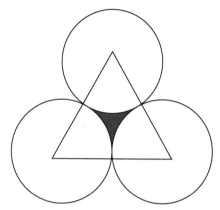

F. 16
G. 52
H. 121
J. 157
K. 173

59. Which of the following equations describes a line that is parallel to a line with equation $-4x + 3y = 24$?

A. $-8x + 6y = 36$
B. $-4x - 3y = 12$
C. $-3x + 4y = 18$
D. $4x + 3y = 9$
E. $8x + 6y = 21$

DRILL 2—PLUGGING IN

32. In a set of 5 numbers, value *A* is removed and replaced with a different number, value *B*. If the mean of the new set is 2 more than the mean of the original set, what is the positive difference between *A* and *B* ?

F. $\dfrac{2}{5}$

G. 3

H. 7

J. 10

K. 25

35. Brian and Miguel decide to have a race. Miguel decides to give Brian a 20-meter lead at the beginning of the race. Brian runs at a speed of $2\dfrac{1}{2}$ meters per second. Miguel runs at a speed of 5 meters per second. If they start running at the same time, how many seconds will it take Miguel to catch Brian?

A. $2\dfrac{1}{2}$

B. 4

C. 8

D. $12\dfrac{1}{2}$

E. 20

36. A marathon director is looking to define the rectangular starting area for an upcoming race. She has determined that she needs 64 square meters of space for the starting area, which will be delineated by rope barriers. What is the minimum length, in meters, of rope needed to enclose the starting area?

F. 8

G. 16

H. 32

J. 40

K. 64

44. If $h(x) = \dfrac{1}{x^2}$ and $j(x) = x + 3$, what is $j(h(x))$?

F. $\dfrac{x+3}{x^2}$

G. $\dfrac{x^2+3}{x^2}$

H. $\dfrac{1}{x^2}+3$

J. $\dfrac{1}{x^2+3}$

K. $\dfrac{1}{(x+3)^2}$

45. Function f is defined as $f(x) = \dfrac{3}{x}$. If $\dfrac{1}{7} < f(a) < \dfrac{1}{6}$, where a is an integer, which of the following lists all possible values of a ?

- **A.** 19 only
- **B.** 20 only
- **C.** 19 and 20
- **D.** 18, 19, 20, and 21
- **E.** There are no possible values of a.

52. On her first 6 rounds of golf this season, Mary has an average of s strokes per round. If Mary wants to decrease her average strokes per round to $s - 3$ strokes, how many fewer strokes than s must she take during the 7th round?

- **F.** 3
- **G.** 7
- **H.** 18
- **J.** 21
- **K.** 25

47. If b is an integer, then the difference of $3b$ and $7b$ is *always* divisible by which of the following?

- **A.** 3
- **B.** 4
- **C.** 7
- **D.** 10
- **E.** 21

53. Let x and y be real numbers. If $(x - y)^2 = -2xy$, it *must* be true that:

- **A.** both x and y are zero.
- **B.** both x and y are negative.
- **C.** both x and y are fractions.
- **D.** either x or y is zero.
- **E.** x is positive and y is negative.

51. What real value of x satisfies the equation $27^{x+2} = \dfrac{3^2}{9^{x-3}}$?

- **A.** -1
- **B.** $\dfrac{2}{5}$
- **C.** $\dfrac{3}{2}$
- **D.** 2
- **E.** 3

56. Let $\text{я}x$ be equal to the average (arithmetic mean) of the first x positive integers. For example, $\text{я}6 = \dfrac{6+5+4+3+2+1}{6} = 3.5$. For all positive integers, x, which of the following statements, if any, are true?

   I. $\text{я}x + \text{я}(x-1) = \text{я}(2x)$

   II. $\text{я}x = \dfrac{x+1}{2}$

   III. $(\text{я}x)^2 = \text{я}x^2$

- **F.** I only
- **G.** I and II only
- **H.** II only
- **J.** III only
- **K.** None

DRILL 3—WORD PROBLEMS AND ADVANCED MATH

24. Pete's Artisanal Pickles sells gourmet pickles at farmer's markets. Two types of machines—sealing machines and labeling machines—are used to jar the pickles. Each sealing machine processes jars at the rate of 30 jars per minute, and each labeling machine processes jars at the rate of 2 jars per second. Pete's Artisanal Pickles is currently using 16 sealing machines. How many labeling machines should be used so that the sealing machines and the labeling machines process the same number of jars in 1 *minute*?

    F. 2
    G. 4
    H. 8
    J. 15
    K. 20

32. In the standard (x, y) coordinate plane, what are the coordinates of the center of the circle with equation $(x + 3)^2 + (y + \sqrt{7})^2 = 4$?

    F. $(\ \sqrt{7},\ \ 3)$
    G. $(-\sqrt{7},\ -3)$
    H. $(\ \ 3, -\sqrt{7})$
    J. $(\ \ 3,\ \sqrt{7})$
    K. $(\ -3, -\sqrt{7})$

36. The graph of $y = \sec x$ is shown in the standard (x, y) coordinate plane below. What is the period of $\sec x$?

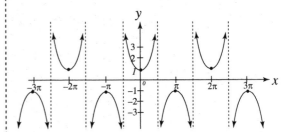

    F. $\dfrac{5\pi}{2}$

    G. 2π

    H. $\dfrac{3\pi}{2}$

    J. π

    K. $\dfrac{\pi}{2}$

44. The number of hours it takes a team of workers to assemble a certain type of machine varies directly with the number of machines and inversely with the square of the number of workers on the team. If c represents the constant of variation, which of the following expressions represents the number of hours it will take n workers to assemble x machines?

F. $\dfrac{cx}{n^2}$

G. $\dfrac{cn^2}{x}$

H. $\dfrac{xn^2}{c}$

J. $\dfrac{c}{xn^2}$

K. cxn^2

49. Each player of a certain game starts on the #10 space of a board with spaces numbered 1 through 150. A player flips a coin and moves forward 6 spaces for each time the coin lands on heads and moves backward 3 spaces for each time the coin lands on tails. Sven's coin landed on heads twice as many times as it landed on tails, moving him to the #100 space on the board. How many times did Sven's coin land on heads?

A. 5
B. 10
C. 15
D. 20
E. 25

50. In the standard (x,y) coordinate plane, when $f \neq 0$ and $g \neq 0$, where does the graph of $h(x) = \dfrac{3x + g}{x + f}$ have a *horizontal* asymptote?

F. $y = -\dfrac{g}{f}$

G. $y = \dfrac{g}{3}$

H. $y = -g$

J. $y = f$

K. $y = 3$

52. The stem-and-leaf plot below shows the scores received on a given test by the 32 students in Mrs. Brown's algebra class. What was the median score on this algebra test?

Stem	Leaf
5	1 2 3 4 6 7
6	3 3 4 5 5 8 9
7	0 1 2 4 6 7 7 7 9
8	0 3 4 4 5 6
9	1 1 2 5

Key: 5 | 1 = 51

F. 72
G. 73
H. 74
J. 76
K. 77

53. Angle R has a measure of $\dfrac{35}{4}\pi$ radians. Angle R and angle S are coterminal. Angle S could have which of the following measures?

A. 12°
B. 36°
C. 45°
D. 90°
E. 135°

56. For all x such that $\cos x \neq 0$, the expression $\dfrac{\csc x \cdot \tan x}{\cos^2 x}$ is equivalent to which of the following?

(Note: $\sec x = \dfrac{1}{\cos x}$; $\csc x = \dfrac{1}{\sin x}$; $\tan x = \dfrac{\sin x}{\cos x}$)

F. $\csc^2 x$
G. $\csc^2 x \cdot \tan x$
H. $\sec^3 x$
J. $\sin x$
K. 1

59. Consecutive terms of a certain geometric sequence have a constant integer ratio between adjacent terms. The product of the first three terms of the sequence is 1,728. Which of the following values CANNOT be the first term of the geometric sequence?

A. 7
B. 6
C. 4
D. 3
E. 2

MATH DRILL ANSWERS AND EXPLANATIONS

Drill 1

28. **F** The question asks for the approximate length, in feet, *from the top of the flagpole to where Mario is standing*. Note that the drawing is a triangle, that the question provides the length of a side, and that $\sin \theta = \dfrac{5}{13}$. Trig functions are ratios, so the measurements are not necessarily 5 and 13. Use the given information about sine and the given measurement to find the missing side, which can be labeled as x. SOHCAHTOA indicates that sine is equal to $\dfrac{opposite}{hypotenuse}$, so $\sin \theta$ also equals $\dfrac{18}{x}$, given the measurements in the question. Therefore, the sine ratios are equal: $\dfrac{5}{13} = \dfrac{18}{x}$. Cross-multiply to get $5x = 18(13)$, which simplifies to $5x = 234$. Divide both sides by 5 to get $x = 46.8$. The correct answer is (F).

37. **D** The question asks for *the area, in square inches, of the circle*. Label the provided figure by drawing the height of the triangle $\overline{YW}$ and marking it congruent to the base. The area of the triangle is given in the question, so write the formula for the area of a triangle, $A = \dfrac{1}{2}bh$, and the area formula for a circle, $A = \pi r^2$, because the area of the circle is what the question asks for. Since the question states that the height and base of the triangle are equal and that the area of the triangle is 72 in^2, plug area = 72 and $b = h$ into the triangle formula to find the height. This becomes $72 = \dfrac{1}{2}h^2$. Multiply both sides by 2 to get $144 = h^2$, and take the square root of both sides to get $h = 12$. The height of the triangle is also the diameter of the circle. Take half the diameter of the circle to find the radius: $r = \dfrac{1}{2}(12) = 6$. Plug this into the formula for the area of a circle: $A = \pi(6^2) = 36\pi$. The correct answer is (D).

39. **B** The question asks *how many hours* it takes for the pump to *fill the pool with water*. According to the information provided, the *pump fills the pool at an average rate of 70 cubic yards per hour*. The unit of cubic yards indicates that the pump is filling a volume. Use the geometry basic approach and write down the volume formula for the pool, a rectangular solid: $V = lwh$. Now determine the volume of the pool with the given measurements: $V = (20)(10)(3) = 600$ cubic yards. The pump can fill 70 cubic yards an hour, so divide the total volume, 600 cubic yards, by the amount the pump can fill the pool in one hour, 70 cubic yards, to determine how many hours it will take the pump to fill the pool from empty: $\frac{600}{70} = 8.57$. Round to the nearest 0.1 hours, as instructed by the question, to get 8.6. The correct answer is (B).

40. **K** The question asks for *the length, in yards, of the longest side of the new pool* that is *geometrically similar to the pool shown* in the diagram. "Geometrically similar" means that the dimensions of the pools have a consistent proportion. Start by drawing another rectangular solid pool and label the height of this new pool $4\frac{1}{2}$ yards. The question asks for the length of the new pool. Label the side that is in the same position as the side that measures 20 yards on the pool in the diagram x, because the text above the diagram states that the length of the original pool is 20 yards. Now set up a proportion that relates both pools to determine the length of the new pool: $\frac{3}{20} = \frac{4.5}{x}$. Cross-multiply to get $3x = (4.5)(20)$; then simplify to $3x = 90$, and divide both sides by 3 to get $x = 30$. The correct answer is (K).

41. **E** The question asks for *the perimeter, in inches, of the quadrilateral ADEC*. Start by labeling $\overline{DE}$ and $\overline{AC}$ as parallel. Then write the formula for the perimeter of a quadrilateral: $P = \textit{sum of the sides}$. Plug in the numbers provided on the diagram to get $P = 5 + 17 + s_3 + s_4$, and simplify to get $P = 22 + s_3 + s_4$. Eliminate (A) and (B) because the remaining sides must have some length, so the perimeter must be greater than 22. The question also states that the triangle ABC is isosceles and that $\overline{DE}$ and $\overline{AC}$ are parallel, which indicates that $\overline{DA} \cong \overline{EC}$. Because $\overline{DA}$ would form the hypotenuse of a right triangle with a height of 8 if a line perpendicular to $\overline{AC}$ was drawn from point D, it can be said that the length of $\overline{DA}$ is greater than 8, and therefore the length of $\overline{EC}$ is greater than 8 is also true. Given this information, it is true that $P > 22 + 8 + 8$, so $P > 38$. Eliminate (C) and (D). The correct answer is (E).

44. **F** The question asks for *the slope of* $\overleftrightarrow{PR}$ given points $P(-5, 6)$ and $R(-3, 12)$. Given two points, the slope of a line is calculated as $\dfrac{y_2 - y_1}{x_2 - x_1}$. Therefore, the slope $= \dfrac{12-6}{-3-(-5)} = \dfrac{6}{-3+5} = \dfrac{6}{2} = 3$. The correct answer is (F).

45. **D** The question asks for *the tangent of the smallest angle in right triangle QRS*. Draw lines connecting point Q to point R, point R to point S, and point S to point Q. Because $\overline{QR}$ is vertical, the distance from point Q to point R is the change in the y-value of the coordinates $R(-3, 12)$ and $Q(-3, 4)$: $12 - 4 = 8$. Because $\overline{QS}$ is horizontal, the distance from point $S(4, 4)$ to point $Q(-3, 4)$ is the change in the x-values: $4 - (-3)$ $= 4 + 3 = 7$. Label these distances on the triangle. SOHCAHTOA indicates that the tangent is $\dfrac{opposite}{adjacent}$, so there is no need to calculate the hypotenuse of this triangle. The question asks for the tangent of the smallest angle, and the smallest angle in a triangle is always opposite the smallest side. Therefore, the question is asking for the tangent of $\angle R$: $\tan R = \dfrac{7}{8}$. The correct answer is (D).

48. **G** The question asks *how many yards due south and how many yards due east* Sherrie's house is from Tommy's house. The question provides the angle at which Tommy travels to Sherri's house in relationship to east and states that Tommy travels 550 yards from his house to Sherri's. Start by drawing a vertical line to create a right triangle: draw a vertical line from the line representing due east to the line representing the direction Tommy traveled to Sherri's house. Label this line s, and label the distance Tommy traveled, 550 yards, on the line indicating Tommy's direction of travel. Note that the question asks about the distance Tommy traveled due south (the length of the vertical leg, s, of the triangle) and the distance he traveled due east (the length of the horizontal leg of the triangle). Given the 33° angle and the length of the hypotenuse of the triangle, use sine $= \dfrac{opposite}{hypotenuse}$ to solve for

s: $\sin 33° = \dfrac{s}{550}$. Solve for s by first multiplying both sides by 550: $s = 550\sin 33°$, and using the provided values to find $s = (550)(0.545) \approx 300$ yards due south. Eliminate (F), (H), (J), and (K), since these all have different values in the *Due south* column. The correct answer is (G).

50. **F** The question asks for *the area, to the nearest square inch, of the shaded region*. Notice that each circle has a wedge within the triangle. The area of the shaded region is the same as the area of the triangle minus the areas of the three wedges. Write the area formulas for a triangle and a circle: $A = \dfrac{1}{2}bh$ and $A = \pi r^2$, respectively. Label the sides of the triangle as 20 inches and each angle within the equilateral triangle as 60°. The question states that the circular stands *are congruent*, or equal, and *tangent* to one another. Since *each vertex* of the triangular *table lies on the center of a circle*, it can be said that half the length of each side of the triangle is equal to the length of the radius of each circle. Therefore, the radius of each circle is $r = 10$ inches. Given this, the 60° angle, and the part-to-whole relationship in circles $\left(\dfrac{angle}{360°} = \dfrac{segment\ area}{area} = \dfrac{arc\ length}{circumference} \right)$, it can be determined that the area of the segment of each circle contained within the triangle is $\dfrac{60°}{360°} = \dfrac{segment\ area}{\left(10^2\right)\pi}$. This can be simplified to $\dfrac{60°}{360°} = \dfrac{segment\ area}{100\pi}$. Cross-multiply to get $6{,}000\pi = 360(segment\ area)$; then divide both sides by 360 to get segment area $= \dfrac{6{,}000\pi}{360} = \dfrac{50\pi}{3}$. Since there

are 3 congruent segments contained within the triangle, multiply $\dfrac{50\pi}{3}$ by 3 to get 50π. This is the area to be subtracted from the area of the triangle in order to determine the area of the shaded region. Next determine the area of the triangle. Draw a height in the equilateral triangle to create a 30°-60°-90° triangle with hypotenuse of 20. In a 30°-60°-90° triangle, the hypotenuse has a measure of $2x$, where x is the length of the shorter leg and $x\sqrt{3}$ is the length of the longer leg. In this case, the height of the equilateral triangle is the longer leg. Solve $2x = 20$ to get $x = 10$. Plug $x = 10$ into $x\sqrt{3}$ to find the height of the equilateral triangle: $10\sqrt{3}$. Now use the height of $10\sqrt{3}$ and base of 20 to find the area of the triangular table: $A = \dfrac{1}{2}\left(10\sqrt{3}\right)\left(20\right) = 100\sqrt{3}$. Determine the area of the shaded region by subtracting the area of the segments from the area of the triangle to get $100\sqrt{3} - 50\pi \approx 16$. The correct answer is (F).

59. **A** The question asks *which of the following equations describes a line that is parallel to a line with equation* $-4x + 3y = 24$. Parallel lines have the same slope, so the slope of the given line must match the slope of the correct answer. Find the slope of each equation by putting the equations into slope-intercept form, or notice that the given line and all the answers are in the standard form of a line, $Ax + By = C$. The slope of a line in standard form is $-\dfrac{A}{B}$. For the equation given in the question, $A = -4$ and $B = 3$, so the slope of the line is $-\dfrac{-4}{3} = \dfrac{4}{3}$. Check the answers to see which choice has the same slope. For the equation in (A), $A = -8$ and $B = 6$, so the slope is $-\dfrac{-8}{6} = \dfrac{8}{6} = \dfrac{4}{3}$. Keep (A). It is not necessary to check the remaining answers because the numbers to determine the slope are provided by the question and answers, and the question only requires that the slopes of the lines match. The correct answer is (A).

Drill 2

32. **J** The question asks for the *positive difference* between *A* and *B*. While the answer choices do contain numbers, it may be difficult to plug in the answers because the answers give only a positive difference between two numbers, not the numbers themselves. Instead, plug in for the numbers in the set. Make the first set of five numbers {1, 2, 3, 4, 5}. Find the mean of that set by using the formula for mean (average): *total* = *average* × *number of things*. There are five numbers in the set, so *number of things* = 5. The *total* is the sum of the numbers: 1 + 2 + 3 + 4 + 5 = 15. Thus, 15 = *average* × 5 and the average is $\frac{15}{5} = 3$. Select one of the numbers as *A*. Make *A* = 5 and remove it from the set. Replace it with *B*. The new set is {1, 2, 3, 4, *B*}. This new set needs to have a mean that is *2 more than the mean of the original set*. Since the original mean was 3, the new mean is 3 + 2 = 5. The new set also has five numbers so *number of things* = 5. Use the formula for mean with the new set, and *total* = 5 × 5 = 25. Solve for *B*: 1 + 2 + 3 + 4 + *B* = 25, so *B* = 25 − 10 = 15. The difference between *A* = 5 and *B* = 15 is 15 − 5 = 10. The correct answer is (J).

35. **C** The question asks *how many seconds it will take Miguel to catch Brian*. Since the question asks for a specific value and the answers contain numbers in increasing order, plug in the answers. Begin by labeling the answers as "*seconds running*" and start with the middle answer, (C), 8. Since Brian runs at a speed of 2.5 meters per second, after 8 seconds Brian will have run 2.5 × 8 = 20 meters. Since Miguel runs at a speed of 5 meters per second, after 8 seconds Miguel will have run 5 × 8 = 40 meters. Check whether this matches the information in the question. Brian's 20-meter run and his 20-meter head start make his total distance run 20 + 20 = 40. This is same as the 40 meters Miguel has run. Thus, it is exactly at this point when Miguel catches Brian. Stop here. The correct answer is (C).

36. **H** The question asks for the *minimum length, in meters, of rope needed to enclose the starting area*. Since the question asks for a specific value and the answers contain numbers in increasing order, plug in the answers. Begin by labeling the answers as "*length of rope*," but because the question asks for the *minimum*, start with the smallest answer, (F), 8. Consider how much area could be enclosed with 8 feet of rope. The rope must consist of two equal lengths and two equal widths, adding up to

the perimeter of the rectangular area. With a total of 8 meters of rope, this means that one length and one width would equal 4 meters. A length of 3 meters and a width of 1 meter would enclose an area of 3 × 1 = 3 square meters. A length of 2 meters and a width of 2 meters would enclose an area of 2 × 2 = 4 square meters. Neither matches the given area of 64 square meters. Try a greater number: (G), 16. One length of rope and one width of rope would be exactly half of that, 8 meters. A length of 2 and a width of 6 would enclose an area of 2 × 6 = 12 square meters. A length of 3 meters and a width of 5 meters would enclose an area of 3 × 5 = 15 square meters. A length of 4 meters and a width of 4 meters would enclose an area of 4 × 4 = 16 square meters. These do not match the given area of 64 meters. Eliminate (G). Try a greater number: (H), 32. One length of rope and one width of rope would be exactly half of that, 16 meters. A length of 8 meters and a width of 8 meters would enclose an area of 8 × 8 = 64 square meters. Therefore, given 32 meters of rope, it is possible to enclose 64 square meters of space as long as each side of the rectangle is 8 meters. Note that even though the question defines the space as *rectangular*, this doesn't mean that it cannot be square. All squares are also rectangles. The correct answer is (H).

44. **H** The question asks for the value of a compound function. In function notation, the number inside the parentheses is the x-value that goes into the function, and the value that comes out of the function is the y-value. There are variables in the answer choices, so plug in. Make $x = 2$. Because compound functions work from the inside out, first plug 2 into the h function: $h(2) = \frac{1}{2^2} = \frac{1}{4}$. Now substitute $\frac{1}{4}$ for $h(2)$ in the j function: $j\left(\frac{1}{4}\right) = \frac{1}{4} + 3 = 3\frac{1}{4}$. This is the target value; circle it. Now plug $x = 2$ into the answer choices to see which one matches the target value. Choice (F) becomes $\frac{(2+3)}{2^2} = \frac{5}{4}$. This does not match the target. Eliminate (F). Choice (G) becomes $\frac{2^2 + 3}{2^2} = \frac{4+3}{4} = \frac{7}{4}$.

Eliminate (G). Choice (H) becomes $\dfrac{1}{2^2} + 3 = \dfrac{1}{4} + 3 = \dfrac{1}{4} + 3 = 3\dfrac{1}{4}$. This matches the target value. Keep (H) but check the other answer choices to make sure. Choice (J) becomes $\dfrac{1}{2^2 + 3} = \dfrac{1}{4 + 3} = \dfrac{1}{7}$. Eliminate (J). Choice (K) becomes $\dfrac{1}{(2+3)^2} = \dfrac{1}{5^2} = \dfrac{1}{25}$. Eliminate (K). The correct answer is (H).

45. C The question asks for *all possible values of a* that fit the given inequality. Since the question asks for specific values and the answers contain numbers in increasing order, plug in the answers. Begin by labeling the answers as "*a*" and start with the middle answer, (C), 19 and 20. In function notation the number inside the parentheses is the *x*-value that goes into the function, and the value that comes out of the function is the *y*-value. Since $f(a) = \dfrac{3}{a}$, then $f(19) = \dfrac{3}{19}$ and $f(20) = \dfrac{3}{20}$. To determine whether these values are between $\dfrac{1}{7}$ and $\dfrac{1}{6}$, either use a calculator or convert the fractions given in the question to equivalent fractions with 3 as the numerator: $\dfrac{1}{7} = \dfrac{3}{21}$ and $\dfrac{1}{6} = \dfrac{3}{18}$. Both $\dfrac{3}{19}$ and $\dfrac{3}{20}$ are between $\dfrac{3}{21}$ and $\dfrac{3}{18}$, making the inequality true. Eliminate all choices that do not include both 19 and 20 as possible values for *a*: eliminate (A), (B), and (E). To determine whether (D) is correct, plug in one of the other values listed. For $a = 21$, $f(21) = \dfrac{3}{21}$, which is equal to $\dfrac{1}{7}$. This is not between $\dfrac{1}{7}$ and $\dfrac{1}{6}$. Eliminate (D). The correct answer is (C).

47. B The question asks which number *the difference* between 3*b* and 7*b* will *always* be *divisible* by. Even though this question has numbers of increasing order in the answer choices, Plugging In the Answers could prove difficult because there is no value given for *b*. Plug in for *b* instead. Make *b* = 3. This makes

$3b = 3(3) = 9$ and $7b = 7(3) = 21$. The difference is $21 - 9 = 12$. 12 is divisible by 3 and 4, but is not divisible by 7, 10, or 21. Eliminate (C), (D), and (E). The word *always* in the question is often a signal that plugging in more than once is necessary. For the second value, try a weird number such as 0, 1, a fraction, or a negative number. Since b must be an integer, try $b = 1$. This makes $3b = 3(1) = 3$ and $7b = 7(1) = 7$. The difference is $7 - 3 = 4$. Since 4 is not divisible by 3, eliminate (A). The remaining value 4 is divisible by 4. The correct answer is (B).

51. **B**   The question asks for the value of x that *satisfies the equation*. Because the question asks for a specific value and the answers contain numbers in increasing order, plug in the answers. Begin by labeling the answers as "x" and start with the middle answer, (C), $\frac{3}{2}$. This could get complicated, so plug in carefully and use a calculator to do the hard work. First, rewrite $\frac{3}{2}$ as 1.5 to make it easier to plug in. The equation becomes $27^{1.5+2} = \frac{3^2}{9^{1.5-3}}$, which simplifies to $27^{3.5} = \frac{9}{9^{-1.5}}$. A negative exponent means to take the reciprocal of the number with a positive exponent, so this becomes $27^{3.5} = 9(9^{1.5})$. Use a calculator to find that this becomes $102{,}275.87 = 243$. This is not true, so eliminate (C). The left side needs to be much smaller, so try a smaller value for x, such as $\frac{2}{5}$ in (B). This can be rewritten as 0.4 and plugged into the equation to get $27^{0.4+2} = \frac{3^2}{9^{0.4-3}}$. This simplifies to $27^{2.4} = \frac{9}{9^{-2.6}}$ or $27^{2.4} = 9(9^{2.6})$. Use a calculator to find that this becomes $2{,}724.4 = 2{,}724.4$. This is true, so stop here. The correct answer is (B).

52. **J**   The question asks *how many fewer strokes than s* Mary must take in her seventh round of golf in order to decrease her overall average from s to $s - 3$ strokes per round. Even though the answer choices are all numbers, it may prove tricky to plug in the answers because, using (C) as an example, 18 *fewer strokes* does not provide actual values for the number of strokes. Instead, consider plugging in for s. Choose a number such that $s > 25$, the greatest listed answer choice. Make $s = 50$. Use the formula for averages, *Total = Average × Number of things*, to find Mary's total number of strokes. If Mary

averaged 50 strokes per round over her first 6 rounds, her *Total* = 50 × 6 = 300. Thus, 300 is equal to Mary's number of strokes for the first six rounds of golf. Mary wants to decrease that average to *s* – 3 or 50 – 3 = 47 strokes per round. Use the formula for averages again to determine what her new total should be after seven rounds. Mary's new average is 47 and her new number of rounds is 7. Therefore, Mary's new total is 47 × 7 = 329. Subtract her old total from her new total to find that Mary must use 329 – 300 = 29 strokes in her seventh round to average 47 strokes per round. Determine how many fewer strokes this is compared to her average over the first 6 rounds: 50 – 29 = 21. The correct answer is (J).

53. **A** The question asks what *must be true* given the expression. Even though the answer choices do not contain numbers, they do offer only limited possibilities. Determine which answer must be true by plugging in the answers. Test (A) by plugging in $x = 0$ and $y = 0$. This makes the equation $(0 - 0)^2 = -2(0)(0)$ or $0 = 0$. This is true. Because x and y could both equal zero, none of (B), (C), and (E) *must* be true. It does not have to be true that x and y are fractions, positive, or negative (zero is neither positive nor negative) when they could each be zero. Eliminate (B), (C), and (E). Choice (D) is true when both x and y equal zero, so try new numbers that fit the requirements of (D). Make $x = 1$ and $y = 0$. The equation becomes $(1 - 0)^2 = -2(1)(0)$ or $1 - 0 = 0$ or $1 = 0$. This is false. Eliminate (D) because it *can* be true, but the question asks which *must* be true. The correct answer is (A).

56. **G** The question asks which of the statements, if any, are true. There are variables in the statements, so plug in. Make $x = 3$. This makes statement (I) become

ꓤ3 + ꓤ(3 − 1) = ꓤ(2 × 3) or ꓤ3 + ꓤ2 = ꓤ6. ꓤ3 equals the average of the first 3 integers, so $ꓤ3 = \dfrac{3+2+1}{3} = \dfrac{6}{3} = 2$. ꓤ2 equals the average of the first 2 integers, so $ꓤ2 = \dfrac{2+1}{2} = \dfrac{3}{2} = 1.5$. ꓤ6 equals the average of the first 6 integers, so $ꓤ6 = \dfrac{6+5+4+3+2+1}{6} = \dfrac{21}{6} = 3.5$. Since 2 + 1.5 = 3.5, statement (I) is true. Eliminate any answer choices that do not contain (I): eliminate (H), (J), and (K). Now try statement (II): $x = 3$ makes statement (II) become $ꓤ3 = \dfrac{3+1}{2} = \dfrac{4}{2} = 2$. ꓤ3 was previously calculated as 2, so statement (II) is true as well. Eliminate (F). The correct answer is (G).

Drill 3

24. **G** The question asks how many *labeling machines* must be use to process the *same number of jars* per minute as the sealing machines. Start by calculating how many jars are currently processed per minute by the sealing machines. If there are 16 machines working at a rate of 30 jars per minute, together they seal 16 × 30 or 480 jars in 1 minute. A labeling machine will process 2 jars per second, and there are 60 seconds in a minute, so it will process 2 × 60 or 120 jars in 1 minute. This rate is $\frac{1}{4}$ the rate of the sealing machines, because $\frac{120}{480} = \frac{1}{4}$, so there must be 4 labeling machines to keep up with the rate of the sealing machines. The correct answer is (G).

32. **K** The question asks for *the coordinates of the center* of a given circle. If the center of a circle is at (*h*, *k*), the formula for the equation for that circle is $(x - h)^2 + (y - k)^2 = r^2$. The *x*-coordinate of the circle is in parentheses with the *x*, and the *y*-coordinate is in parentheses with the *y*. Therefore, (F) and (G) can be eliminated, because they switch the *x*- and *y*-coordinates. The signs in the circle equation in the question are both positive, so they should still match in the credited response. Choice (H) can now be eliminated, since the numbers in that answer have opposite signs. Finally, the equation of a circle has *x* <u>minus</u> the *x*-coordinate of the center. The equation in the question has addition, which means there must have been subtraction of a negative *x*-coordinate. The two negatives cancel each other out to become a positive. The correct answer should have two negative values as a result, not two positive values. The correct answer is (K).

36. **G** The question asks for the *period of sec x*. Period is defined as the distance required for a function to make one full cycle, or how long before it starts to repeat itself. Start at the origin and look at the function to the right of the *y*-axis. First, the graph slopes up, like the right side of a parabola, between *x* = 0 and the asymptote, or dashed line, at $x = \frac{\pi}{2}$. Between the asymptotes at $x = \frac{\pi}{2}$ and $x = \frac{3\pi}{2}$, it looks like an upside-down parabola. Between $x = \frac{3\pi}{2}$ and *x* = 2π, the graph looks like the left side of a parabola. At *x* = 2π, it starts sloping up again like the right side of a parabola. Since this is the point where it starts to repeat itself, the period is 2π. The correct answer is (G).

44. **F** The question asks for an expression for the number of hours it takes n workers to assemble x machines. When two things vary directly, as one variable increases the other also increases. Plug in values for the different variables; then change the value for the number of machines to determine if it varies directly with the number of hours. Try $c = 2$, $n = 3$, and $x = 4$. For (F), the number of hours with these values is $\dfrac{2 \times 4}{3^2} = \dfrac{8}{9}$. If the number of machines (x) is increased to 5, the new value is $\dfrac{2 \times 5}{3^2} = \dfrac{10}{9}$. This value increased, so (F) could be the credited response. Now try (G) using the same values. The first set of values gives $\dfrac{2(3)^2}{4} = \dfrac{18}{4}$, and the second set gives $\dfrac{2(3)^2}{5} = \dfrac{18}{5}$. This is smaller than the first value, so (G) can be eliminated. The values for (H) are $\dfrac{4(3)^2}{2} = \dfrac{36}{2}$ and then $\dfrac{5(3)^2}{2} = \dfrac{45}{2}$, so (H) could be the credited response. The values for (J) are $\dfrac{2}{4(3)^2} = \dfrac{2}{36}$ and then $\dfrac{2}{5(3)^2} = \dfrac{2}{45}$, so (J) can be eliminated. The values for (K) are $(2)(4)(3^2) = 72$ and then $(2)(5)(3^2) = 90$, so (K) could be the credited response. Now check the remaining answer choices by varying the value for n. If the number of hours varies inversely with the square of n, the number of hours will decrease with an increasing n. For the initial values of $c = 2$, $n = 3$, and $x = 4$, (F) was equal to $\dfrac{8}{9}$. If $n = 5$, (F) becomes $\dfrac{2 \times 4}{5^2}$ or $\dfrac{8}{25}$. The value for (F) got smaller, whereas (H) and (K) both get larger when the value of n is increased. The correct answer is (F).

49. **D** The question asks for the number of *times Sven's coin* landed *on heads*. When asked for a specific amount and given numbers in the answer choices, use PITA. Start with (C) and assume that Sven's coin landed on heads 15 times. This would mean that his coin landed on tails half as many times as that, or 7.5 times. It is not possible to flip a coin 7.5 times, so (C) cannot be the credited response. It is now clear that an even number is needed, so (A) and (E) can also be eliminated. Try the value in (D) and assume

Sven's coin landed on heads 20 times and tails 10 times. He moved forward 6 spaces for each coin toss that resulted in heads, so he moved forward 20(6) or 120 spaces. He started on the #10 space, so that would move him to the (10 + 120) or #130 space. He moved backward 3 spaces for each coin toss that resulted in tails, so he moved back 10(3) or 30 spaces. From the #130 space, this would move him back to the (130 – 30) or #100 space. The question states that Sven did end up on the #100 space, so the correct answer is (D).

50. **K** The question asks for the *horizontal asymptote* of a function. An asymptote is a line that a graph approaches but does not (usually) reach. A horizontal asymptote can occasionally be crossed, but a graph of an equation will usually reveal the line that is the boundary of the *y*-value. To graph this function on a calculator, however, values need to be set for *f* and *g*. Given these variables in the question and answer choices, plug in numbers for *f* and *g*, following the restriction that 0 is not used. Try $f = 1$ and $g = 2$. Now the function is $h(x) = \dfrac{3x + 2}{x + 1}$ or $y = \dfrac{3x + 2}{x + 1}$. Graphed on a calculator with a window of 10 units in all directions from the origin, the resulting image looks like this:

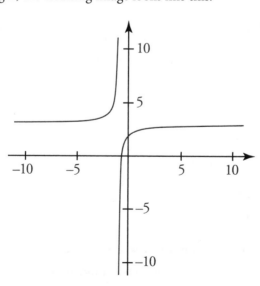

The graph gets close to, but does not seem to reach the horizontal line at $y = 3$. Choice (K) looks like the credited response, but check the other answers to make sure that none of them also equals 3. Choice (F) is $y = -\frac{2}{1}$ or -2, (G) is $y = \frac{2}{3}$, (H) is $y = -2$, and (J) is $y = 1$. None of these are $y = 3$, so they can be eliminated. The correct answer is (K).

52.   **G**   The question asks for the *median score* on an algebra test. Each of the numbers on the stem-and-leaf plot under the Leaf heading represents one score on the test. To find the median of this list of scores, the middle number needs to be determined. Start by crossing off 4 scores from the top row of the list and 4 scores from the bottom of the list, like this:

Stem	Leaf
5	~~1 2 3 4~~ 6 7
6	3 3 4 5 5 8 9
7	0 1 2 4 6 7 7 7 9
8	0 3 4 4 5 6
9	~~1 1 2 5~~

Continue in this manner, crossing off the same numbers of scores from the front and back ends of the list, until the middle of the list is reached.

Stem	Leaf
5	~~1 2 3 4 6 7~~
6	~~3 3 4 5 5 8 9~~
7	~~0 1~~ 2 4 ~~6 7 7 7 9~~
8	~~0 3 4 4 5 6~~
9	~~1 1 2 5~~

If there were an odd number of scores on the list, the single score in the middle would be the median. With an even number of scores, the median is the average of the middle two scores. In this case, the middle two numbers are 72 and 74, so the average is 73. The correct answer is (G).

53.   **E**   The question asks for the *measure of angle S,* which is *coterminal* with *angle R.* The question gives the measure of angle R in radians, but the answers contain degree measures. Start by converting $\dfrac{35}{4}\pi$ radians into degrees. The unit circle is 2π radians and a circle has $360°$, so $2\pi = 360°$ and $\pi = 180°$. Therefore, $\dfrac{35}{4}\pi$ radians $= \dfrac{35}{4}(180°) = 1{,}575°$. "Coterminal," or having the same terminal angle, means that the angle measures are equivalent on the unit circle. From a measure of $1{,}575°$, it is necessary to go down to the much smaller measures in the answer choices. So, subtract $360°$ from $1{,}575°$ as many times as is needed to hit one of the answer choices. $1{,}575° - 360° = 1{,}215° - 360° = 855° - 360° = 495° - 360° = 135°$. Therefore, $1{,}575°$ and $135°$ are coterminal, and the correct answer is (E).

56.   **H**   The question asks for the expression that is *equivalent* to the given expression, and the question and answers contain trigonometric functions. One way to solve a tricky trig question like this would be to get everything into terms of sine and cosine before trying to simplify it. A better approach on most tricky trig problems is to plug in a value for x and to rely on the calculator to do the hard work. Pick a value like $x = 20°$ and plug in, making sure the calculator is in degrees, not radians. Taking it in bite-sized pieces to avoid errors, calculate that $\csc 20° = \dfrac{1}{\sin 20°} = 2.924$ (approximately), $\tan 20° = 0.364$, and $\cos^2 20° = (0.940)^2 = 0.884$. Therefore, $\dfrac{\csc x \cdot \tan x}{\cos^2 x} = \dfrac{(2.924)(0.364)}{(0.884)} = 1.204$. Now plug in $x = 20$ on each of the answer choices to see which one equals approximately 1.204. Choice (K) definitely does not, so it can be eliminated. For (F), $\csc 20° = 2.924$, so $\csc^2 20° = (2.924)^2 = 8.550$. This is not 1.204, so (F) can be eliminated. Choice (G)

can be rewritten as $(\frac{1}{\sin^2 20°})(\tan 20°) = (\frac{1}{(0.342)^2})(\tan 20°) = (8.55)(0.364)$ = 3.112, so (G) can also be eliminated. Choice (H) equals $\frac{1}{\cos^3 x} = \frac{1}{(0.939)^3} = $ 1.204, so (H) seems to be the credited response. Check (J) just to be certain; sin 20° = 0.342, which is not 1.204, so (J) can be eliminated. The correct answer is (H).

59. **A**   The question asks for a number that *CANNOT be the first term of a geometric sequence.* A geometric sequence is a series of numbers in which each term after the first is obtained by multiplying by the same number, which could be positive, negative, or fractional. For example, 3, 6, 12 is a geometric sequence because each term is multiplied by 2 to get the next term. Similarly, the ratio between adjacent terms is the same because $\frac{12}{6} = \frac{6}{3} = 2$. To check if each of the answer choices could be the first term of the given geometric sequence, plug in the answers. The constant must be positive because the product of the 3 terms is positive. For (A), assume 7 is the first term and multiply it by a small, positive integer, such as 2. The sequence in this case would be 7, 14, 28, and the product would be 2,744. This is too big, but there can't be a sequence with a ratio of 1, so there is no way to make it smaller. Therefore, (A) contains the number that cannot be the first term. Choice (B) works if the sequence is 6, 12, 24, (C) works with 4, 12, 36, (D) works with 3, 12, 48, and (E) works with 2, 12, 72. The correct answer is (A).

Part IV
ACT Reading

Chapter 15
Introduction to the ACT Reading Test

To pursue a perfect or near-perfect score on the Reading Test, you have to employ superior critical-thinking and time-management skills. To go from good to great, you have to be flexible and willing to try a variety of approaches to find the best strategy for you. The passages change on every ACT, so you have to be willing to adapt to variations and switch up strategies mid-test and even mid-passage when one isn't working.

We'll teach you how to evaluate the order in which you work the passages. We'll also review strategies for working the passages and distinguishing among close answers, all to help you pursue perfection on the Reading Test.

WHAT'S ON THE READING TEST

On the Reading Test, you have 35 minutes to work through four passages and a total of 40 questions. ACT selects excerpts from books and articles to create one long passage or two shorter passages. For each test, they choose four new passages, but the topics are always chosen from the same content areas of study, and they always come in the same order: Literary Narrative, Social Science, Humanities, and Natural Science. The passages are roughly the same length, usually 700–900 words, and each is followed by 10 questions.

The passages feature authors and topics that the ACT writers judge typical of the type of reading required in first-year college courses. And your goal, according to ACT, is to read the passages and answer questions that prove you understood both what was "directly stated" as well as what were the "implied meanings."

HOW TO CRACK THE READING TEST

If you are pursuing a perfect or near-perfect score, you likely are already doing a very good job of reading the passages and finding both the directly stated and implied meanings. To go from good to great, evaluate your current approach and determine whether (and how) it can be improved.

Pick the Best Order of the Passages for You

You can work the passages in the order ACT presents, *if you like that order*. But there is no rule that says you have to do them in ACT's order, and we recommend working the passages in an order that works best for you and makes best use of the time constraints.

Now, Later

We recommend working first the passages you like best and/or typically perform best on. A tough passage can easily steal too much time from the others, and if you rush through the rest (or even run out of time), you're giving up points you otherwise could have banked.

If you have already taken a fair number of practice tests, then you're ready to analyze your performance:

- Regardless of where they are in your order, do you consistently do the best on social science and natural science? If so, then consider starting with those two.

- Do you usually prefer the literary narrative and humanities to the social science and natural science? Do you consistently earn more points on those passages? If so, consider completing both before tackling the other two.
- Do you rarely read fiction outside of school? If so, then the literary narrative is unlikely to be a smart choice to do first.

Here is some additional information about the four categories to help you reflect on your own Personal Order of Difficulty (POOD).

Literary Narrative

Facts may matter less than do the setting, the atmosphere, and the relationships between characters. The plot and dialogue may even be secondary to the characters' thoughts and emotions, not all of which will be directly stated. In fact, the questions are more likely to involve identifying the implied meanings than what was directly stated.

If you like to read fiction for school assignments or for pleasure, you may find the literary narrative one of the easier passages. If you don't like to read fiction, you may find the passages unclear and confusing.

Social Science

Social science passages should remind you of the papers you write for school. The organization will flow logically with clear topic sentences and well-chosen transitions to develop the main idea. The author may have a point of view on the subject or may simply deliver informative facts in a neutral tone.

Humanities

Humanities passages are nonfiction, but if they are memoirs or personal essays, they may feel similar to the literary narrative passages. The narrative may use a more organic development instead of a linear one, and the tone will be more personal and perhaps more emotional than the more objective tones found in social and natural science. In other cases, the humanities passage has the same objective tone and organization as the science passages, differing only in featuring a topic related to the arts.

Natural Science

Natural science passages feature a lot of details and sometimes very technical descriptions. Similar to the passages on social science, natural science features a linear organization with clear topic sentences and transitions to develop the main idea. The author may or may not have an opinion on the topic.

Subscores
On your official score report, ACT groups your performance on literary narrative and humanities under an Arts/Literature subscore, and your performance on social science and natural science under a Social Studies/Science subscore. The subscores don't connect mathematically to the Reading score or the composite, but the groupings may help you think about your own order.

The next time you take a practice Reading Test, incorporate this analysis and adjust your order and analyze the results. With enough practice and self-analysis, you will be able to determine your Personal Order of Difficulty (POOD).

Need More Practice?

1,523 ACT Practice Questions provides 6 tests' worth of Reading passages. That's 24 passages and 240 questions.

When Good POOD Goes Bad

Each ACT features all new passages, and certain characteristics may vary enough to affect the difficulty of a passage. Pay attention to the particulars of each test and be willing to adapt your order for that day's test.

- **Paragraphs:** about 8–12 medium-sized paragraphs is better than a few very long paragraphs or a lot of very short paragraphs.
- **Questions:** the more line references, the better
- **Answers:** short are better than long

Need Even More Practice?

The Princeton Review's *English and Reading Workout* has 4 more full-length Reading Tests.

Danger Signs

The passages all run roughly the same number of words (700–900), and each features 10 questions followed by four answer choices. But the way the passages, questions, and answers *look* can provide valuable clues that you should use to determine that day's order.

Paragraphs

Which passage would you rather work, one with eight to twelve medium-sized paragraphs or one with three huge paragraphs? The overall length is the same, but the size and number of the paragraphs influences how easily you can navigate the passage and retrieve answers as you work the questions.

Some literary narrative passages can feature too many paragraphs, with each paragraph an individual line of dialogue. Too many paragraphs can make it just as difficult to locate the right part of the passage to find answers.

Ideally, a passage should feature eight to twelve paragraphs, with each paragraph made up of five to fifteen lines.

Questions

The questions that accompany a passage aren't written in an order that follows the progression of ideas in the passage. In other words, the first question might be about the end of the passage, and the fifth question might be about the beginning of the passage. Some, but not all, of the questions include line references. Line references (and paragraph references) are maps, pointing to the precise part of the passage to find the answer. You waste no time getting lost, hunting through the passage to find where to read. Therefore, a passage with only one or two line- or paragraph-reference questions will be more challenging than one that features four, five, six, or more (eight is the most we've ever seen).

Answers

Long answers usually answer harder questions, and short answers usually answer easier questions. A passage with lots of questions with short answers is likely to be an easier passage.

Use Your Eye, Not Your Brain

There's no guarantee that the four passages will be uniform in number or length of paragraphs, or that there will be an equal number of line-reference or short-answer questions. Especially as a high scorer, you'll need to be prepared to tackle any passage.

Look at the passages to evaluate the paragraphs, line references, and answer choices. Don't thoughtfully ponder and consider each element, and don't read through the questions.

Use your eye to scan the paragraphs, look for numbers amidst the questions, and scan the length of answer choices. If you see lots of warning signs on what is typically your first passage, leave it for Later. If you see manageable paragraphs, line references, and lots of short answers on the passage you typically do Later, consider bumping it up to second, maybe first. This should take no more than two seconds.

> **The Blurb**
> The blurb at the top of the passage will provide the title, author, copyright date, and publisher. The title may not make the subject clear, but it's always worth checking to see whether it does. The information in the blurb may also affect the passage's place in your order.

The Questions

Remember that the questions aren't written in an order that follows the progression of ideas in the passage, nor are they in any order of difficulty from easiest to hardest. You shouldn't work the questions in the order given just because ACT numbered them in order. Instead, work the questions in an order that makes sense for you.

Now Questions

Work Now the questions that are easy to answer or easy to find the answer to.

Later Questions

Work Later the questions that are both harder to answer and harder to find the answer to.

Easy to Find/Harder to Find

A question with a line or a paragraph reference comes with a map, showing you where in the passage to find the answer. Questions that come with a great lead word can also make finding the answer easy. Lead words are the nouns, phrases, and sometimes verbs that are specific to the passage. They're not the boilerplate language like "main idea" or "the passage characterizes."

Look at the following questions. All the lead words have been underlined.

11. Mark Twain probably would have said that lawyers:

12. The author states that maritime law is unique in that:

13. According to the passage, the primary danger steamboats posed was:

35. Which of the following statements most accurately summarizes how the passage characterizes opiates and benzodiazepines?

Lead words are words and phrases that can be found in the passage.

Great lead words are proper nouns, unusual words, and dates.

Your eye can spot great lead words in the passage just by looking and without reading. They leap off the page. In Chapter 16, we'll teach you how to use lead words as part of the basic approach.

Easy to Answer/Harder to Answer

A question that is easy to answer often simply asks what the passage says, or as ACT puts it, what is explicitly stated. In ACT's words, these questions require the use of "referring" skills to find the answer in the passage. The correct answer will be barely paraphrased, if at all. Most answers are also relatively short: that's why many questions with short answers reliably predict an easier passage.

Questions that are more difficult to answer are typically those that require "reasoning" skills: these questions are based on what is stated in the passage, but the correct answer may be a paraphrase of what was stated. The answer choices may also be longer. Reasoning questions include questions that ask about what is "implied" or "suggested," as well as questions about the main idea, the author's purpose, or what someone would agree or disagree with.

Pace Yourself

It would be logical to assume that you should divide the 35 minutes evenly across four passages, spending precisely eight minutes and 45 seconds on each passage. In reality, you will likely spend more time on one or two of the passages and less time on the others. To earn a perfect or near-perfect Reading score, you can neither rush and risk misreading, nor can you belabor one or two questions when more are waiting.

> Focus on the number of raw points you need, and don't get stuck on one or two tough questions.

Don't spend more than 10 minutes on one passage, and try to leave *at least* six minutes for the last passage. In Chapter 18, we'll teach you different strategies to improve your time-management skills.

Be Flexible and Aggressive

Flexibility is key to your ACT success, particularly on the Reading Test.

Get out of a passage on which you've already spent too much time, cutting yourself off at 10 minutes on any given passage. Force yourself to guess on the question you've been rereading for minutes, make smart and swift guesses on any questions still left, and move on.

We're not saying this is easy. In fact, changing your own instinctual behavior is the hardest part of cracking the Reading Test. Everyone has made the mistake of ignoring that voice that's screaming inside your head to move on, and we've all answered back "But I'm almost there and if I take just a little more time, I know l can get it."

You may in fact get that question. But that one right answer likely cost you two to three others. And even worse, you had probably already narrowed it down to two answer choices. You were down to a fifty-fifty chance of getting it right, but instead of guessing, you wasted more time to prove the one right answer.

In Chapter 18, we'll show you how to use that time more effectively to begin with and what to do when you're down to two choices. But both skills depend on the Process of Elimination, or POE.

POE

POE is a powerful tool on a multiple-choice, standardized test. On the Reading Test, you may find several Now questions easy to answer and be able to spot the correct answer right away among the four choices. There will be plenty of tough Reasoning questions, however, whose answers aren't obvious, either in your own words or among the four choices. You can easily fall into the trap of rereading and rereading to figure out the answer. Wrong answers, however, can be more obvious to identify. They are there, after all, to hide the right answer. In fact, if you can cross off all the wrong ones, the right answer will be waiting there for you. Even if you cross off only one or two, the right answer frequently becomes more obvious.

Process of Elimination

Each time you eliminate a wrong answer, you increase your chance of choosing the correct answer.

We'll spend more time with POE in the following chapters. Use POE to escape the death-spiral questions that will hold you back.

Summary

- There are always four passages and 40 questions on the Reading Test.

- The passages are always in the same order: Literary Narrative, Social Science, Humanities, Natural Science.

- Each passage has 10 questions.

- The passages are all roughly the same length, usually 700–900 words.

- Follow your POOD to pick your own order of the passages.

- Look for passages to do Now whose categories and topics you like best or find easier.

- Be aware of danger signs that could indicate a harder passage: fewer, longer paragraphs or lots of short paragraphs; few line-reference questions; many questions with long answers.

- Pace yourself. Don't let one tough passage or question derail you.

- Be flexible. Be ready to adapt your order, leave a tough passage, or guess on a tough question.

- Use Process of Elimination to cross off wrong answers and save time.

Chapter 16
The Basic Approach and Beyond

To earn a perfect or near-perfect score on the Reading Test, you need an efficient strategy. In this chapter, we'll discuss our 6-Step Basic Approach to working the passages, questions, and answers.

THE 6-STEP BASIC APPROACH

You may have already developed a strategy that works well for you, but you want to find a way to answer the handful of questions that are keeping your Reading score down. We urge you to read through this chapter and try our 6-Step Basic Approach. You may find that you like the entire strategy better than your own, or you may pick and choose certain elements to incorporate and enhance your current approach.

Note: because this book has smaller pages than the ACT test booklet does, the sample passages take up more lines than they will on the ACT. Therefore, the usual 5- to 10-line window will appear longer in this book. Often, the appropriate window is about one paragraph long, so you can use that as a guide as you work the following examples.

To learn about the ACT Reading Basic Approach in more detail, check out another Princeton Review title, *ACT Prep*.

Step 1: **Preview.** Check the blurb and map the questions. Star questions with line references, and underline lead words—words that actually appear in the passage.

Step 2: **Work the Passage.** Spend 2–3 minutes reading the passage. Look for and circle the lead words from the questions.

Step 3: **Select and Understand a Question.** Use your POOD to find Now and Later questions. Restate the question to make sure you know what you are looking for.

Step 4: **Read What You Need.** Most questions require 5–10 lines. Find that window and read it carefully. Read with the question in mind, which will help with efficiency.

Step 5: **Predict the Correct Answer.** Find something in the text that answers the question. Underline it. Do not try to analyze or paraphrase. Stick with what's actually stated in the text.

Step 6: **Use Process of Elimination.** Find the best answer by eliminating three bad ones. "Bad" answers are either inconsistent with your prediction or contain one of ACT's common traps.

Reading, Skimming, and Scanning

When you Work the Passage in Step 2, you may read quickly, or you may skim or scan the passage, according to what works best for you. Be aware that they are three distinct approaches.

Reading needs your brain on full power: you're reading words, and your brain is processing what they mean and drawing conclusions. Reading is watching the road, searching for directional signs, and glancing at the scenery, all for the purpose of trying to figure out where the road is leading.

Skimming means reading only a few words, maybe just the first sentence of each paragraph. Skimming is reading only the directional signs and ignoring the scenery.

Scanning requires your eyes more than your brain: let your eyes move over the passage, looking only for specific words. Scanning is looking for Volkswagen Beetles in a game of Slug Bug.

There is more information on these approaches in Chapter 18. For the passage on page 247, pick one strategy to try:

1. Read the passage, taking no more than 2–3 minutes,
2. Skim by reading only the first sentence of each paragraph, or
3. Scan for the lead words only.

Referral Questions

Referral questions are usually easy to answer because they ask what was directly stated in the passage. Read the question carefully to Understand the Question. Once you find the window to read, carefully Read What You Need and Predict the Correct Answer. The correct answers to Referral questions typically match the text closely; use Process of Elimination to get rid of answers that don't match the prediction. Questions 1, 4, 7, and 8 in the following passage are Referral questions.

How to Spot Referral Questions

- Questions that begin with "According to the passage"
- Questions that ask what the passage or author states
- Questions with short answer choices

Reasoning Questions

Reasoning questions ask about what is implied. Although the answer may not be stated word-for-word, you can (and should!) still underline evidence in the paragraph that answers the question. Find the window to read, carefully Read What You Need, and Predict the Correct Answer. Don't create your own interpretations that leap too far away from what is stated; instead, make your prediction based on the text. The answers to Reasoning questions may be paraphrases of what was stated in the text, so use Process of

How to Spot Reasoning Questions

- Questions that use *infer, means, suggests*, or *implies*
- Questions that ask about the purpose or function of part or all of the passage
- Questions that ask what the author or a character in the passage would agree or disagree with
- Questions that ask you to describe all or part of the passage
- Questions with long answer choices

Elimination and match paraphrased answers back to what is actually stated in the text. Questions 2, 3, 5, 9, and 10 in the following passage are Reasoning Questions.

Use a Comparison Process

After you eliminate the answer choices that don't match your prediction, you may sometimes find yourself stuck between two remaining choices. When this happens, use a comparison process. Compare the remaining answers

- to each other. Look for differences between the choices so you know what to focus on.
- to the question. Look for answer choices that answer the wrong question.
- to the passage. Look for differences between the answer choice and the passage.

As you compare, look for what might be wrong with each answer choice, rather than trying to justify each one.

Try out the Basic Approach on the following passage. For now, skip questions 1 and 6. (We'll discuss how to approach them later in this chapter.) If you have trouble finding the answer for one of the questions, come back to it after working easier-to-find questions. When you finish, check your answers with those given on the page following the questions. You may want to mark the passage pages so you can find them easily.

Passage I

LITERARY NARRATIVE: This passage is adapted from the short story "Goodbye Gretchen" by Katherine Craig (©2003 by Northeast Review).

I remember very clearly the first time I saw Gretchen. It was early fall, just after Labor Day when the weather still felt like summer, but school was in session and the evenings were getting darker.
5 She was inside the house, peeking out at me from behind the ancient lace curtains as I watered my tomatoes. Over the next several weeks, she got slowly braver: I saw her standing inside the screen door watching me, then peering over the fence. I
10 never related very well to children; my own had long ago moved away, and we spoke on the phone only a few times a year, rarely saw each other. Because of my general discomfort, I didn't try to speak to her. Looking back, I realize that probably made her
15 feel more comfortable around me.

Eventually, Gretchen worked up the courage to venture over to my yard, and I put her to work. It wasn't so much because I needed the help as I didn't know what else to do, and she did make my
20 chores easier. She was watchful and deliberate, a quick learner. I came to rely on her to do most of the weeding, since bending down was easier on her young back than on mine. She was careful to pull the roots all the way out, not just pull the
25 tops off the plants and leave the roots in the soil to grow again. Her small hands could easily reach between the wires of the tomato cages to retrieve the ripe fruits growing in close to the stalk, and she followed me around the yard as I watered,
30 making sure the hose wasn't kinked and keeping it carefully out of the garden beds.

As the autumn progressed and the evenings got darker, Gretchen began helping me inside the house also. It was a natural progression, from pick-
35 ing cucumbers and tomatoes to canning pickles and stewing tomatoes into sauce.

Gretchen's clothes were ill-fitting, and sometimes in need of mending, so once garden-ing season was over, I started giving her sewing
40 lessons. We hemmed her pants and sewed on buttons. I taught her to embroider flowers to make

the patches look prettier. We fell into a natural rhythm of domesticity.

I hadn't thought that I minded living alone,
45 but during that year I looked forward to the time when Gretchen got home from school. Gretchen was mostly quiet as we went about our work, but sometimes she would tell me about school. She described her teacher, Ms. Kanaley, as "amiable."
50 The girls in her class who teased her about her second-hand clothes were "spiteful," and the ones who were nice to her were "gracious." I was always struck, when she did talk, by how well-spoken she was. Her vocabulary was better than mine, but her
55 speech wasn't affected. Everything that came out of her mouth was spoken with a solemnity that made me listen carefully to her.

As the winter wore on, Gretchen and I be-gan making a quilt together. It was to be for the
60 bed in what used to be my daughter's bedroom. Gretchen picked out the pattern and the colors for the quilt, and we started to refer to the room as hers, since her quilt was going to go on the bed. I never thought, though, that she would take all
65 our talk so seriously.

Gretchen and her mother had moved in next door so Gretchen could attend school in a better district. In the spring, her mother told her that they had to move—she had tried, but
70 just couldn't make ends meet living there. It might have been wonderful to have Gretchen move in with me. But when she asked me, I could only think of the years when my own children were teenagers, which had been like
75 walking through a minefield: sometimes it was calm and beautiful, but I never knew when the next explosions were coming. Gretchen wasn't far from that age, and even just imagining a teenager living with me again made me long for
80 the solitude I hadn't even lost.

"It would be easier on you if Mom and I lived here," Gretchen said, "you're always saying there's too much space for just you. We'll help you with the housework. If we lived here, you could
85 teach me to cook for you." We were sitting in the living room, each of us on one side of the quilting

frame. I quickly glanced up at her pale, serious face. She was twirling a lock of her thin, brown hair nervously around her index finger. I didn't
90 know how to respond to this plea, so I looked back down and just cleared my throat instead. But I wasn't really looking at the quilt, and I stabbed my thumb with the needle hard enough that it drew blood. "I'll go get you a Band-Aid,"
95 Gretchen said in a small, deflated voice. "You don't want to get blood on your quilt."

1. The narrator suggests all of the following EXCEPT that she:

   A. did not require help with her chores.
   B. had a poorer vocabulary than Gretchen did.
   C. saw her children only a few times a year.
   D. might have enjoyed having Gretchen live with her.

2. It can most reasonably be inferred from the passage that the narrator interprets Gretchen's statement "I'll go get you a Band-Aid" (line 94) to mean which of the following?

   F. "I care more about the quilt than you do."
   G. "You don't want us to move in."
   H. "I'm glad I asked you."
   J. "You're grateful for the offer."

3. When the narrator mentions "a natural rhythm of domesticity" (lines 42–43), she's most nearly referring to:

   A. unusual acts of spite made by young children against perceived outsiders.
   B. seasonal cycles of planting, harvesting, and canning foods.
   C. renting rooms to friends who have fallen on hard times.
   D. regular chores typically coordinated with a partner.

4. The narrator speculates that one reason for Gretchen's comfort with her might have been that:

   F. the narrator didn't try to speak to Gretchen because of the narrator's own discomfort.
   G. the girls at Gretchen's school had told Gretchen the narrator could be trusted.
   H. Gretchen and the narrator's children had been friends, which made the narrator a maternal figure for Gretchen.
   J. the narrator knew how to communicate with Gretchen because of the narrator's positive experience with her own children.

5. The passage reveals that when Gretchen's mother announced that they had to move, Gretchen asked the narrator if she and her mother could move in. The narrator indicates that she viewed this request as:

   A. possibly sarcastic, which left the narrator feeling hurt.
   B. somewhat impulsive, which explains the narrator's uncertainty.
   C. completely welcome, which left the narrator speechless.
   D. somewhat surprising, which explains the narrator's struggle to respond.

6. As it is used in line 75, the word *minefield* most nearly means:

   F. war zone.
   G. tense situation.
   H. pressure cooker.
   J. booby trap.

7. The narrator claims that since her children moved away, her living situation had been marked by:

   A. comfortable solitude.
   B. lonely isolation.
   C. overwhelming chores.
   D. social obligations.

8. As the narrator reflects on the year spent with Gretchen, the narrator realizes that she:

    F. resented the time Gretchen's company took up and kept her away from her household chores.

    G. criticized Gretchen too much, and now regrets driving her away.

    H. appreciated it at the time, but now is grateful that she has her privacy back.

    J. enjoyed it, but was unaware that Gretchen thought seriously about moving in.

9. The references to *calm* and *explosions* in lines 76–77 are most likely intended to suggest that at the time, the narrator felt:

    A. guilty that she preferred Gretchen's company to that of her own children.

    B. appreciative that Gretchen and her mother would make her feel less lonely.

    C. worried about the conflicts and challenges a teenager in the house would bring.

    D. suspicious that Gretchen was trying to take advantage of her.

10. In the context of the passage, the concluding two sentences (lines 94–96) are most likely meant to suggest:

    F. a mutual benefit for two people has been acknowledged.

    G. an earnest offer of help has been eagerly accepted.

    H. a painful rejection is being handled with grace.

    J. a longtime rift has been healed.

SELF-ANALYSIS

The answers to the questions are 2. (G), 3. (D), 4. (F), 5. (D), 7. (A), 8. (J), 9. (C), 10. (H). How did you do? If you missed more than one question or spent a long time, analyze your approach on this passage and consider what changes you can make the next time.

- Did one question take up more time than the rest?
- Did you do the questions in the order given instead of answering Now questions first?
- Did you answer the questions from memory instead of Reading What You Need and Predicting the Answer based on the text?
- Did you find yourself rereading selections of text multiple times to identify a correct answer?
- Did you find yourself torn between two answers?

Here's How to Crack the Questions
—The explanations for Questions 1 and 6 are given in the next sections.—

Question 2 In lines 81–85, Gretchen gives reasons that it would be advantageous if Gretchen and her mother lived here with the narrator. In lines 89–91, the narrator says that she *didn't know how to respond to this plea* and that she didn't answer. When Gretchen says, *"I'll go get you a Band-Aid,"* Gretchen's voice is described as *small* and *deflated*. This suggests that the narrator believes Gretchen is disappointed because she thinks the narrator will not let Gretchen and her mother live with her. Choice (F) is not related to the topic of Gretchen and her mother moving in, which is the focus of the conversation in this paragraph. Choices (H) and (J) have a positive tone, which doesn't match the description of Gretchen's small, deflated voice. The correct answer is (G).

Question 3 Lines 21 through 43 describe how Gretchen and the narrator worked on chores together, including gardening, canning, and mending clothes. Lines 42–43 state, *We fell into a natural rhythm of domesticity,* suggesting that the natural rhythm is related to what the two characters did, rather than the seasonal cycles mentioned in (B). The correct answer is (D).

Question 4 The lead words *Gretchen's comfort* don't appear in the passage exactly, but those lead words in the question should make you circle *comfortable* in line 15. The correct answer is supported by lines 13–15. The correct answer is (F).

Question 5 Gretchen's request to move in is relatively easy to find in lines 81–85. However, the evidence for the correct answer spans several paragraphs, from line 64 through the end of the passage, which means question 5 may be easier to work after you've gotten more familiar with the passage by working other questions. The answers to Questions 2, 8, and 10 also support the correct answer for question 5. The correct answer is (D).

Question 7 The narrator mentions her children moving away in lines 10–11, but she mentions her children again in lines 72–77 and the answer to Question 7 is in lines 77–80. If you didn't quickly find the evidence you needed to answer question 7, it would be wise to come back to it after working easier-to-find questions. The correct answer is (A).

Question 8 The lead words *past year* do not appear in the passage, but *that year* appears in line 45. Lines 44–46 support the statement that the narrator enjoyed the time spent with Gretchen. Lines 64–65 support the statement that the narrator did not realize that Gretchen thought seriously about moving in. The correct answer is (J).

Question 9 The correct answer is supported by lines 72 through 80, which describe what the narrator thought of when Gretchen asked to move in with her. The narrator describes how unpredictable life with her own teenage children had been, and the words *calm* and *explosions* emphasize the unpredictability. Then she states, *Gretchen wasn't far from that age* and indicates that imagining living with a teenager made her long for *solitude*. The correct answer is (C).

Question 10 The correct answer to question 10 is supported by the answers to Questions 2 and 9 as well as by lines 66–96. In the last two paragraphs, Gretchen asks to move in with the narrator, and the narrator does not answer her. Gretchen takes the narrator's lack of response to mean that she does not want Gretchen and her mother to move in. In lines 94–96, Gretchen does not react to the perceived rejection; instead, she simply offers to help the narrator, who has injured herself. The correct answer is (H).

If you missed any of these questions, examine the answers you chose. What is the difference between your choice and the correct answer? What drew you to the wrong answer? What makes the correct answer the "best" answer?

Now, let's look at the remaining question types.

Vocabulary-in-Context

Question 6 in the preceding set is a Vocabulary-in-Context question. Vocabulary-in-Context questions ask you to determine the meaning of a word or phrase as it's used in context. The difficulty of the vocabulary can vary, but most of these questions test secondary meanings of relatively common words.

You don't need to read a full window of 5–10 lines for Vocabulary-in-Context questions, but you do need to read at least the full sentence to determine the word's meaning in context. First, cover the answer choices so you don't get caught by a trap answer. Then cross out the word or phrase in the passage and substitute your own word.

6. As it is used in line 75, the word *minefield* most nearly means:

Lines 72–77 state, *But when she asked me, I could only think of the years when my own children were teenagers, which had been like walking through a minefield: sometimes it was calm and beautiful, but I never knew when the next explosions were coming.*

What word or phrase would you use to replace *minefield*? _____

Perhaps you wrote down something along the lines of "emotional or upsetting environment." Your prediction doesn't need to be anything fancy—just capture the meaning in your own words. Now, move to the answers and use POE to eliminate choices that don't match your prediction. The correct answer has to reflect the way that the word is used in the passage—beware of trap answers that are valid definitions of the word in the question but that don't match its meaning in context.

    F. war zone.
    G. tense situation.
    H. pressure cooker.
    J. booby trap.

Choices (F) and (J) are related to the literal meaning of *minefield*, but they don't match the meaning of the word in the context of the narrator's family life. Choice (H) is another metaphor that might describe the situation, but it isn't the meaning of the word *minefield*. The correct answer is (G).

Later Questions

Do Later the questions that are difficult to answer and whose answers are hard to find. These may include questions that have neither a star nor any underlined lead words, as well as questions whose lead words are difficult to find. The later you do such questions, the easier they become. While working the Now questions, you'll either stumble across the hard-to-find lead words or gain a better sense of the passage's structure.

General questions that ask about the passage as a whole, such as main idea or primary purpose questions, should also be done Later. Now that you are more familiar with the passage, let's try Question 1.

    1. The narrator suggests all of the following EXCEPT that she:
        A. did not require help with her chores.
        B. had a poorer vocabulary than Gretchen did.
        C. saw her children only a few times a year.
        D. might have enjoyed having Gretchen live with her.

The question doesn't provide any line reference or lead words. Furthermore, it's a negative question, and it can be easy to forget about the NOT and choose an answer that **is** suggested by the passage. The combination of these challenges makes this question a good Later question.

To find the evidence you need, look up lead words from each answer choice. Confirm whether each answer choice is or is not suggested. Rather than cross out wrong answers, jot down a "Y" for "yes" or an "N" for "no" next to each answer. Then you will clearly be able to see which answer choice is the odd one out.

Choice (A) is suggested in line 18. Choice (B) is suggested in line 54. Choice (D) is suggested in lines 70–72. Choice (C) is **not** suggested; it is a misreading of lines 9–12, which state that the narrator *spoke on the phone only a few times a year* with her children, and that she *rarely saw* them. The correct answer is (C).

> **The Pencil Trick**
> When you have to look harder for a lead word, use your pencil to sweep over each line from beginning to end. By keeping your pencil moving, you will keep your brain from actually reading and will let your eyes look for the word.

In the following chapters, we'll address in greater depth both critical reading and time-management skills. After all, success on the Reading Test requires polishing both sets of skills. But applying the 6-Step Basic Approach can help you with both.

Summary

- o Use the 6-Step Basic Approach.
  - o Step 1: **Preview.** Check the blurb and map the questions. Star line and paragraph references and underline lead words.
  - o Step 2: **Work the Passage.** Finish in 2–3 minutes. Use skimming or scanning and finish in 2–3 minutes. Look for and circle lead words.
  - o Step 3: **Select and Understand a Question.** Do Now the questions that are easy to answer or whose answers are easy to find.
  - o Step 4: **Read What You Need.** Most questions require a window of 5–10 lines.
  - o Step 5: **Predict the Correct Answer.** If possible, underline evidence for the answer in the text.
  - o Step 6: **Use Process of Elimination.**

Chapter 17
Critical-Reading Skills

In this chapter, we'll help you hone your critical-reading skills to crack the most challenging of difficult text. We'll also build on your mastery of the 6-Step Basic Approach by teaching you advanced POE (Process of Elimination) strategies.

CRITICAL READING

By now, your use of the 6-Step Basic Approach and your personal order of difficulty (POOD) of both passages and questions should make you feel more confident on the Reading Test. But you also may still be struggling with time and feel that you just can't work fast enough to get to enough questions.

Critical-reading skills and time-management skills are entwined on the ACT, and it's likely that when you struggle with time, it's less because you don't *read* fast enough and more that you can't *read and understand* fast enough. You probably waste a lot of time when you read and reread a window of text, or even an entire passage, trying to figure out what it's saying. When you're stuck on a question, you likely reread the window of text several times. You may have even eliminated two answers, but when you're still not sure what the correct answer is, what do you do? You read the window yet again, desperate to figure out the meaning and correct answer.

We've all been there. Part of what makes standardized tests so evil is how they encourage us to listen to our worst instincts. You can't treat the Reading Test as you would a school assignment, and you can't fall prey to your own panicked responses. You have to develop both strategies and skills specific to *this* test.

Active Reading

The key to developing better reading skills is to read *actively*. Getting lost in even a small window of text that makes no sense is like getting lost on unfamiliar roads. You wouldn't stare down at the yellow line, would you? Instead, you would look around for landmarks and road signs, trying to figure out where you are and where the road is going.

Passage, Interrupted

This chapter uses a natural science passage and questions, but the passage will not be presented in its entirety nor in order. The blurb contains some useful additional information.

Passage IV

NATURAL SCIENCE: This passage is adapted from the article "Who's Domesticating Whom?" by Rachel Hunter (©2002 by Wilson's Quarterly).

Hunter is reviewing the book *The Botany of Desire: A Plant's-Eye View of the World* by Michael Pollan.

Topic Sentences and Transition Words

When you're lost in a tough section of text, use topic sentences and transitions as your landmarks and road signs. Use the topic sentence to identify the main point of a paragraph. Look for transitions to see whether ideas are heading in the same direction or opposite directions.

Let's see how this works. Read the following topic sentence.

> Most people define domesticated species from a typically anthropocentric context.

What's going to come next in the paragraph? The author could provide examples of *domesticated species* under this definition, explain why people use such a definition, or state that most people are wrong and there is a better definition. You would be safe anticipating any of those outcomes, but the anticipation is the key. Don't sit back and wait to see where the road is going. Lean forward and look for the fork in the road or the detour sign telling you to turn around. In other words, look for transitions.

Let's look at some choices for our domesticated-species sentence.

- If the next words were *For example*, what does that tell you is coming next? You'd expect to see examples of the species and how they've been defined.

- If the next words were *In other words*, what does that tell you is coming next? You'd expect to see a restatement, most likely a clearer version of the author's point.

- If the next word were *However*, what does that tell you is coming next? You'd expect to see a contradiction to this belief, possibly one the author herself agrees with.

Transitions play a key role in active reading. Look for transitions to announce additional points, contradictory points, cause-and-effect relationships, examples, or conclusions.

For more on transitions, see page 60.

Modifiers

Like transitions, modifiers are important in active reading. Nouns and verbs reliably provide the facts in a statement, but authors use modifiers to communicate their points of view.

Look at the adverbs in the previous sentence and see how they helped shape the point: *Reliably* means you can infer that nouns and verbs *almost always* give facts. *Necessarily* modifies the verb phrase *don't provide*. Without it, you could infer that nouns and verbs never give you the point. Adjectives and adverbs are just as useful as transitions, conveying the author's opinion on what would otherwise be a statement of fact.

Consider the first topic sentence again.

> Most people define domesticated species from a typically anthropocentric context.

How does the adverb *typically* affect *anthropocentric context*? The author implies that this should be expected. What does the choice of using *most people* imply? At the very least, some other people think differently, and it's fair to presume the author is one of them. After all, if she agreed with this definition, wouldn't she have just written a sentence providing this fact?

> Domesticated species are defined from an anthropocentric context.

Without the modifiers, this sentence is a neutral statement of facts. The author's deliberate choices of *most people* and *typically* allow us to infer her opinion on this stance and anticipate her own viewpoint to come.

Pronouns

Transitions and modifiers do not have a monopoly on conveying meaning and connections. Certain pronouns, used alone or as a modifier when paired with a noun or other modifiers, provide clear maps from one idea to another. Consider the following topic sentence.

> This problem of monoculture is not unique to the potato; a similar situation is described in the case of the apple.

This problem of monoculture directly identifies the topic of the prior paragraph, and the author characterizes the topic as a *problem*. Moreover, the phrase *this problem of monoculture* applies to the *similar situation* of the apple. The topic sentence allows us to infer that the rest of the paragraph will discuss how this problem of monoculture applies to the apple. Furthermore, the use of the pronoun *this* in front of the noun makes clear that monoculture was discussed and perhaps defined in the preceding paragraph.

The pronouns *another, it, this, that,* and *such* can be very useful road signs. These pronouns indicate that the subject has been discussed previously. Consider the following examples and what you can infer.

Such a technique has its advantages.

What's the technique? It must have been explained in the preceding sentence. The following sentences will show its benefits.

> *It's tempting, but it's wrong.*

It was explained in the preceding sentence, likely in a very positive manner (it's "tempting"). But, the next sentence will explain why *it* is wrong.

Translation

When you're struggling to make sense of a window of confusing text, look for transitions and modifiers to help you determine the main point. You may be in the thick of a body paragraph with the topic sentence in the rearview mirror, or the topic sentence fails to illuminate the main point of the paragraph. Instead of focusing on every single word, use the transitions, modifiers, and pronouns to get the general direction of points and the connections between them.

Let's look at a tough paragraph and see how this works.

Pollan is not a botanist; he is a journalist who has written extensively on food and food production, tracing the human relationship with food from farm and garden to table and plate. Pollan himself is a gardener, and in his latest book on his favorite subject, he describes an afternoon
5 in his garden planting potatoes. He realizes that both he and the bees that are busily pollinating an apple tree nearby are performing essentially the same evolutionary role. That is, the bees promote certain varieties of apples based on useful features. Many people would find such a notion absurd, but we have no trouble believing that humans cultivated certain
10 varieties of potatoes based on their desirable traits. Pollan makes a convincing case that we are more like the bees than we have been accustomed to think: in his case, the potato adapted to its particular size and flavor so that humans would plant it and disseminate its genes. In the case of the bees, the apple trees developed perfectly symmetrical blossoms and
15 sweet scents to entice the bees to pollinate it.

Here's How to Crack It

You may have struggled to understand the middle part of the paragraph and even opted to reread the whole paragraph, but a second time through probably still failed to clarify the author's meaning

Focus on key modifiers, transitions, and pronouns. *Same* indicates a comparison between humans and bees, while the adverb *essentially* softens the similarity a bit. The transition *that is* leads into a restatement of the point. *Such* a notion about bees that we would find *absurd* is the claim that they promoted certain apple trees. The transition *but* leads into our having *no trouble* having the same notion about humans. The similarity between bees and humans is reinforced in the next sentence, *we are more like the bees*. Moreover, this sentence includes the author's blessing: she calls Pollan's case *convincing*. The parallel structure of *in his case* and *in the case of the bees* reasserts the similarity and in fact introduces specific examples of that *same evolutionary role*. The potato used humans. The apple trees used bees.

ACT BOOK CLUB

Critical thinking also extends to knowing more about the test-writers themselves. You may find the passages dry and boring, but the folks at ACT would not agree with you. They have gone out of their way to select passages whose topics they find interesting and worthy of being read. They choose authors whose work they respect.

Thus, when it comes time to write questions and correct answers, the ACT test-writers will not make these chosen authors look bad by putting rude, silly, or offensive words in their mouths. The topics may include some challenging facts and ideas, but they are unlikely to be divisive or controversial. In the nonfiction passages, the authors may be critical or supportive of their subject, but they will state their opinions professionally and respectfully. Correct answers, therefore, must use the same level of diplomacy and respect to paraphrase the authors' ideas.

- Topics are interesting and worthy.
- Authors are professional and respectful.
- Correct answers are not rude, silly, or offensive.

Use this knowledge to eliminate at least one wrong answer below. If you've retained the brief information we've gleaned so far about the passage and what the author thinks of Michael Pollan, you may be able to eliminate one more or identify the correct answer. If not, stay tuned to the end of the chapter when the answer will be provided.

---

31. Which of the following best describes how the passage's author describes Pollan?

  A. A well-intentioned environmentalist willing to challenge the accepted practices of industrial food production
  B. A trained botanist attempting to replace the practice of monoculture with genetically modified foods
  C. A knowledgeable journalist able to use his story-telling skills to promote the importance of biodiversity
  D. A cynical author willing to shock readers in efforts to promote his book

Here's How to Crack It

Choice (D) is out. It's offensive both to Michael Pollan and the passage's author if it's not true. In the unlikely event that the passage actually did discuss such an author, the correct answer would phrase it in a more tactful way. Choice (B) is also out. The paragraph cited for the Translation exercise stated the opposite. See the last part of this chapter for confirmation of the correct answer.

ADVANCED POE SKILLS

In an ideal situation, you would read a question, read the window of text looking for your prediction, and then work through the answer choices to find the best match, using POE to get rid of those that don't.

But situations are seldom ideal on the Reading Test. When you don't quite understand the window and therefore have no clue about the prediction, go straight to working the answers. You can reread your window to spot transitions and modifiers; do this in conjunction with Process of Elimination.

The Art of Wrong Answers

If you worked for ACT, you'd have to sit in a cubicle all day writing test questions. The easy part of the job is writing the correct answer (in respectful language, of course). You may even know the correct answer before you write the question. The harder part is coming up with three wrong answers. If you didn't write great wrong answers, everyone would get a 36. So you have to come up with temptingly wrong answers.

Let's take a look at some ways to make wrong answers.

Read the following question, correct answer, and text. We don't care about the right answer in this exercise, so you can read it before you read the window.

> **35.** The main point of the fourth paragraph (lines 1–45) is that:
>
> **A.** some species may play a role in their domestication by developing traits that make them useful to humans.
>
> > In the introduction to his new book, *The Botany of Desire,* Michael Pollan points out that today there are fifty million dogs in the United States alone and only ten thousand wolves. Pollan uses this fact to question the standard understanding of domestication. He argues that
> > 5 dogs have the evolutionary advantage over wolves because they have developed a survival strategy that involves making humans desire their company. The idea that domestication is something for which humans are unilaterally responsible and that we impose on other species he calls a "failure of imagination."

Our goal here is to examine *why* the three wrong answers are wrong.

> **B.** humans developed an evolutionary strategy by making themselves desirable to dogs.

Look carefully at lines 6–7. Choice (B) took tempting words out of the passage and garbled them. The passage does not support this answer.

> **C.** the evolutionary strategy of dogs has been more successful than that of wolves.

Lines 2–3 indicate that there are many more dogs than wolves, so you could infer that the dogs have developed a more successful strategy. But (C) is incorrect because the example of dogs is used to support the main point but is not itself the main point of the paragraph.

D. bees developed an evolutionary strategy dependent on the desirable traits of apples trees.

Bees and apple trees are not mentioned in this window and have instead been taken from a different window. Because this question asks about the main point of the fourth paragraph, any choice that references facts or points from different windows is wrong.

Answers can be wrong because they don't match what the passage says, because they answer the wrong question, or because they're not even found in the right window. But no matter how tempting or obvious wrong answers are, they are all easier to understand than 5 to 10 lines of text from the passage, simply because they're shorter. So when you're stuck on tough questions that reference tough windows, rely on the answers and POE.

Work Backwards from the Answers

Instead of rereading the window to try to understand it, read the answer choices for their meaning. Then see if you can match that meaning back to part of the passage.

- Look for lead words or phrases in the answer choices.
- Determine whether the words or meaning match words or meaning in the window.
- Use POE to cross off choices that don't match what's in the window.

Let's see how this works. Read the following question and window.

Even before he gets to the era of humans and domestication of plants in the grand scheme of biological history, Pollan maintains that, without angiosperms—plants that produce fruit, thereby inducing animals to do the work of spreading their seeds—mammals would not have evolved
5 as they have, and the reptiles that had no need of delicious plants and fruits would likely still rule Earth. Thus, the co-evolutionary relationship between plants and mammals began hundreds of millions of years ago. There is no reason to think that the human relationship to plants is appreciably different than that of a squirrel burying acorns or a bee
10 pollinating an apple tree.

37. It can reasonably be inferred that the author provides the example of angiosperms (line 3) in order to:

Take the answer choices one at a time. In each choice, we've identified a lead word or phrase in the answer by making it bold. Can you match these words, or a paraphrased meaning of them, in the window of text?

    A. argue that **mammals developed traits more useful to plants than to reptiles**.

The paragraph suggests that mammals were more useful to plants than were most reptiles, but it does not mention specific traits developed by mammals, and it does not discuss the relationship between mammals and reptiles at all.

    B. reveal which traits made reptiles **lose their dominance to mammals**.

Would likely still rule Earth is a good paraphrase of *lose their dominance* and *that had no need of delicious plants and fruits* could be the trait, or lack thereof, that disadvantaged reptiles. But this doesn't give us a reason for including the example of angiosperms.

    C. explain why **dinosaurs became extinct**.

The passage never mentions dinosaurs, so (C) can't be right.

    D. illustrate that the evolution of mammals **depended on useful traits developed by plants**.

The ability of angiosperms to produce fruit and get mammals to spread their seeds is a *useful trait*. Moreover, *depended on* is a good paraphrase of *co-evolutionary relationship between plants and mammals*. Choice (D) is the correct answer.

Try the next two examples. Choose your own words or phrases out of each answer to work backward with. Does the answer match the passage?

○

This problem of monoculture is not unique to the potato; a similar situation is described in the case of the apple. The first grafted apple trees to arrive in America did not fare well. But thanks to the efforts of John Chapman (aka Johnny Appleseed), who is the main focus of Pollan's
5 apple chapter, many thousands of apple trees were planted from seeds, allowing genetic variation to provide species that would thrive in the new environment. But with modern industrial-scale food production and marketing, fewer and fewer varieties of apples are grown today, and genetic variation is quickly dwindling. In the end, Pollan urges us
10 to pay attention to our co-evolutionary role in agriculture and strive to preserve biodiversity, rather than rely on the idea that human (and chemical) ingenuity will always come to the rescue.

32. How does the passage's author characterize the genetic variation of apples within the context of modern food production?

  F. Threatened, to the point that several new varieties of apples planted today fail to thrive
  G. Declining, to the point that relatively few varieties are planted
  H. Declining, in that varieties derived from genetically modified seeds will replace the varieties descended from the seeds sown by Johnny Appleseed
  J. Threatened, in that several varieties of apples could soon be extinct

33. Based on the passage, Pollan would most likely say that relying on human ingenuity is more a matter of:

  A. being practical than of being naïve.
  B. dismissing scientific facts than of learning from evolutionary history.
  C. hoping for a solution to a problem than addressing the causes.
  D. accepting hysteria than of remaining optimistic.

Here's How to Crack Questions 32 and 33

For Question 32, the four answer choices all begin with a word that is a good paraphrase of *dwindling*. *Fail to thrive* in (F) misuses *thrive*, used to describe the trees grown from Johnny Appleseed. *Few varieties planted* in (G) is accurately placed in the paragraph and confirms (G) as the correct answer. *Genetically modified seeds* in (H) is not mentioned in the paragraph. *Extinct* in (J) cannot be supported by the passage.

For Question 33, *practical* and *naïve* in (A) may be possibilities, but they are in the wrong order. *Human ingenuity* is what Pollan discourages; thus, *naïve* can't match what he is encouraging. *Evolutionary history* in (B) could refer to *our co-evolutionary role in agriculture* but *dismissing scientific facts* is almost opposite to *(chemical) ingenuity*. *Hoping for a solution* in (C) matches well with *come to the rescue*, and (C) is the correct answer. In (D), *remaining optimistic* is in the wrong place, a better paraphrase of what Pollan discourages rather than what he encourages.

PULL IT ALL TOGETHER

Try using all of your critical-reading skills on the next question.

Many pet dogs would stand no chance of survival in the wild. Though pugs and poodles are descended ultimately from wolves, they bear little resemblance to their wild cousins. Archaeological remains indicate that somewhere between 15,000 and 30,000 years ago, wolves began to be
5   domesticated; that is, they began to live with and become dependent on humans. As this relationship became more common, people chose those animals with the most desirable traits to breed, and the obedient and loyal *Canis lupus familiaris* (domestic dog) was born.

36. The main purpose of the first paragraph is to:

   F. provide an example to introduce a concept that the rest of the passage will examine.

   G. list the desirable traits that made humans domesticate dogs.

   H. pose a theory that the rest of the passage will disprove.

   J. explain how the process of domestication benefits biodiversity.

Here's How to Crack It

The correct answer is (F). Dogs and wolves are an example of the concept of domestication, which is examined in the rest of the passage. Choice (G) is incorrect because the paragraph does not *list the desirable traits*. Choice (H) is tempting because the rest of the passage discusses Pollan's point that dogs played some role in their domestication (see Question 35), but *disprove* is too strong. Choice (J) is incorrect because the paragraph does not *explain* anything, much less address *biodiversity*.

Agreement

Question 36 above was easier to answer because of the knowledge gained from working the prior questions. No matter how well you may read a passage, you learn the main points better as you work the questions. The questions, after all, all come from the same passage and it only makes sense that they should agree with one another.

Take another look at Question 31, now paired with another question.

31. Which of the following best describes how the passage's author describes Pollan?
    A. A well-intentioned environmentalist willing to challenge the accepted practices of industrial food production
    B. A trained botanist attempting to replace the practice of monoculture with genetically modified foods
    C. A knowledgeable journalist able to use his story-telling skills to promote the importance of biodiversity
    D. A cynical author willing to shock readers in efforts to promote his book

39. As a piece of writing, Pollan's book is judged by the author to be:
    A. inscrutable to all but trained experts in the field of botany.
    B. revolutionary in its challenge of traditional understandings of domestication.
    C. simplistic in an effort to attract gardeners and casual readers.
    D. accessible and enjoyable in its mixture of anecdote and history.

Here's How to Crack Questions 31 and 39

From several questions and selections of text, we have proof that the author approves of Pollan. One selection of text explicitly gave praise to his writing skills.

> Pollan has a deep grasp of and appreciation for the principles of evolution and botany, **yet** he tells his stories in an entertaining and easily understandable manner.

This is the proof for (C) in Question 31 and (D) in Question 39. If you chose (A) for Question 31, the selection of (D) for Question 39 should make you change your answer. Keep your radar up as you make your way through the questions. Make sure your answers agree, and look for the Golden Thread.

The Golden Thread

Place yourself again in the cubicle of an ACT test-writer. When you determine which details to test in a question, you would likely choose the important ones, those that support the main point. Thus, the main idea runs throughout the correct answers of at least a few of the specific questions, like a golden thread that ties the questions together.

---

34. It can reasonably be inferred from the passage that by titling his book *Botany of Desire,* Pollan was trying to suggest that plants:

    F.   have the same feelings as mammals.

    G.   played some role in their own domestication.

    H.   have been cultivated as part of natural selection.

    J.   are dependent on humans for their evolution.

Here's How to Crack It

Look at the answers to Questions 35 and 37. These answers identify (G) as the correct answer for Question 34. The paragraph we used in the translation exercise provides the proof from the passage for (G), but so do the answers to the other questions, and in a more concise fashion.

Summary

- Use critical-reading skills to crack difficult passages and windows of passages.

- Use topic sentences, transitions, modifiers, and pronouns to help translate confusing windows of text.

- Eliminate answer choices that are rude, silly, or offensive.

- Work backward with answer choices. Try to match the answer to the passage instead of the passage to the answer.

- Correct answers should agree with one another.

- Look for the Golden Thread of the main idea as it appears in correct answers to at least a few of the specific questions.

Chapter 18
Time-Management Skills

The ACT Reading Test offers 35 minutes to answer 40 questions on four passages. To earn a perfect or near-perfect score, you have to use your time efficiently, pacing yourself to go slowly enough to avoid careless errors and quickly enough to get to all questions. You also need strategies to use when pacing doesn't go as planned.

READING WITHOUT TIME LIMITS

For school, most of your reading is done with no time limits, at least theoretically. You have assignments of chapters, essays, and articles that you read, reread, highlight, and notate out of class. You may even make flashcards. In class, group discussions and even lectures from the teacher help you grasp the significance, meaning, and context of what you have read. You may need to "show your understanding" in a quiz, test, in-class essay, or paper, but you have usually had plenty of time to work with the text to develop a thorough understanding.

Outside of school, serious readers take time to process what they've read and form an opinion. As a college student, you'll be asked not only to read but also to think about what you've read and offer an opinion. Any professor will tell you that understanding takes thought, and thought usually takes time, more than 35 minutes.

This Isn't School

In school, you have been rewarded for your ability to develop a thorough, thoughtful grasp of the meaning and significance of the text. But in school, you have the benefit of time, not to mention the aid of your teachers' lectures, class discussions, and various tools to help you not only understand but also remember what you've read. On the ACT, there is a time limit, which means you have none of those tools available. And on the Reading Test, it's dangerous to approach the passages as if you do.

You don't earn points from reading the passage. You earn points from answering the questions correctly. Even strong readers can take too much time reading the passage, and everyone has made the mistake of wasting time by rereading confusing, dense text.

PACING

Practice, Practice, Practice
1,523 ACT Practice Questions provides 6 tests' worth of Reading passages. That's 24 passages and 240 questions.

To work four passages in 35 minutes, you can divide the time in several different ways. It might seem logical to spend eight minutes and 45 seconds on each passage, but reality on the Reading Test is seldom that neat.

There is no single pacing strategy that works best for all students. Some do best by investing the greatest amount of time on the two passages on which they typically earn the most points. Others can tackle their strongest passages in less time and give more time to the passages that they usually find more challenging. And on any given test, the topic or features such as the size and number of paragraphs and the number of line-reference questions can vary widely and have a significant impact on your pacing. The best way to determine *your* best pacing plan is to try various approaches and see which one helps you earn the most points most consistently.

Sample Pacing Strategies

These are general guidelines. Every time you do a practice Reading Test, analyze your performance, tracking how much time you spent on each passage and where you lost points—and why. Find the pacing strategy that works best for you.

Strategy 1

First passage: *9–10 minutes*
Second passage: *9–10 minutes*
Third passage: *7–8 minutes*
Fourth passage: *7–8 minutes*

Strategy 2

First passage: *6–7 minutes*
Second passage: *7–8 minutes*
Third passage: *10 minutes*
Fourth passage: *11 minutes*

Be Flexible

Our best advice is to be flexible. Just as you develop a typical order of the passages, you need to develop a typical pacing strategy. But be prepared to adapt both on each Reading Test if you have to.

THE 6-STEP BASIC APPROACH

Let's look at how to incorporate pacing into the 6-Step Basic Approach. Remember, each step is designed to help you use your time effectively.

> Step 1: **Preview.** Check the blurb and map the questions.
> Step 2: **Work the Passage.** Spend 2–3 minutes reading the passage.
> Step 3: **Select and Understand a Question.** Use your POOD to find Now and Later questions.
> Step 4: **Read What You Need.** Most questions require 5–10 lines.
> Step 5: **Predict the Correct Answer.** Try to find text in the passage that answers the question.
> Step 6: **Use Process of Elimination.** Get rid of answers that do not match the prediction.

When you preview the questions, you learn the main idea of the passage and know what to look for. Whether you read or skim the passage, you will both comprehend better and complete in less time and will avoid wasting time on unimportant details. Apply the critical-reading skills we covered in Chapter 17 to work steps 3–6. Read what you need to confirm or find an answer. Work backward with the answers when you are confronted with difficult, dense text.

Pacing the Basic Approach

If you invest eight to nine minutes on a given passage, do so wisely. This is how we suggest using the time.

> Step 1: **Preview.** *15–30 seconds*
> Step 2: **Work the Passage.** *2–3 minutes*
> Steps 3 through 6: **Work the Questions and Answers.** *6 minutes*

When you struggle with time, there are several steps that could be eating up the minutes.

Step 1: Preview

To move at the fastest speed when you preview, you can't read the questions. Let your eye *look* for lead words and numbers. Don't let your brain *read*. Or, in other words, *scan*. Ignore common question words like "main idea," "in order to," or "author suggests." Those words won't show up in the passage, so just let your eye move right past them.

Time yourself to see if you can preview the following blurb and questions in 15–30 seconds.

Passage II

SOCIAL SCIENCE: This passage is adapted from the article "Turning Trees Green Again" by Liza Clement (©2012 by Sustainability Quarterly).

11. It can most reasonably be inferred that the author's reason for including a variety of concerns surrounding the harvesting and processing of trees is to:

12. The passage's description of the Forest Stewardship Council reveals that the project lists one of its successes as the:

13. The main idea of the eighth paragraph (lines 73–86) is that:

14. The passage indicates that illegal logging may result in:

15. The passage states that certification programs have positively impacted all of the following EXCEPT:

16. The passage indicates that compared to products made from reclaimed lumber, conventionally made wood products are somewhat more:

17. The passage notes that companies that engage in illegal logging overlook the fact that:

18. The passage refers to *patina* as a product of:

19. The passage indicates that Detroit offers programs that train workers to reclaim lumber because in that city:

20. The last paragraph leaves the reader with the clear impression that awareness of environmental and social impacts has:

 **Step 2: Work the Passage**

This step should take no more than three minutes, and you should not be trying to read the passage thoroughly. Your only goal is to find as many of your lead words as you can and circle them.

If you struggle to work the passage in three minutes, there are ways to adapt the Basic Approach. You can incorporate these adaptations as a regular strategy, or you can use them if your pacing strategy goes awry on a particular test.

BASIC APPROACH ADAPTATIONS

Your approach does not need to be uniform for all four passages on every test. The key to flexibility is having a few different strategies in your toolbox and knowing when to use them.

Read the Topic Sentences

Read only the first sentence of each paragraph. You may find fewer lead words, but you will give yourself more time to spend on working the questions and answers and can find lead words then. Below, the first version of the passage removes the temptation to read the whole passage. On pages 278–279, you'll have the same passage in its entirety along with the 10 questions and their answer choices. For now, apply the critical-reading skills you honed in Chapter 17 and let the topic sentences and transitions help you anticipate the content and organization of the passage.

> Products made of wood surround us in our daily lives. Blah blah blah blah blah Blah blah blah blah blah Blah blah blah blah blah Blah blah blah blah blah Blah blah blah blah blah Blah blah blah blah blah Blah blah blah blah blah Blah blah blah blah blah Blah blah blah blah blah Blah blah blah blah blah Blah blah blah blah blah Blah blah blah.

> There has been a growing interest in recent years in organic food, and the "farm to table" and locavore movements that focus on getting to know the people and places that produce the food we eat, but many people don't realize that they can be making similar efforts when it comes to wood. Blah blah blah blah blah Blah blah blah blah blah Blah blah blah blah blah Blah blah blah blah blah blah blah blah Blah blah blah blah blah blah Blah blah blah blah blah Blah blah blah blah blah Blah blah blah Blah blah blah blah blah Blah blah blah blah blah.

In response to such concerns, several organizations and governments have established policies and certification processes for sustainably harvested wood and wood products. Blah blah blah blah blah Blah blah blah blah blah Blah blah blah blah blah Blah blah blah blah blah blah blah blah blah Blah blah blah blah blah blah Blah blah blah blah blah blah blah Blah blah blah blah blah Blah blah blah blah blah Blah blah blah blah blah.

The FSC has ten principles about growing and harvesting lumber designed to protect both ecosystems and communities. blah blah blah blah Blah blah blah blah blah blah Blah blah blah blah blah Blah blah blah blah blah Blah blah blah blah blah blah Blah blah blah blah blah blah blah Blah blah blah blah blah blah Blah blah blah blah blah blah Blah blah blah blah blah Blah blah blah blah blah Blah blah blah blah blah.

Through its certification program for cooperatives, the FSC is helping to make real change in national policy on forest management and logging. blah blah blah blah Blah blah blah blah blah blah Blah blah blah blah blah Blah blah blah blah blah Blah blah blah blah blah Blah blah blah blah blah.

"Despite initial skepticism in many quarters that certification could bring about genuine benefits for people and forests," says Andre Giacini de Freitas, executive director of FSC, "FSC has grown and matured with exceptional success." blah blah blah blah blah Blah blah blah blah blah blah Blah blah blah blah blah Blah blah blah blah blah Blah blah blah blah blah Blah blah blah blah blah.

Consumers of furniture and building products have an even more conservation-minded option than certified wood: recycled lumber is increasingly used for flooring, paneling, furniture, and cabinetry. Blah blah blah blah Blah blah blah blah blah blah Blah blah blah blah blah Blah blah blah blah blah Blah blah blah blah blah Blah blah blah blah blah.

Reclaimed lumber is labor-intensive on the demolition end: workers pry boards out of buildings one at a time and remove screws and nails from them. blah blah blah blah Blah blah blah blah blah blah Blah blah blah blah blah Blah blah blah blah blah Blah blah blah blah blah blah Blah blah blah blah blah.

As our awareness of the long-term environmental and social impacts of everyday products grows, so too do the efforts to make those products more sustainable.

Steps 3 through 6: Work the Questions and Answers

You should have spent no more than four minutes *total* on Steps 1 and 2. Spend no more than six additional minutes to work the questions and answers on pages 281–282, Remember to do the questions in an order that makes sense to you.

Passage II

SOCIAL SCIENCE: This passage is adapted from the article "Turning Trees Green Again" by Liza Clement (©2012 by Sustainability Quarterly).

Products made of wood surround us in our daily lives. Our houses and furniture are made of it; the paper that surrounds us in the form of books and magazines, junk mail and flyers, and
5 tissues and toilet paper are all made from wood. Although worldwide consumption of wood and paper products is on the rise, consumption in the United States is more than three times that in other developed countries. American consumption of
10 paper products alone averages 886 pounds per person annually.

There has been a growing interest in recent years in organic food, and the "farm to table" and locavore movements that focus on getting
15 to know the people and places that produce the food we eat, but many people don't realize that they can be making similar efforts when it comes to wood. Although trees take longer to reach harvestable maturity than corn or tomatoes do,
20 their harvest and processing brings up many concerns similar to those related to industrial farming. Illegal logging is hazardous to the environment because it destroys wildlife habitats and biodiversity, contributes to global warming,
25 and threatens food and water supply. Companies that engage in such practices are not taking into account the long-term effects of their actions: by haphazardly cutting down old-growth trees in sensitive ecosystems, they are destroying the
30 future possibility of harvesting more lumber from the same areas.

In response to such concerns, several organizations and governments have established policies and certification processes for sustainably
35 harvested wood and wood products. One of the best-known of these organizations is the Forest Stewardship Council (FSC), which was started in 1993 after the previous year's Earth Summit failed to establish international policies to halt
40 deforestation. The FSC provides both forest management certification, for those who harvest trees, and chain-of-custody certification, for companies that process and sell lumber and wood products.

The FSC has ten principles about growing
45 and harvesting lumber designed to protect both ecosystems and communities. Participating forests and logging operations that abide by the principles earn FSC certification. Currently, about 10 percent of forests worldwide are certified
50 by FSC or another sustainability program, and participation in the programs is growing quickly. A large international packaging company is increasing the percentage of FSC-certified fiber it uses every year, with the end goal of using
55 exclusively FSC-certified fibers. "It's in our best interest," says a spokesperson for the company, "to help ensure the long-term viability of the raw materials our business depends on."

Through its certification program for coop-
60 eratives, the FSC is helping to make real change in national policy on forest management and logging. For example, a growers' cooperative in Indonesia composed of individuals who provide sustainable teak for outdoor furniture was started
65 in 2005 with 196 individual members. Today, that cooperative has grown to 744 members. Its success has led the Indonesian government to assign the co-op to the management of state-owned teak plantations. Now local growers of
70 other crops in high international demand, such as cocoa and cashew nuts, are also seeking similar kinds of certification based on the success of the teak cooperative.

"Despite initial skepticism in many quarters
75 that certification could bring about genuine benefits for people and forests," says Andre Giacini de Freitas, executive director of FSC, "FSC has grown and matured with exceptional success." Though critics say that certification has little
80 meaning, a study of the effects of certification programs on U.S. forests found that organizations seeking certification made on average 14 significant changes to their social, environmental, and/or economic practices.

85   Consumers of furniture and building products have an even more conservation-minded option than certified wood: recycled lumber is increasingly used for flooring, paneling, furniture, and cabinetry. Recycled wood has the patina that
90 only age and wear can provide, keeps useable materials out of landfills, and also provides a story. Consumers are willing to pay a little bit more for flooring that came from the old high-school gym, or beautifully weathered paneling
95 from an old barn.

    Reclaimed lumber is labor-intensive on the demolition end: workers pry boards out of buildings one at a time and remove screws and nails from them. But this is seen as a win-win
100 situation for many. In communities such as Detroit, which has a large stock of abandoned buildings to demolish, a program trains people to deconstruct buildings and make new products from the reclaimed wood. This program benefits
105 the community by providing jobs and job training, by removing urban blight, and by promoting the city of Detroit to consumers who purchase products made from the recycled wood. Every piece of reclaimed lumber is stamped with the
110 address of the building from which it was taken. To consumers who want to know the social and environmental effects of their purchases, the extra cost of such products is worthwhile.

    As our awareness of the long-term environ-
115 mental and social impacts of everyday products grows, so too do the efforts to make those products more sustainable.

11. It can most reasonably be inferred that the author's reason for including a variety of concerns surrounding the <u>harvesting and processing of trees</u> is to:

  A. urge readers not to buy teak furniture.
  B. present to readers the need for the sustainability efforts discussed in the passage.
  C. prompt readers to contemplate investing in recycled wood production.
  D. inspire readers to invent new solutions to the problems of wood production.

12. The passage's description of the <u>Forest Stewardship Council</u> reveals that the project lists one of its <u>successes</u> as the:

  F. improved practices in harvesting and processing wood.
  G. reduced consumption of paper products.
  H. establishment of international policies on deforestation.
  J. improved quality of recycled wood products.

☆ **13.** The main idea of the eighth paragraph (lines 96–113) is that:

  A. products made from reclaimed lumber are becoming increasingly expensive to purchase.
  B. the process of reclaiming lumber illustrates the benefits of logging old-growth trees.
  C. the process of reclaiming lumber poses great dangers to workers.
  D. the process of reclaiming lumber can offer social and economic benefits.

14. The passage indicates that <u>illegal logging</u> may result in:

  F. old-growth trees losing their patina.
  G. food and water supplies being threatened.
  H. much of the lumber being wasted.
  J. trees reaching maturity at later ages.

15. The passage states that <u>certification programs</u> have positively impacted all of the following EXCEPT:

  A. growers' cooperatives for teak, cocoa, and cashew nuts.
  B. ecosystems and communities of some U.S. forests.
  C. an international packaging company.
  D. workers in Detroit.

16. The passage indicates that compared to products made from reclaimed lumber, conventionally made wood products are somewhat more:

   F. difficult to recycle.
   G. labor-intensive to demolish.
   H. dangerous to workers.
   J. affordable to purchase.

17. The passage notes that companies that engage in illegal logging overlook the fact that:

   A. overharvesting may limit the availability of future growth in the same areas.
   B. most paper products are made from trees harvested legally.
   C. sensitive ecosystems are being destroyed.
   D. international policies permit deforestation.

18. The passage refers to *patina* as a product of:

   F. teak furniture.
   G. old-growth trees.
   H. age and wear.
   J. certified wood.

19. The passage indicates that Detroit offers programs that train workers to reclaim lumber because in that city:

   A. landfills are filled with old wood products.
   B. many abandoned buildings are being demolished.
   C. trained carpenters are in short supply.
   D. reclaiming lumber is less labor-intensive.

20. The last paragraph leaves the reader with the clear impression that awareness of environmental and social impacts has:

   F. increased over time.
   G. struggled to grow.
   H. decreased substantially.
   J. remained flat.

Score and Analyze Your Performance

The answers are 11. (B), 12. (F), 13. (D), 14. (G), 15. (D), 16. (J), 17. (A), 18. (H), 19. (B), 20. (F). How did you do with regard to accuracy and time? If you were unable to get all of the questions right using only six additional minutes, analyze where you spent your time and consider what changes you can make next time.

Do Now Questions 13 and 20 because both have line references. Question 19 is a Referral question and has a great lead word (*Detroit*), which you should have found in the eighth paragraph when you answered Question 13. The same paragraph features the lead words in Question 16. Question 12 also has great lead words, and while it may require a window spanning a few paragraphs to answer it (lines 32–73), that work allows you to answer Question 15 immediately afterward, even though it's a negative question.

Do Later questions that are neither easy to answer nor easy to find the answers for.

Questions 14 and 17 are Referral questions that have the same lead words (*illegal logging*) and can be answered from the same window found in the last third of the second paragraph (lines 22–31).

Question 18 has a lead word that is unusual (*patina*), but it still may be difficult to find. Since you haven't run into it answering any of the prior questions, look first in the paragraphs you haven't read, and you'll find it in the seventh paragraph (lines 85–95). Do Question 11 last.

The Pencil Trick
When you have to look harder for a lead word, use your pencil to sweep each and every line from beginning to end. This will keep your brain from reading and let your eye look for the word.

As You Go

As You Go is another adaptation to working the passage. It's a slight adjustment of the 6-Step Basic Approach. This strategy works well for many students, and it can be a good option for all students when a passage has five line/paragraph references or more.

> Step 1: **Preview.** Check the blurb. Underline lead words. Mark the passage with the questions with line references.
>
> Steps 2–5: **Work the Passage and Questions.** Read the passage and work the questions as you go.
>
> Step 6: **Use Process of Elimination.**

Step 1: Preview

When you map the questions, just underline the lead words in those questions. For the questions with line or paragraph references, map the passage. Write the question number in the margin next to the appropriate lines on the passage.

Steps 2–5: Work the Passage and Questions

Read the passage, but answer the questions you marked in the margin as you go. Resume reading until the next question marked in the margin. As you read, keep an eye out for the lead words you underlined in the questions. When you spot a question's lead words, stop and do the question.

Step 6: Use Process of Elimination

Whether you work the passage up front and the questions later or work the passage and questions as you go, good use of POE will save you time and help you get every question right.

> Work the following passage As You Go. Once you've finished, think about which strategy for working the passage is best for you. Do you do better working the passage Up Front or As You Go?"

Passage III

HUMANITIES: This passage is adapted from the memoir *Under the Jujube Trees: Growing up in India* by Amrita Mehra (©2002 by Amrita Mehra).

My days as a schoolgirl in Jaipur had a distinct rhythm to them. My mother would wake my sisters and me early and guide us to the bathroom for our morning beauty routine. We would splash
5 on our faces the fresh milk that was delivered directly from the barn to us, inhaling its grassy, sweet aroma and rubbing the yellowish blobs of fat into our skin.

After completing the beauty routine and
10 then brushing our teeth, we would dress in our matching starched blue pinafores, then report to the dining room for breakfast.

In the winter, we would bundle ourselves in our matching tweed coats, and my mother would
15 carefully inspect us, making sure the black bows of our braids were perfectly symmetrical, and our shiny, stiff leather shoes tightly double-knotted. I imagined us as a chain of identical paper dolls standing side by side, our hands and the edges of
20 our coats touching. She would also inspect my father, brushing imaginary pieces of lint from his 3-piece suit and straightening his tie. On these days I felt more like a British schoolgirl from one of the stories we read at school than like a
25 Hindu girl in northern India.

My father would leave to walk to the textile factory where he was the manager as my sisters and I piled into the back seat of the car that would take us to our Catholic school. My mother stood
30 in the doorway waving, resplendent in her perfectly pressed sari, elegant wool shawls draped around her instead of the Western-style overcoats the rest of us wore.

For holidays, our family would return to
35 Delhi, to my grandfather's house where my many aunts and uncles and cousins lived. The house was outside the city gates, in an orchard. Here, among my extended family, I felt freed from the constraints of life in Jaipur. This was
40 not only because of the long days at school—

there were many rules to be followed, and the nuns were very strict—but also because of the starched blue uniforms and the tight braids we wore every day. Everything in Jaipur seemed
45 regimented and confining.

By contrast, grandfather's house, which we called by its address, Number 12, was relaxed and free. Here I didn't have to wear braids, and I could wear boys' shorts and spend my afternoons
50 climbing trees in the orchard with my many cousins. The transition to life in Delhi made me feel the way I imagined a caged tiger would feel upon being set free to once again prowl the forest.

Although there were many more people
55 around Number 12 than at our house in Jaipur, there was far less supervision. All of us children were largely left to roam about on our own. This was especially true on the hot afternoons, when the adults would retreat inside the house for naps.

60 Some days, we would venture down to the Yamuna River, which ran along the edge of my grandfather's property, to fish and swim. Other days, we would raid the guavas. The older cousins would climb the small trees, pick the hard, unripe
65 fruits, and quarter them with pocket knives. They would hand wedges of guava down to the younger children, and we would eat them greedily after dipping them in salt mixed with cumin and red chilies. The tartness of the guava was highlighted
70 by the contrast with the spicy salt, leaving fireworks on our tongues.

Perhaps my favorite time at my grandfather's house was when there was a family wedding. Several days before the festivities began, scores more
75 relatives would arrive, along with the caterers. The women would be in a flurry of preparing clothing and flower garlands. The caterers, meanwhile, would be bustling about in their tent, a myriad of magical aromas wafting out to give us a hint
80 of the feasts to come.

Amidst all the chaos, the children would run back and forth from indoors to outdoors, keeping tabs on the progress of the different groups. Sometimes my mother would assign me

85 a task: "Go and tell the gardener we need more jasmine." Outside, if we were lucky, the caterers would allow us a taste of spicy lamb meatballs or tart tamarind chutney.

Most of the marriages were arranged, and
90 the bride and groom had often not met each other before the wedding. The bride always looked beautiful in her richly embroidered, bright red *lehenga*, her face covered by a veil. I always found myself holding my breath at the moment
95 at which the veil was lifted. Once, the veil had revealed a cousin in tears, making no effort to hide her disappointment in her new husband. More often, the veil revealed a face as radiant as the ornaments the bride wore.

100 The double life I lived as a child, in Jaipur and in Delhi, has fundamentally shaped me as the person I am today. I keep different parts of my life compartmentalized in my mind: work goes in one area, family in another, and so on. The thought
105 of those places that feel free and unconstrained the way my grandfather's house did help me cope with the parts that are more burdensome.

21. The point of view from which the passage is told is best described as that of:

A. an adult recounting various experiences of her childhood.

B. an adult relating in third person the thoughts and events of her childhood.

C. a young girl discussing being a servant in Number 12.

D. a young girl explaining how she uses fantasy and daydreaming to escape her regimented daily life.

22. In the passage, which of the following activities is NOT mentioned as one for which the author's mother was present?

F. Getting ready for a wedding

G. Spending holidays at Number 12

H. Standing for inspection before school

J. Raiding orchards for guava

23. In the passage, the author compares herself to:

  I. a caged tiger.
  II. a British schoolgirl.
 III. a boy.

A. I and II only

B. I and III only

C. II and III only

D. I, II, and III

24. The author most likely describes her clothes as *starched* and her braids as *tight* in line 43 to suggest:

F. she felt relaxed and free to spend time unsupervised in Delhi.

G. she was proud to attend school looking her best.

H. she felt constrained by following strict rules in Jaipur.

J. she felt feminine at school because she wore boys' shorts on holidays.

25. In the fifth and sixth paragraphs (lines 34–53), the author draws a contrast primarily between the:

A. regimented life she led in Jaipur and the relaxed freedom of holidays spent at Number 12.

B. relationship she had with her sisters and the one she had with her cousins.

C. preparation adults made for a wedding and the relaxation enjoyed by children.

D. the academic challenge of school in Jaipur and the unsupervised playtime in Delhi.

26. The author uses the phrase "report to" in line 11 to suggest that:

F. the author and her sisters rush through their morning beauty routine in order to make it to breakfast on time.

G. the author's mother pays careful attention to the appearance of her husband and daughters.

H. the author's father leaves for work without his daughters if they are late.

J. the author and her sisters dress in a manner of their choosing rather than in one chosen by their mother.

27. The statement "I always found myself holding my breath at the moment at which the veil was lifted" (lines 93–95) most strongly suggests that the author was:

- **A.** disappointed in the appearance of the bride.
- **B.** concerned about the bride's reaction.
- **C.** imagining her own wedding.
- **D.** radiant with happiness.

28. The details the author recounts of her childhood adventures with her cousins are based most often on which physical sense?

- **F.** Taste
- **G.** Sight
- **H.** Sound
- **J.** Touch

29. When the author writes that she "imagined us as a chain of identical paper dolls" (line 18), she is most likely making the point that:

- **A.** she felt constrained by the formality of her school uniform.
- **B.** she and her sisters dressed precisely and similarly.
- **C.** she and her sisters disappointed their mother with their appearance.
- **D.** she wished she wore a sari instead of a Catholic school uniform.

30. In the context of the passage, the phrase *compartmentalized in my mind* (line 103) can most nearly be paraphrased as:

- **F.** divided in loyalties between work and family.
- **G.** kept work and family concerns separate.
- **H.** sorted a list of priorities.
- **J.** suffered mental confusion.

Score and Analyze Your Performance

The answers are 21. (A), 22. (J), 23. (A), 24. (H), 25. (A), 26. (G), 27. (B), 28. (F), 29. (B), 30. (G). How did you do in accuracy and time? If you were unable to get all of the questions right or used more than 10–11 minutes, analyze where you spent your time and consider what changes you can make next time. Here is some general advice that may help you pinpoint where you can save time.

Stop and do Now Questions 26 and then 29. Resume reading until you get to the questions in the 5th and 6th paragraphs, Questions 24 and 25. In your search for the lead words in the Roman numerals, spot both *British schoolgirl* and *caged tiger* after working the first four questions, and try Question 23. Eliminate (B) and (C). If you spotted *boys' shorts* and knew that the phrase failed to live up to a comparison to *a boy*, you have the correct answer. If not, return to this question after you've finished the passage and find no comparison to a boy.

Continue reading and stop and do Question 28 when you spot another mention of *cousins* with a more specific description of *adventures*. Answer Question 27 based on the second-to-last paragraph. Finish the passage and do Question 30. Do Questions 21 and 22 last.

DUAL READING PASSAGES

You will also see a "Dual Passage" on the Reading Test. Like the "Dual Passages" found in the Science Test (see Chapter 23, Dual Science Passages), this set of passages features multiple viewpoints, with questions asked about each passage individually and then together. Because you'll be comparing in addition to analyzing, these passages require a bit more reading, but they are also susceptible to more strategic thinking.

Here's the strategy we'll be using for Dual Passages.

1. **Preview.** Read the blurb and map the questions as you would in a typical passage. Do a quick count of how many questions are asked about each passage.

2. **Work the Popular Passage.** If one passage has more questions than the other, work that one first. Take the questions that ask only about that passage and work them according to the sequence of line references, working the passage As You Go through the questions.

3. **Work the Other Passage.** Before you jump to the questions that deal with both passages, work the other passage the same way you worked the first. Reorder the questions by line reference and work the passage As You Go through the questions in the new order.

4. **Work the Questions that Deal with Both Passages.** By this point, you've hopefully got a good sense of what unites the passages. Answer the questions that deal with both passages, and make sure that these answers agree with the others regarding each individual passage!

A Note on the Golden Thread

As you may have noticed, correct answers seem to repeat in a lot of ACT passages. You may find that if you get one answer, you can get three more with the same information. We call this phenomenon the "Golden Thread," named for some main idea or topic that threads through many of the answer choices.

On Dual Passages, it's more important than ever to find the Golden Thread. If you think about it, the questions that ask about both passages are really just variations on the theme, "What do these two passages have to do with each other?"

As you read through the two passages separately, try to answer this question, even if only in a vague way. Any answers you can generate for this "Golden Thread" question will help you throughout parts of the rest of the passage.

Here is what one of the passages will look like. Note how kindly ACT has separated the questions for you.

HUMANITIES: Passage A is adapted from the essay "From West Orange to Paris and Back" by Ashley C. Throckmorton. Passage B is adapted from the essay "Train Robberies and Magic" by Abigal Colorado Tintype.

Passage A by Ashley C. Throckmorton

While it may be impossible to know when the history of the cinema properly begins, there is no question that it had its first real flowering in the late-nineteenth and early-twentieth centuries. The
5 history of photography goes back much further— to the 1830s at least—but the history of cinema properly began when the technological advance- ments caught up with the theoretical advance- ments in photography. English photographer
10 Eadweard Muybridge was the first to figure out how to take photographs in rapid enough suc- cession as to produce the illusion of movement. First created in 1877, his series of photographs of "animal locomotion" (a running horse in
15 Muybridge's case) look like early film strips, as they seem to capture the horse's movement in minute intervals.

Around this same time, Thomas Edison invented one of the most popular technologies
20 of the century: the phonograph. In 1888, Edison wanted a visual component to add to the now near- universal phonograph, and he commissioned one of his lab assistants, William Dickson, to do so. Dickson incorporated the work of Muy-
25 bridge and others into a series of mechanisms that could both record motion pictures and then "play" them back. The tangible result of this process was the Kinetoscope, which would, with internal battery power, "play" the pictures
30 in rapid enough succession that they produced the illusion of continuous movement. Edison established a Kinetograph studio in West Orange, NJ, where he and his assistants made short pieces for the Kinetoscope, usually portraying simple
35 actions like kisses or individual dances. As the phonograph had before it, the Kinetoscope took the world by storm.

Inspired by Edison's invention, two French brothers, Auguste and Louis Lumière, sought to
40 make it more available for public consumption. To that end, they invented the first commercially viable projector, the *cinématographe*, which made the single-viewer mechanism of the Ki- netoscope available to many viewers at once.
45 Where the Kinetoscope could weigh more than 1,000 pounds, the *cinématographe* weighed only 20. As a result, the Lumières were able to shoot much larger scenes and did not require the stability of a particular studio as Edison had. Their most
50 famous film, "The Arrival of a Train at La Ciotat Train Station," was just that, and while it may be dull by contemporary standards, this simple 50-second film thrilled and amazed audiences.

Here, from the hands of nearly a half-century
55 of inventors, was the birth of the cinema. We have them to thank when we go to the movies or even, one could argue, watch videos on our computers and video-chat on our phones. Indeed, if we are able to suspend our disbelief for just a
60 moment, we can put ourselves back in that early cinema moment. Watch the Lumière film of the arriving train in just the right mood, and it can fill you with the same wonder that overtook the original audiences.

Passage B by Abigal Colorado Tintype

65 While the history of the cinema is inconceiv- able without the efforts of Thomas Edison and the Lumière brothers, they in fact contributed little more than the invention of a technology. After all, when we think of the cultural force
70 that the cinema has become, we do not refer to the miniature documentary curiosities of the Kinetoscope. Without this mechanism, the cinema would have been impossible, but Edison and the Lumières are no more responsible for the history
75 of the cinema than a dairy farmer is responsible for a delicious milkshake.

The real birth of the cinema began in the early years of the twentieth century. With the technology that had been given to him, a French
80 magician named Georges Méliès started to exper- iment. As a magician, Méliès saw the new film

cameras as working in his professional favor: he saw the cinema as producing illusions along the lines of those he created on the stage. In the nearly
85 500 films he produced between 1896 and 1913, Méliès not only showed the artistic capabilities of "trick" cinema. He also created some of the first and most complex narrative films ever to be seen on screen: *A Trip to the Moon* (1902) was
90 14 minutes long and had 30 scenes.

　　Around this same time, a former Edison employee, the American Edwin S. Porter, was creating some narrative films of his own. Porter worked as a projectionist for the Edison company,
95 where he would arrange fifteen-minute programs from a series of short films. This assembly no doubt inspired Porter to think of how a narrative film could be assembled, and Porter was the first to see that scenes could be portrayed
100 from multiple perspectives at once. Inspired by but departing from Méliès's theatrically staged narrative films, Porter found a new way, one that was only available in the cinema. In *The Great Train Robbery* (1903), Porter used a technique
105 that has since been dubbed "parallel editing," which enabled him to tell the story of both the train robbers and the train passengers, themselves in different places for much of the film's action, at what seemed to be the same time.

110 　　Therefore, while the contributions of Edison and the Lumières are indispensable, the cinema as we know it today began a few years later with Porter and Méliès. Indeed, the cinema has its cultural power today because of its *artistic*
115 achievements, not merely its technological ones. Edison and the Lumières may have provided the canvas, but Porter and Méliès were the first to use that canvas to create real art.

Questions 21–24 ask about Passage A.

---

21. According to information in the second paragraph (lines 18–37), the early film camera was related to the phonograph in that the camera was:

A. conceived as a technology to accompany the sounds produced by the phonograph.

B. designed to replace the phonograph within fifteen to twenty years.

C. inspired by the work of Eadweard Muybridge, the inventor of the phonograph.

D. limited by its weight and size in the same way that the phonograph was.

22. According to Throckmorton, a primary advantage of the *cinématographe* over the Kinetoscope was that the *cinématographe* was:

F. invented in France, where inventors could take proper credit for their inventions.

G. mobile in a way that the Kinetoscope was not and could therefore capture new subjects on film.

H. able to shoot films that were as much as fifty seconds longer than Kinetoscope films.

J. intimate for the viewer in a way that the Kinetoscope's large projections could not be.

23. The word "play" (line 27) is set off in quotation marks in order to signify that the:

A. Kinetoscope was invented before movies were considered fun to watch.

B. *cinématographe* was the first film technology to use electricity.

C. films produced by the Kinetoscope were intended mainly for children.

D. technology used still photographs to produce the illusion of motion.

24. According to Throckmorton, why do contemporary viewers have Edison and the Lumières "to thank" (lines 55–56)?

F. Edison and the Lumières created some of the first and most thrilling narrative films of the nineteenth century.

G. Edison and the Lumières popularized the inventions of William Dickson and Eadweard Muybridge.

H. Edison and the Lumières contributed to the invention of a technology that is now almost universally accessible.

J. Edison and the Lumières contributed major parts to the invention of the computer and smartphone.

Questions 25–27 ask about Passage B.

---

25. When Tintype states that Edison and the Lumières "provided the canvas" but that Méliès and Porter were the first "to create real art" (lines 116–118), she most nearly means that:

A. the narrative innovations of Porter and Méliès would have been possible without the work of Edison and the Lumières.

B. the narrative innovations of Porter and Méliès were less significant in the history of science than the work of Edison and the Lumières.

C. the technological innovations of Edison and the Lumières were not supposed to be used to create narrative films.

D. the technological innovations of Edison and the Lumières enabled the early cinematic achievements of Porter and Méliès.

26. According to Tintype, Porter and Méliès are the true inventors of the cinema because they:

F. made the first blockbuster films that made significant amounts of money.

G. proposed that films should be longer than a few seconds.

H. introduced the artistic elements that made cinema a cultural force.

J. predicted that films would one day be universally accessible.

27. Tintype compares Edison and the Lumières to "a dairy farmer" (line 75) in order to suggest that:

A. those who produce the raw material do not necessarily deserve credit for what is done with that raw material.

B. people who cannot invent significant technologies should consider work in industries where they will be more useful.

C. scientific innovators maximize their use of resources in order to produce things that people find interesting or necessary.

D. some of the most interesting technological innovations come from those who work in the field of agriculture.

Questions 28–30 ask about both passages.

---

28. The accounts of Throckmorton and Tintype are similar in that they believe:

F. Porter and Méliès were the true inventors of film as a storytelling medium.

G. cinema's greatest achievements would not have been possible without the work of Edison and the Lumières.

H. the history of film would have been much different if the Lumières had perfected their camera before Edison perfected his.

J. Méliès's background in magic suited him especially well for work in the illusionistic medium of cinema.

29. What is the main component of Tintype's essay that is not addressed in Throckmorton's essay?

   A. Technological innovation
   B. Particular films
   C. Camera size
   D. Narrative storytelling

30. Throckmorton would most likely see *A Trip to the Moon* as:

   F. a copy of a Lumière film produced ten years earlier.
   G. superior to Porter's *The Great Train Robbery*.
   H. an extension of earlier technological innovations.
   J. the subpar work of an amateur magician.

How to Work Through a Dual-Passage Reading Section

STEP **1** » ## Step 1: Preview

As the blurb indicates, these passages are adapted from a couple of essays. It doesn't tell much more than that. Lead words include *early film camera, phonograph, cinématographe, Kinetoscope, Edison, Lumière, Méliès, Porter,* and *A Trip to the Moon.*

A quick count will show that there are more questions about Passage A than there are about Passage B. Let's do Passage A first!

STEP **2** » ## Step 2: Work the Popular Passage

Before you start reading, rearrange the questions in the order of their appearance in the passage. When there aren't line references, use lead words to determine the order in which to work the questions. In this case, it looks like the questions will appear in the passage in roughly this order: 23, 21, 22, 24.

Read through the passage and stop as you come to the lines in each question. Now that you've ordered the questions, you don't have to worry about missing anything.

Use the techniques you've learned throughout these reading chapters! POE still applies and bad answers are just as bad here as they are in any other passage.

STEP **3** » ## Step 3: Work the Other Passage

Rinse and repeat! These questions will fall roughly into this order: 27, 25, 26. Work through these questions, always looking to eliminate bad answers.

STEP **4** » ## Step 4: Work the Questions that Deal with Both Passages

By this point, you have hopefully noticed what unites these passages. Before you get to the questions that deal with both passages, make sure to jot down a sentence or two about what you see as the "Golden Thread" that unites the two passages.

Try it for these passages we've just read. You probably came up with something like this:

Passage A (Throckmorton) sees Edison and the Lumières as the inventors of the cinema because they invented the cameras. Passage B (Tintype) sees Edison and the Lumières as important but sees Méliès and Porter as the inventors because they made it a narrative form.

Now let's look again at those questions that deal with both passages. Use the Golden Thread whenever possible!

28. The accounts of Throckmorton and Tintype are similar in that they believe:

  F. Porter and Méliès were the true inventors of film as a storytelling medium.
  G. cinema's greatest achievements would not have been possible without the work of Edison and the Lumières.
  H. the history of film would have been much different if the Lumières had perfected their camera before Edison perfected his.
  J. Méliès's background in magic suited him especially well for work in the illusionistic medium of cinema.

Here's How to Crack It

Remember, we want something that both authors talk about. Porter and Méliès were only mentioned in the second passage, so (F) and (J) can be eliminated. Then, (H) can be eliminated because neither passage discusses what would be different if the inventors' timelines had been different. We need an answer that encapsulates both passages, and only (G) does so.

29. What is the main component of Tintype's essay that is not addressed by Throckmorton?

  A. Technological innovation
  B. Particular films
  C. Camera size
  D. Narrative storytelling

Here's How to Crack It

Throckmorton is all about the technology aspect of the cinema. Tintype is all about the narrative and artistic aspects of the cinema. As a result, Throckmorton is much more interested in (A) and (C) than Tintype is, so those can be removed. Then, because a quick glance at the italics will show that both authors mention particular films, you can also eliminate (B). But you may have arrived at the answer already using the Golden Thread: the best answer is (D), because only Tintype is interested in the narrative and artistic aspects of the cinema.

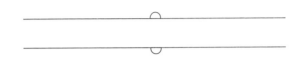

30. Throckmorton would most likely see *A Trip to the Moon* as:

- **F.** a copy of a Lumière film produced ten years earlier.
- **G.** superior to Porter's *The Great Train Robbery*.
- **H.** an extension of earlier technological innovations.
- **J.** the subpar work of an amateur magician.

Here's How to Crack It

Keep that Golden Thread in mind! Throckmorton is all about the technology. Tintype is all about the art. Therefore, even though Throckmorton doesn't talk about *A Trip to the Moon*, she would almost certainly be interested in something *technological* about it, not anything about its artistic merits, thus eliminating (G) and (J). Even (F) doesn't quite address the technological aspects of the film, so that can also be eliminated. After all, Throckmorton says that the work of Edison and the Lumières was foundational: she doesn't say that other people copied their particular films. As a result, only (H) can work.

Score and Analyze Your Performance

We've already discussed the trickier questions that combine elements of both Passage A and Passage B, but don't forget that the questions about each individual passage are worth just as many points. Go back and check your work: 21. (A), 22. (G), 23. (D), 24. (H), 25. (D), 26. (H), 27. (A). If you're getting these questions wrong, you might want to review Chapter 16, "The Basic Approach and Beyond."

BE FLEXIBLE

We started this chapter with the exhortation to be flexible and we'll repeat it here. The techniques and strategies we've outlined are designed to give you options of how to replace or adapt your own strategy. When you are answering almost every question correctly, it can be difficult to change what's working for you so well. But to achieve a perfect or near-perfect score on the Reading Test, you have to both tweak a few things and be ready to switch gears when your typical approach isn't working on a particular test.

When you take a Reading Test for practice, try some of the different strategies we've covered. Always be willing to analyze your performance and evaluate what you can change. The more you practice different techniques, the easier it will be to adapt when the particulars of a challenging test demand a change.

We're not saying this is easy. In fact, changing your own instinctual behavior is the hardest part of cracking the Reading Test. Everyone has made the mistake of ignoring that internal voice that's screaming to move on, and we've all answered back "But I know I'm almost there and if I take just a little more time, I know I can get it." Know your strengths, know your weaknesses, know when to adapt, and know when to just guess and move on.

In closing, here are a few guidelines to help you think about your specific challenges with time management and pacing yourself.

SPEND TIME WISELY

To use your time most effectively, know where to invest time and where to save it. Rushing in crucial places is just as damaging as wasting time.

The Passage

Most students waste the bulk of their time reading (and rereading) the passage, disconnected from working the questions. Some students can read and process the whole passage, and then move on to the questions, making good predictions of the answers and knowing where to look to confirm an answer, if needed. If that's not you, spend no more than two to three minutes reading or skimming the passage. Do not reread any sentence or paragraph. Let topic sentences and transitions help to confirm the important points. Save your time to spend on a question that references difficult text, not on your initial read of the passage.

The Questions

When you Preview, *look* for lead words to underline and line/paragraph references to star, but don't spend time *reading* the questions. However, when you work the questions, slow down and read the questions carefully. Don't rush and then answer incorrectly because you misread the question. If you struggle with a window of text, use topic sentences, transitions, modifiers, and pronouns to decipher the point and predict the answer.

Work questions in an order that makes sense, doing Now questions that are easy to answer or whose answers are easy to find. Do questions that are difficult to answer and whose answers are difficult to find Later.

If you struggle to find lead words on some Later questions, it's important to *look* for and find them before you lock into reading for comprehension. Do not read the passage again to try to find them. Work on the paragraphs you haven't read, and use the pencil trick.

The Answers

Do not rush reading through the answers. You can choose a wrong answer because you missed that it was only half right. But half right is all wrong. Work backward with the answers when you struggle with the window of text needed to answer a question.

Adapt

If your pacing strategy goes awry, read just the topic sentences in Step 2. If it goes really off base and you have five minutes for your last passage, skip Step 2 entirely. Go straight to Step 3 and Work the Now questions. Look for the Golden Thread on the most general questions saved for last.

If a passage has five or more line/paragraph references, try As You Go.

Summary

- Use the 6-Step Basic Approach to save time.
  - Step 1: **Preview.** Check the blurb and map the questions in 15–30 seconds. Star line and paragraph references and underline lead words.
  - Step 2: **Work the Passage.** Finish in two to three minutes. Look for and circle lead words.
  - Steps 3–5: **Work the Questions.** Do Now questions that are easy to answer or whose answers are easy to find. Read what you need in a window of 5 to 10 lines to find your answer. Save for Later questions that are both hard to find and hard to answer.
  - Step 6: **Use Process of Elimination.** Use POE to find your answer, particularly on Reasoning questions. Work backward with the answers on challenging questions.

- Skim and scan when you work the passage. If necessary, read just the topic sentence of each paragraph.

- Read windows of text when you work the questions.

- Do not reread the passage in Step 2.

- Do not reread a window of text in Step 4 without working backward with the answers.

- Use As You Go when a passage has five or more line/paragraph references.

- Break up Dual Passages into their component parts.

- Be ready and willing to adapt when your strategy is not working.

Chapter 19
Reading Drills

Use the drills and explanations in this chapter to hone your Reading approach. Drill 1 is a literary narrative passage, and Drill 2 is a natural science passage.

DRILL 1

LITERARY NARRATIVE: This passage is adapted from the novel *Prima Ballerina* by Laurie Sigel (©2008 by Laurie Sigel). Alicia Alonso (born 1921) is a Cuban ballet dancer.

After the revolution, her life had become different in many ways, but the ballet was the thing that stood out in vivid color among her faded black-and-white memories of early childhood.
5 Going to school was strange enough. Her older sister hadn't gone, because girls didn't, and her brother didn't, because they couldn't afford the fees. Under the new regime, however, not just poor children, but even poor girls went to school.

10 Nevertheless, school was at least something she had known about. That cold, bright day in January of 1967, when she boarded a rusty, sputtering bus for a class field trip to the *Palace of the Galician Centre* to see Alicia Alonso dance
15 *Giselle,* felt like a rebirth to her, as if she were emerging from her cocoon into a new and bigger world. She couldn't believe she was going to actually walk into such a stately building, and was half-afraid that the marble statues keeping
20 watch over the entrance would come to life and forbid her to enter. Enter she did though, and the grandness of the interior forced her into a hush, as if she were in the Cathedral, not a theater. She tried to walk quietly, but her hard-soled school
25 shoes insisted on asserting their presence on the shiny floor and the immense marble staircase that curved insistently upward, seemingly to heaven.

Years later, Isabel Moreno would go to that theater many times, confidently clicking her high-
30 heeled shoes on the same staircase, but that day as a schoolgirl, she hadn't known such places existed. She sat gingerly on the edge of her seat, afraid to lean back into the luxurious plush red upholstery. Then, when the music started and the
35 dancers appeared, she couldn't lean back because she was so mesmerized by what was happening on stage. The elegance of the ballerinas in their pointe shoes was unlike anything she had seen; the dancers' movements, impeccably controlled
40 and flawlessly in time with the music, transported Isabel to the joyful and yearning world of peasant girls celebrating the bountiful harvest and young love. She knew those feelings, but had never been able to imagine or express them as perfectly as
45 the dancers did.

After that performance, Isabel had begged her mother to let her try out for the ballet school—she felt as though her life would never have meaning unless she could be one of those
50 dancers on stage. She wasn't accepted, and wept for weeks afterwards. Even as an adult, every time she went to the ballet she felt that overwhelming sadness again that became so powerful it felt strangely joyful. The *pas de deux* of Siegfried
55 and Odette in Act 2 of *Swan Lake* seemed to her a more truthful presentation of the awakening of love than anything she would experience in real life. When Cinderella had to leave the ball at the end of Act 2 for fear of being discovered as her
60 dress turned back to rags, Isabel felt keenly the anxiety of living a relatively comfortable life, so far removed from the poverty of her childhood.

Isabel's son, Alejandro, had been trying to get her to come visit Miami for years, but she had
65 never accepted, claiming that the paperwork was too complicated, that she couldn't take the time off from the hospital. Alejandro had tried to entice his mother with visits to the Miami Ballet, but Isabel wasn't interested. The dancers in Miami
70 weren't as good as the Cuban dancers, she'd say. Eventually, Alejandro realized he had to tempt her with something she couldn't see in Havana. When he called Isabel to say he had purchased tickets to see Mikhail Baryshnikov in Miami, it
75 was as if she were the mechanical doll Coppélia suddenly brought to life. She needed to see the legendary Russian dancer who had defected from the Soviet Union and abandoned classical ballet for modern dance with a fierceness that
80 overcame her hesitations about paperwork and vacation time.

The program started with a short solo dance by Baryshnikov, and he was a marvel of unas- suming, fluid grace. Isabel had often thought that
85 male dancers were too assertively athletic, that the ballerinas were the real stars of the show. But that evening, in that short, simple dance, Isabel

understood that the classical Cuban ballet she so
loved was only one small part of the expressive
90 possibility of dance. She was transported back
to that first day at the ballet when she was a
schoolgirl, and she felt that same sense of wonder
that she hadn't known about this heartbreakingly
beautiful art form before. When the first dance
95 ended, she was too stunned to clap. Alejandro
touched her arm lightly, worried that Isabel hadn't
liked it. After a moment, Isabel turned to her son,
tears now leaking out of the corners of her eyes,
and embraced him warmly. *"Gracias, mi hijo,"*
100 she whispered, "thank you, my son."

1. The point of view from which the passage is
told is best described as that of:

A. a son who understands his mother's
thoughts.
B. a narrator who relates events from the
perspective of Alejandro.
C. a school girl seeing classical ballet for the
first time.
D. an impartial narrator who understands
what the characters are thinking.

2. The passage establishes all of the following
about Isabel EXCEPT that she:

F. had wanted to be a dancer when she was a
child.
G. could identify with some of the issues that
Cinderella faced.
H. felt that *Swan Lake* accurately portrayed
the process of falling in love.
J. enjoyed performing.

3. Which of the following statements best characterizes Alejandro's relationship with his mother,
as it is presented in the passage?

A. He feels isolated from her.
B. He hopes to become a dancer to please her.
C. He would like his mother to visit him.
D. He is hesitant to spend time with her.

4. In the passage, lines 11–17 primarily serve to:

F. suggest that the theater building was more
important to Isabel than the ballet performance.
G. describe the experience of going to the
Cathedral.
H. imply that the fear Isabel felt prevented her
from enjoying the ballet.
J. provide details that show how new and
strange an experience it was.

5. Isabel's reaction to the *Giselle* performance is
most clearly reflected in the way Isabel:

A. "tried to walk quietly" (line 24).
B. "couldn't lean back" (line 35).
C. "wept for weeks afterwards" (lines 50–51).
D. "embraced him warmly" (line 99).

6. The passage indicates that Alejandro ultimately
decided to buy the tickets to see Baryshnikov
because Alejandro:

F. decided to take a chance on an obscure
dancer.
G. thought his mother loved Baryshnikov.
H. was unable to get tickets to the Miami
Ballet.
J. realized that Baryshnikov was unlikely to
perform in Cuba.

7. The phrase *insistently upward* (line 27) is most
likely included in the passage to suggest that
Isabel:

A. was awed by the grandeur of the theater.
B. believed the staircase led to heaven.
C. became tired climbing the stairs.
D. was afraid of heights.

8. The statement in lines 51–54 most nearly means
that Isabel:

F. was ashamed of the poverty of her child-
hood.
G. thought her feelings could only be ex-
pressed through ballet.
H. believed she would never experience love.
J. was deeply moved by ballet performances.

9. The statement "she hadn't known such places existed" (lines 31–32) most directly refers to the fact that Isabel:

A. was unaware that there was anything like the *Palace of the Galician Center* in Cuba.

B. had never traveled to the country to celebrate the bounty of the harvest.

C. wore only shoes with no heels before she became an adult and started shopping at fancier shoe stores.

D. had heard stories about what the interior of the Cathedral looked like but had never visited it herself.

10. According to the passage, the event that made Isabel feel "as if she was the mechanical doll Coppélia suddenly brought to life" (lines 75–76) was:

F. the time her son called to say he had tickets to see Baryshnikov.

G. traveling to Miami to see Baryshnikov dance.

H. going to the see Alicia Alonso perform when she was a school girl.

J. attending the Miami Ballet's performance of *Giselle*.

DRILL 2

NATURAL SCIENCE: This passage is adapted from the article "The Microbial World Within" by Janet Fisher (©2013 by Science Monthly).

"I'm not your typical new dad," says biologist Rob Knight. "When the baby's diaper needs changing, I'm always excited to do it." Knight runs a lab that is part of the American Gut project,
5 through which thousands of people have paid to send in samples of their feces to be analyzed, and his sixteen-month-old daughter's diapers play an important role in his research.

"I know it sounds a bit crazy that people
10 pay to send us their poop, but we're using a crowd-funding model to both help pay for the research and get a wide variety of samples," explains Knight. As for his daughter's diapers, he's been studying the way her microbiome,
15 the make-up of bacteria and other microbes in her digestive tract, has been changing since she was born.

Humans have around 100 trillion microbes living on and in them, typically of several hun-
20 dred different species. They are not visible to the naked eye, but all together they account for about three pounds of a person's weight. Recent research indicates that they have a huge influence on our health.

25 What Knight and his colleagues do with the feces samples they receive from around the country is analyze the genetic material present to establish what kinds of microbes live in the donors' guts. They combine the genetic informa-
30 tion with data from a survey that donors fill out and enter all the information in a giant database. Their goal is to have enough samples to be able to start to decode the influence of lifestyle on the characteristics of a microbiome. The survey
35 asks donors questions about their diets, where they live, whether they have pets, and even how frequently they wash their hands, all of which can affect the numbers and kinds of bacteria present in a person's digestive tract.

40 Microbes were first discovered in the seventeenth century, but not extensively studied until Louis Pasteur began formulating his germ theory in the nineteenth century. Even then, the focus of microbial research mainly had to do
45 with pathogens, the microbes that make us sick.

The technique used by Knight for analyzing the genetic makeup of microbes wasn't widely used until the 1980s. This genetic analysis allows scientists to see all the different strains of microbes
50 that are present in a microbiome, the vast majority of which are beneficial. The understanding of just how many there are is leading to new research in treatments for chronic health problems such as obesity, cardiovascular disease, and even cancer.

55 For example, several studies have found that obese mice that are given transplants of intestinal colonies from lean mice lose weight. There is growing evidence to suggest that inflammation may be behind cardiovascular disease, diabetes,
60 and other such conditions. Patrice Cani at the Université Catholique de Louvain in Brussels has been studying the role of microbes in maintaining a healthy epithelium, the lining of our digestive system that is supposed to allow nutrients through
65 to the bloodstream, but keep toxins out.

Cani's research has shown that mice fed a high-fat diet have lower numbers of the microbes that help keep the epithelium healthy, which means that more toxins are able to make their
70 way into the bloodstream. In turn, the toxins lead to general inflammation, which eventually leads to metabolic syndrome, the precursor to diseases such as diabetes.

Microbes may also play a role in our mental
75 health: the bacteria in our guts produce neuro-chemicals, including serotonin, which helps to regulate mood, sleep, and appetite and can affect memory and learning. For this reason, our digestive tract is sometimes referred to as
80 our "second brain."

A study conducted by Dr. Premysl Bercik at McMaster University studied the effect of changing the composition of shy mice's gut bacteria by feeding them a specially designed mix of
85 antibiotics. "Their behavior completely changed," Bercik says. "They became bold and adventurous."

The question of how to regulate the microbes in our guts for optimal health is one that can't
90 be answered until scientists have a better picture of what constitutes a healthy microbiome. This is part of the goal of the American Gut Project, and other scientists are going even further. María Gloria Dominguez-Bello, a microbiolo-
95 gist at New York University, travels to remote areas of the world to collect samples from peoples who have had very little contact with the Western world.

Dominguez-Bello has found that the micro-
100 biomes of people who have never had antibiotics or processed food are far more diverse than the typical Western microbiome, and the people they come from have a very low rate of allergies, asthma, and chronic conditions such as diabetes and
105 cardiovascular disease.

It's too early for microbiologists to promise that regulation of a patient's microbiome will be able to cure chronic health conditions, but the research is quickly gaining traction, and some
110 patients with gastro-intestinal disorders are already being treated with "fecal transplants" from healthy donors.

Though there is still much to be learned about the relationship between our bodies and
115 the teeming colonies of unseen organisms living within them, scientists are optimistic about the paths such research is leading them down.

1. The main idea of the passage is that:

   A. a healthy microbiome can help a person maintain a healthy weight.
   B. scientists are just beginning to understand how important our intestinal microbes are to our overall health.
   C. taking a specially designed mix of antibiotics can affect serotonin levels, which will improve mental health.
   D. new understandings of beneficial microbes have led scientists to believe that old notions of germ theory are incorrect.

2. The passage's mention of scientists' efforts to "decode the influence of lifestyle on the characteristics of a microbiome" (lines 33–34) most nearly refers to their efforts to:

   F. determine how important pets are in maintaining a healthy microbiome.
   G. track how a baby's microbiome develops over time.
   H. analyze the genetic material of the beneficial microbes in a feces sample.
   J. understand how choices in diet and living conditions affect intestinal microbes.

3. Which of the following is NOT mentioned in the passage as something that scientists believe is influenced by intestinal microbes?

   A. Mental health
   B. Lifestyle
   C. Metabolic syndrome
   D. Diabetes

4. Rob Knight's statement in line 1 is based mainly on the assumption that most people:

   F. understand the importance of studying a baby's microbiome.
   G. believe changing diapers is an important skill.
   H. don't think the contents of a baby's diaper are worthy of study.
   J. enjoy hearing stories about the experiences of new fathers.

5. Within the passage, the eleventh and twelfth paragraphs (lines 88–105) primarily serve to:

A. prove a connection between a Western lifestyle and chronic cardiovascular disease.
B. indicate the importance of introducing antibiotics to remote areas of the world.
C. explain one way in which scientists are trying to establish what a healthy intestinal microbiome looks like.
D. resolve a disagreement among scientists about which strains of bacteria should be present in a healthy microbiome.

6. The passage indicates that all of the following contribute to intestinal microbes' influence on metabolic syndrome EXCEPT:

F. a high-fat diet.
G. diabetes.
H. an unhealthy epithelium.
J. toxins that lead to inflammation.

7. According to the passage, how do intestinal microbes affect mental health?

A. Intestinal microbes produce neurochemicals that can regulate moods.
B. Serotonin affects the brain function of intestinal microbes.
C. The second brain is regulated by the neurochemicals that also regulate intestinal microbes.
D. Antibiotics can change the serotonin levels produced by the microbes in an adventurous person's intestines.

8. According to the passage, research in intestinal microbiomes is:

F. promising; fecal transplants have already helped some patients.
G. promising; scientists have found a cure for metabolic syndrome.
H. unpromising; scientists don't have enough information to make such research useful.
J. unpromising; the effects of lifestyle choices on microbiomes is unclear.

9. The passage indicates that the diversity of bacteria living in a person's gut is directly related to:

A. the person's age.
B. the health of the person's epithelium.
C. how many pets the person has.
D. whether the person has ever taken antibiotics.

10. According to the passage, which of the following was the focus of early microbe studies?

F. Babies
G. Pathogens
H. Obesity
J. Genetics

READING DRILLS ANSWERS AND EXPLANATIONS

Drill 1

1. **D** Choice (D) is correct because the passage is written in the third person, and is mostly about Isabel. Choices (A) and (C) are incorrect because the story is told about Isabel and Alejandro, but is in the third person. It is not told by either of them in the first person. Choice (B) is incorrect because the narrator treats Alejandro and Isabel the same way.

2. **J** This is an EXCEPT question, so the answer choice that does not appear in the passage is correct. Choice (J) is correct because the story does not mention Isabel ever performing. Choice (F) is incorrect because the passage describes how *Isabel had begged her mother to let her try out for the ballet school.* Choice (G) is incorrect because the passage states that *When Cinderella had to leave the ball...Isabel felt keenly the anxiety of living a relatively comfortable life, so far removed from the poverty of her childhood.* Choice (H) is incorrect because the passage says that...*the pas de deux...seemed to her a more truthful representation of the awakening of love....*

3. **C** Choice (C) is correct because the passage states that *Isabel's son, Alejandro, had been trying to get her to come to Miami for years.* Although the fact that Isabel didn't go visit her son might lead the reader to believe that Alejandro feels isolated from her, there is no direct support for (A) in the passage. Choice (B) is incorrect because there is no mention of whether Alejandro is—or hopes to become—a dancer. Choice (D) is incorrect because the passage says that Alejandro wanted Isabel to come visit him, and there is no indication that he was hesitant about wanting to spend time with her.

4. **J** At the beginning of these lines, the experience of going to the theater is described as feeling to Isabel *as if she were emerging from her cocoon into a new and bigger world.* The rest of the excerpt describes her first impressions of going into the theater, and thus best supports (J), the correct answer. Choices (F) and (H) are incorrect because Isabel did enjoy the ballet, and there is no indication that the building was more important. Choice (G) is incorrect because the Cathedral is used as a simile; it is not the building described.

5. **B** Isabel's experience at the performance of *Giselle* is described in the second and third paragraphs, which means that the correct answer must come from that part of the passage. Choice (B) is the correct answer because it most directly refers to

her reaction to the performance. Choice (A) is incorrect because it describes Isabel's experience walking into the theater, but not her reaction to the performance. Choice (C) is incorrect because it describes Isabel's reaction to not getting into ballet school, and (D) is incorrect because it describes her reaction to seeing Baryshnikov dance.

6. **J**   Choice (J) is the correct answer because the passage states that Alejandro bought tickets to see Baryshnikov when he *realized he had to tempt her with something she couldn't see in Havana*. Choice (F) is incorrect because the passage refers to Baryshnikov as *the legendary Russian dancer*, so he is not unknown. Choice (G) is plausible, but there is no direct support for it in the passage. Choice (H) is incorrect because the passage states that *Alejandro had tried to entice his mother with visits to the Miami Ballet*.

7. **A**   Choice (A) is the correct answer because the phrase in question appears in a part of the passage that describes how *stately* and *grand* Isabel thought the theater was. Choice (B) is incorrect because it is too literal a reading of the phrase *seemingly to heaven*. There is no evidence in the passage to support (C) or (D).

8. **J**   The phrase in question describes an *overwhelming sadness* Isabel felt that *became so powerful it felt strangely joyful*. The descriptions of strong emotions give support to (J), the correct answer. Choice (F) is incorrect both because it refers to a sentence later in the same paragraph and because there is no evidence that Isabel was *ashamed*. Choice (G) is incorrect because it takes an idea from an earlier sentence from the same paragraph, *she felt as though her life would never have meaning unless she could be one of those dancers*, and mixes it up with the idea of emotions in the sentence in question. Choice (H) may sound as though it might be a good choice, but the passage says that Isabel felt a dance was *a more truthful presentation of the awakening of love than anything she would experience in real life*, not that she would *never experience love*, so it is incorrect.

9. **A**   The words *such places* in the phrase in question most directly refer back to *that theater*, or the *Palace of the Galician Center*, which lends support to (A), the correct answer. Choice (B) is incorrect because, while *peasant girls celebrating the bountiful harvest* are mentioned, they are characters in the ballet; Isabel did not actually travel to the country. Choice (C) is incorrect because, while the passage describes Isabel *confidently clicking her high-heeled shoes*, there is no mention of any shoe stores. Choice (D) is incorrect because the Cathedral is used in the previous paragraph as a simile, but the passage does not address whether she had ever visited it.

10. **F** Isabel felt like Coppélia when Alejandro *called Isabel to say he had purchased tickets to see Mikhail Baryshnikov in Miami*, so (F) is the correct answer. Choices (G) and (H) are both things that happened to Isabel, but not in connection with the phrase in question. Choice (J) is incorrect because Isabel never attended a performance of *Giselle* at the Miami Ballet.

Drill 2

1. **B** Choice (B) is the correct answer because it most accurately represents the passage as a whole, which describes a promising new field of scientific research. Choice (A) is incorrect because it is only one small detail in the passage. Choice (C) is incorrect because, while the passage mentions both *serotonin* and *antibiotics*, it never directly states that individuals would benefit by taking antibiotics to increase serotonin levels; even if it did, it does not address the main idea of the passage. Choice (D) is incorrect because, while the fifth paragraph mentions *germ theory*, there is no indication in the passage that *old notions of germ theory are incorrect*.

2. **J** The fourth paragraph describes how the scientists are combining genetic information with answers from a survey into one large database, which best supports (J), the correct answer. Choices (F) and (H) are incorrect because they refer only to small parts of the project described in the fourth paragraph. Choice (G) is incorrect because it refers to the wrong part of the passage.

3. **B** When answering a NOT question, remember that answer choices that appear in the passage are incorrect. Choice (B) is the correct answer because lifestyle is mentioned in the fourth paragraph as something that can affect intestinal microbes, not the other way around. Choice (A) is incorrect because it is described in the ninth and tenth paragraphs. Choices (C) and (D) are incorrect because they are described in the seventh and eighth paragraphs.

4. **H** The first paragraph states that Knight's *daughter's diapers play an important role in his research*, which gives support to (H), the correct answer. While (F) is related to the subject of the first two paragraphs, it is not relevant to how Knight is *not your typical new dad*. Choices (G) and (J) are incorrect because there is no support for either one in the passage.

5. **C** The beginning of the eleventh paragraph states that *the question of how to regulate the microbes in our guts for optimal health is one that can't be answered until scientists have a better picture of what constitutes a healthy microbiome*, and then goes on to

describe research related to that idea. Therefore, (C) is the correct answer. Choice (D) is incorrect because there is no indication of a conflict. Choice (A) is incorrect because, while the passage mentions that *the microbiomes of people who have never had antibiotics or processed food are far more diverse than the typical Western microbiome* and that these same people *have a very low rate of...chronic conditions such as diabetes and cardiovascular disease*, there is no indication of *proof* that a *Western lifestyle* causes cardiovascular disease. Choice (B) is incorrect because the passage never indicates that antibiotics should be introduced to remote areas of the world.

6. **G** When answering an EXCEPT question, remember that answer choices that appear in the passage are incorrect. Choice (G) is the correct answer because diabetes is a result of metabolic syndrome, not something that influences it. Choices (F), (H), and (J) are all incorrect because they are described in the eighth paragraph as factors that contribute to metabolic syndrome.

7. **A** The ninth paragraph states *the bacteria in our guts produce neurochemicals, including serotonin, which helps to regulate mood*, which makes (A) the correct answer. Choice (B) is incorrect because, according to the passage, intestinal microbes *produce serotonin*, but there is no indication that the microbes have brain functions that are affected by the serotonin. Choice (C) is incorrect because, while the passage mentions *the second brain* and *neurochemicals*, the neurochemicals *regulate mood, sleep, and appetite*, not intestinal microbes. Choice (D) is incorrect because, while the passage mentions behavior changing after taking antibiotics, it is the behavior of *shy mice* that changes, not an *adventurous person*.

8. **F** The last paragraph states that *scientists are optimistic* about research in intestinal microbiomes. Choice (F) is correct because it accurately reflects this optimism, and because paragraph thirteen uses the example of fecal transplants as a positive development in the research. Choice (G) is incorrect because there is no evidence of a *cure for metabolic syndrome*. Choices (H) and (J) are incorrect because there is no evidence that the research is *unpromising*.

9. **D** Diversity of microbiomes is discussed in the twelfth paragraph, which states that *the microbiomes of people who have never had antibiotics or processed food are far more diverse than the typical Western microbiome*. Choice (D) is therefore the correct answer. Choices (A), (B), and (C) are all incorrect because none of those factors are discussed in relation to *diversity of bacteria*.

10. **G** The fifth paragraph states that when microbes were *first discovered*, they were *extensively studied* and mentions that *the focus of microbial research mainly had to do with pathogens, the microbes that make us sick*. Choice (G) is therefore the correct answer. Choices (F), (H), and (J) are all incorrect because they are not discussed in the relevant part of the passage.

Part V
ACT Science

Chapter 20
Introduction to the ACT Science Test

The ACT Science test is always the fourth section, after the Reading test and before the optional Writing test. Fatigue can negatively affect even the best students by then. Even if the Science test were first, many students find it somewhat intimidating and feel that they need to crack open their freshman bio textbooks. But this is not a test of science facts: it is instead a test of how well you look up and synthesize information from tables, graphs, illustrations, and passages. To maximize your score on the Science test, you need to work the passages in a personal order of difficulty. We'll teach you how to order the passages, and we'll teach you how to employ a strategic and efficient approach that will earn you your highest possible score.

HOW TO CRACK THE SCIENCE TEST

The Science Test on the ACT is, initially, one of the most intimidating things you will see on a standardized test. After all the standardized-test basics of English grammar, math, and reading comprehension, science seems to require something else entirely. It can test subjects ranging from biology to chemistry to ecology, from classes you've had and classes you haven't, and it does so with a specificity that none of the other parts of the ACT demand.

But we're here to tell you that, with a little shift in perception, you will find that ACT Science is one of the easiest sections on the test and one in which you can receive some of your most significant improvements. It all comes down to one simple, counterintuitive idea:

> Don't try to understand the science. Just get the points.

This may seem like an oversimplification, but follow along in the next few chapters, and you'll see exactly what we mean.

Believe it or not, you actually apply this strategy in reading all the time, whether you've been using our techniques or not. Let's say, for example, that you get a passage on the Reading Test about bear-baiting in the 1500s and 1600s. If you had to work only with your outside knowledge of this subject, you'd probably be in pretty bad shape. A question like this would be pretty impossible:

1. Which of the following does the passage include to demonstrate the popularity of bear-baiting in the 1600s?
   A. Biological records of the evolutionary history of bears
   B. Evidence that both commoners and royalty enjoyed the sport
   C. Parliamentary legislation that freed bear-baiters from significant restrictions
   D. Indications that the sport eventually became popular in France as well

Even if you're an expert on the subject (and why would you be?), this question is nearly impossible to answer without the passage. And you know that, on the Reading Test, every-thing you need *must* be in the passage.

Here's the relevant section:

Someone walking the streets of London from about 1550 to 1700 would have seen any number of bear-gardens, arenas designed for exactly this purpose of bear-baiting. The main bear-garden in London was the Paris Garden, which stood until 1670. A pole would be set at the edge of a pit, and a bear would be tormented (or baited) by dogs and humans alike until it was exhausted or killed. While the sport may seem wildly inhumane to us today, the English of this era had no such qualms about animal cruelty. Not only were the seats around the pit always full of spectators, Henry VIII had a pit constructed in Whitehall, and Elizabeth I overruled an attempt by Parliament to outlaw the sport on Sundays.

Now we know that the answer is (C), for which evidence is given in the last sentence of the paragraph.

It may seem like we just completed a fairly obvious exercise, because of course that's how Reading works on the ACT. The topic of a Reading passage is almost irrelevant because everything we need to know about it will be contained within the passage itself. We don't need to understand or retain any of what we've read—we just have to get the points and move on.

So what's different about questions like these?

2. According to the data in Experiment 1, as the number of molecules increases, the concentration of the compound:

   F. increases only.
   G. decreases only.
   H. remains constant.
   J. varies, but with no general trend.

3. Suppose the experimenters discovered a new compound, Compound E, which contains 700 million molecules. Which of the following would most likely be the concentration of that compound, in mass percent?

   A. 22
   B. 36
   C. 75
   D. 90

As with the previous question, you likely have no idea how to answer these. But remember how we approached the example from Reading. Even though we had no previous knowledge of bear-baiting in the 1600s, we could answer the question easily because the information was given in the passage. *The same is true in Science.* For more than 90% of the questions, all the information that you need will be given in the passage itself.

Let's look at those questions again, this time with the aid of Table 1 from Experiment 1.

Table 1		
Compound	# of molecules (millions)	Concentration (mass %)
A	500	26
B	800	40
C	1200	60
D	2000	81

2. According to the data in Experiment 1, as the number of molecules increases, the concentration of the compound:

   F. increases only.
   G. decreases only.
   H. remains constant.
   J. varies, but with no general trend.

3. Suppose the experimenters discovered a new compound, Compound E, which contains 700 million molecules. Which of the following would most likely be the concentration of that compound, in mass percent?

   A. 22
   B. 36
   C. 75
   D. 90

Here's How to Crack It

Now, the relationships are much clearer. We can see from the chart that as "# of molecules" increases, so too does "concentration," meaning that the correct answer to Question 2 is (F).

We can use the same relationship in Question 3. We know that as "# of molecules" increases, so too does "concentration." Therefore, if Compound E contains 700 million molecules, its concentration will fall between that of Compound A (with 500 million molecules) and Compound B (with 800 million molecules). In other words, the concentration will need to fall between 26 and 40, as only (B) does.

Let's pause for a moment to realize how little traditional "science" we've just done. Not only did we simply pull the information from the table, but also the concepts being tested were essentially irrelevant to the points we earned. Table 1 features "# of molecules" and "concentration," but we didn't use this information at all except to match what's in the question with what's in the introduction. If this table had said "# of froyo toppings" and "units of deliciousness," we wouldn't have treated the information any differently.

This no-science approach usually works on the most seemingly scientific of questions, like this one:

---

4. Based on the information in the passage, which of the following is a possible chemical formula for an ethanolamine?

   F. $HO—(CH_2)_2—NH_3$
   G. $HO—(CH_2CF_2)_2—CH_3$
   H. $H_3C—(CH_2)_4—NH_3$
   J. $H_3N—(CH_2CHCl)_2—NH_3$

Here's How to Crack It

In the passage from which this is taken, there is no indication of how chemical compounds are formed and nothing that lists ethanolamine's chemical formula. However, the first line of the passage reads as follows:

> Ethanolamines *are compounds that contain both alcohol (—OH or HO—) and amine (—NH₃, —RNH₂, —R₂NH, or —R₃N) subgroups.*

It may seem that we still haven't illuminated much about this question, because you may not know the names of the molecules listed. But whatever the molecules are called, we know that the answer will need at least one from the first group and one from the second group.

With this information alone, we can eliminate (H) and (J), which do not contain either an OH or an HO. Then we can see that (F) must be correct because it contains NH_3, which is listed as one of the amines.

———————————————⌒———————————————

If there was any "science" at all in how we tackled Question 4, it was the science of Process of Elimination (POE), which is the cornerstone of approaching the Science Test on the ACT.

POE AND LEARNING THE PASSAGE FROM THE QUESTIONS

Because there is so little actual science on the ACT, we'll need to employ one of our cornerstone techniques frequently on the Science Test: POE. Even if we cannot pluck the data directly from the charts or tables, we can get to the correct answer almost every time with POE.

Above all, ACT Science is about your ability to recognize patterns and make logical deductions about them. Even when you're not working with numbers or trends specifically, the things you'll need to see in each chart or table are based on the numbers or trends within those charts.

Let's look at an example. Glance over the passage and Question 17, then go right to the explanation of how to crack such a question.

Passage III

Osmotic pressure (Π) is the amount of pressure, in atm, required to maintain equilibrium of a solvent across a semipermeable membrane. At a constant temperature, osmotic pressure is dependent only on a solute's ability to dissociate or ionize in the solvent (*van 't Hoff factor*, *i*) and the concentration of solute particles. The osmotic pressure is determined by the equation:

$$\Pi = iMRT$$

M represents the concentration (in molarity, *M*), *R* is the ideal gas constant (0.0821 L atm mol^{-1} K^{-1}), and *T* (300 K) is the temperature in Kelvin (K). The value of *R* is assumed to be a constant for all osmotic pressure calculations.

The dissociation of a solute depends on its unique chemical properties. The van 't Hoff factors for some common substances are displayed in Table 1. Higher van 't Hoff factors correlate with greater dissociation or ionization. The effect of the van 't Hoff factor on the osmotic pressure may be seen in Figure 1.

Table 1	
Substance	van 't Hoff factor *
sucrose	1.0
NaCl	1.9
$MgCl_2$	2.7
$FeCl_3$	3.4
*values at 300 K	

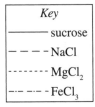

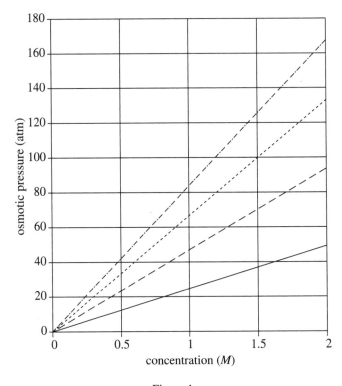

Figure 1

17. A scientist recently discovered a compound that ionizes readily in solution ($i = 3.8$) and results in low osmotic pressure. Are the findings of this scientist consistent with Figure 1 ?

    A. Yes, because $FeCl_3$ causes higher osmotic pressure than does sucrose.

    B. Yes, because sucrose causes higher osmotic pressure than does $FeCl_3$.

    C. No, because $FeCl_3$ causes lower osmotic pressure than does sucrose.

    D. No, because sucrose causes lower osmotic pressure than does $FeCl_3$.

Here's How to Crack It

There's a lot going on in this question, not only because we may be unsure from the passage what *i* refers to, but also because, as we will soon find, the question refers to Figure 1 but actually requires Table 1 as well.

That said, let's start with Process of Elimination. Each answer features a "Yes" or "No" and a reason. While we might be inclined to think that a "Yes" or "No" answer is the first thing we should determine, this is not the case. Whenever ACT gives multiple-part answers, you can use POE to attack any part.

In this case, the "Yes"/"No" question is a little more complex, but the reasons are very simple. We can see from Figure 1 that the reasons in (A) and (D) are correct, and the reasons in (B) and (C) are incorrect. Regardless of the first part of each answer, we can eliminate (B) and (C). We now have a 50% chance of guessing the correct answer, and we haven't done much of anything relating to the question itself.

With the remaining parts of the question, let the question guide the information you need. The question refers to *i*, so use that italicized symbol as a lead word. The first paragraph states that *i* is the symbol for van 't Hoff factor. This value appears in Table 1: sucrose has the lowest, and $FeCl_3$ has the highest. Then, on Figure 1, $FeCl_3$ has the highest osmotic pressure, where sucrose has the lowest osmotic pressure. We can therefore infer that a higher *i* means a higher osmotic pressure. This doesn't agree with the statement made in Question 17, so we can choose "No," and the answer is (D).

───────────────── ◯ ─────────────────

Let's pause for a moment to go over what we've just done. This is a relatively difficult question, and you may suspect that this explanation made it seem easier than it actually was. All we've done, though, is apply a few basic principles that we will always apply throughout the Science Test:

- Don't try to understand the science.
  - In answering Question 17, do we have a clearer sense of why concentration should increase osmotic pressure? Or why *i* should influence osmotic pressure?
  - Do we know what "osmotic pressure" refers to?
  - Do we even know how to pronounce "van 't Hoff factor"?
  - No to all of the above! But we got the point anyway.
- Use POE.
  - More parts in a question mean more opportunities for POE.
  - If you can't answer the question directly, use POE to attack the reasons.

- Let the questions teach you about the passage.
  - You may not have initially seen the relationship between Table 1 and Figure 1.
  - You may not have known what i referred to, but you didn't have to until Question 17 required it.
  - In general, it's easier to find specific information than general information, so let the questions focus your attention for you.
    - What's an easier question to answer with this figure?
      - What does i refer to?
      - What is "van 't Hoff factor" and how does it work?

Let's try another passage in which we will apply these three basic principles. This is one of the more difficult passages we've seen.

Passage IV

The *Citric cycle* is an essential process used to transform carbohydrates, lipids, and proteins into energy in aerobic organisms. If yeast is unable to produce *succinate*, it cannot survive. The Citric cycle steps leading to the creation of succinate in yeast are shown in Figure 1. Each step in this cycle is catalyzed by an enzyme, which is essential to overcome the energy barrier between reactant and product. In the first step, Enzyme 1 is the enzyme, citrate is the reactant, and isocitrate is the product.

citrate $\xrightarrow{\text{Enzyme 1}}$ isocitrate $\xrightarrow{\text{Enzyme 2}}$ α-ketoglutarate $\xrightarrow{\text{Enzyme 3}}$ succinyl-CoA $\xrightarrow{\text{Enzyme 4}}$ succinate

Figure 1

Experiment

A scientist grew four strains of yeast on several different growth media. Each strain was unable to produce succinate because it lacked one of the enzymes required for the reaction pathway shown in Figure 1. Table 1 shows the results of the scientist's experiment: "Yes" indicates that the strain was able to grow in the basic nutrition solution (BNS) + the particular chemical. An undamaged strain of yeast would be able to grow in the basic nutrition solution without any additional chemical. If a strain was able to grow in a given growth medium, then it was able to produce succinate from the additional chemical added to the basic nutrition solution.

Table 1				
Growth medium	Yeast strain			
	W	X	Y	Z
BNS				
BNS + isocitrate	Yes			
BNS + α-ketoglutarate	Yes	Yes		
BNS + succinyl-CoA	Yes	Yes	Yes	
BNS + succinate	Yes	Yes	Yes	Yes

If certain genes are damaged, the essential enzymes cannot be produced, which means that the reactions that the enzyme catalyzes cannot go. Table 2 lists the genes responsible for the enzymes in the steps of the Citric cycle leading to succinate production in yeast. If an enzyme cannot be produced, then the product of the reaction that enzyme catalyzes cannot be synthesized and the reactant in that reaction will become highly concentrated. If a gene is damaged, then it is notated with a superscript negative sign, as in $Cat3^-$; if a gene is not damaged it is notated with a superscript positive sign, as in $Cat3^+$.

Table 2	
Gene	Enzyme
Cat1	Enzyme 1
Cat2	Enzyme 2
Cat3	Enzyme 3
Cat4	Enzyme 4

There are no obvious trends here, so let's go straight to the questions. There's no use trying to understand what's happening in the passage because we'll learn what we need from the questions themselves.

17. Based on the information presented, the highest concentration of isocitrate would most likely be found in which of the following yeasts?

A. Yeast that cannot produce Enzyme 1
B. Yeast that cannot produce Enzyme 2
C. Yeast that cannot produce Enzyme 3
D. Yeast that cannot produce Enzyme 4

Here's How to Crack It

Typically, when we see words like "highest," we're looking to the figures and tables. No clear relationship exists in the tables here, however, so let's pay attention to the other key words: *isocitrate*, *yeast*, and *Enzyme* (from the answer choices).

Enzymes 1–4 appear with *isocitrate* in Figure 1. The meaning of this figure is not entirely clear, but we can make a few simple inferences from it. Enzyme 1 is above isocitrate, and Enzyme 2 is below it, so one of these is likely to be the answer, thus eliminating (C) and (D). Then, use the arrows. Enzyme 1 seems to lead to isocitrate, but if Enzyme 2 were not there, the flow would be broken, and the arrows would stop at isocitrate. We can infer, then, that this would create a large amount of isocitrate, or a high concentration, making (B) the correct answer.

18. According to the information in the passage and Table 2, a strain of yeast that is Cat1$^+$ Cat2$^-$ Cat3$^-$ Cat4$^+$ CANNOT produce:

   F. Enzyme 1 and Enzyme 2.
   G. Enzyme 1 and Enzyme 4.
   H. Enzyme 2 and Enzyme 3.
   J. Enzyme 3 and Enzyme 4.

Here's How to Crack It

The "Cat"s appear in Table 2, so that's a purrfect place to start right meow. Each Cat seems to match up with an Enzyme of the same number.

Start by using POE. Cat1 and Cat4 have a +, and Cat2 and Cat3 have a −. Therefore, the pair of answers will have to refer to one or another of these pairs, eliminating (F) and (J). Now, skim the passage for a reference to + or −. The passage states that *if a gene is damaged, then it is notated with a superscript negative sign.* Therefore, Cat2 and Cat3 are damaged, so the enzymes that cannot be produced are Enzymes 2 and 3. The correct answer is (H).

19. Which of the following statements best describes the relationships between citrate, isocitrate, and α–ketoglutarate as shown in Figure 1 ?

    A. Isocitrate is a product of a reaction of α-ketoglutarate, and α-ketoglutarate is a product of a reaction of citrate.

    B. α-ketoglutarate is a product of a reaction of isocitrate, and isocitrate is a product of a reaction of citrate.

    C. α-ketoglutarate is a product of a reaction of citrate, and citrate is a product of a reaction of isocitrate.

    D. Citrate is a product of a reaction of isocitrate, and isocitrate is a product of a reaction of α-ketoglutarate.

Here's How to Crack It

The question refers to Figure 1 and uses a chemistry term ("product"), which you probably know, but which you don't actually need to know to answer the question.

Use POE and follow the arrows. α-ketoglutarate and citrate don't come into contact at all, so eliminate any answer that puts them into contact: (A) and (C). Then, follow the arrows: citrate first, then isocitrate, then α-ketoglutarate, as (B) indicates.

20. Strain X was most likely unable to synthesize:

    F. isocitrate from citrate.

    G. α-ketoglutarate from isocitrate.

    H. succinyl-CoA from α-ketoglutarate.

    J. succinate from succinyl-CoA.

Here's How to Crack It

"Strain X" appears in Table 1, and while it seems like we might need to read the passage to see what's going on here, we don't. Look for patterns within the table. The most obvious one here is the downward staircase of the word "Yes." That's all.

Let the POE begin. The pattern of "Yes" in column X breaks off between "BNS + isocitrate" and "BNS + α-ketoglutarate," so this must be where Strain X is "unable" to do something and should get us close to the answer. Choice (F) doesn't mention α-ketoglutarate, (H) doesn't mention isocitrate, and (J) doesn't mention isocitrate or α-ketoglutarate, which means that all of these answers can be eliminated. Choice (G) is therefore the correct answer.

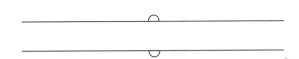

21. One of the growth media shown in Table 1 was a control that the scientist used to demonstrate that all four strains of yeast had genetic damage that prevented the reactions shown in Figure 1, the reactions that are responsible for the synthesis of succinate. Which growth media was used as a control?

    A. BNS
    B. BNS + succinate
    C. BNS + isocitrate
    D. BNS + succinyl-CoA

Here's How to Crack It

The word "control" is among those very few science terms that you should know for ACT Science. A control is something that is held constant in an experiment and something against which the results of the experiment can be tested. In this case, the control is pretty clear, in that "BNS" is common to every growth medium. So, BNS must be the control, as (A) suggests.

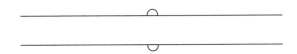

22. For each of the four strains of yeast, W–Z, shown in Table 1, if a given strain was able to grow in BNS + succinyl-CoA, then it was also able to grow in:

    F. BNS.
    G. BNS + isocitrate.
    H. BNS + α-ketoglutarate.
    J. BNS + succinate.

Here's How to Crack It

As with Question 20, it might seem that we need to read the passage in order to be able to answer the question. But again, we need to do no such thing. Whereas in Question 20 we were looking for a difference, we are now looking for a similarity ("also able to grow in"). Let's use the "Yes" columns again, and look for the row that is most similar to succinyl-CoA. Keep it simple! "BNS + succinyl-CoA" has three "Yes" columns. The only other one that has at least three is "BNS + succinate," which has four. On this information alone, (J) must be correct.

We have just completed a very difficult ACT Science passage by doing almost no science at all. But that's what the Science Test is all about: not science, points.

You may be thinking…

Didn't I buy the Advanced book? If I stopped thinking in my honors classes at school, I'd get terrible grades. Why are these people telling me I shouldn't use science on a science test? If I only used the figures on my AP bio test, I'd get a 1, if that!

The answer is simple: this is not your science class at school, and it's not an AP science test. Science on the ACT is a unique entity, and we've developed a strategy that can help to maximize your ACT Science score.

And don't forget: willingness to change your method of test-taking is the only way to get a big score improvement. ACT knows how the average student takes this test because the test-writers know what is taught in schools. What we're showing you how to do, though, is to think like those who write the test rather than those who take it.

The best test takers are those who can CHOOSE how they will take the test. If you learn the tricks specific to the ACT, you'll be miles ahead of those who take the test the way they think they're supposed to.

OUTSIDE KNOWLEDGE

Now that we have convinced you of science's unimportance, we should admit that ACT does test some very basic outside knowledge. We realize that, if you've purchased this book, you're looking to get a very high score, and you need to correctly answer most or all of the questions in order to do so. You'll probably encounter one or two outside-knowledge questions per test, and in fact, you should be able to get most of the way through these with POE.

The cornerstone of the outside knowledge you need on ACT Science is The Scientific Method. The Scientific Method may not even seem like outside knowledge because it is something we use from our very first interactions with science in any form.

Think about the following scenario:

> One day, you wear a new sweater, use a new skin lotion, and eat strawberries. The next day, you wake up with a skin rash. How do you figure out what gave you the rash?

If you answered something like, "Go one day with the new sweater but no lotion and no strawberries. Then go one day with the lotion but no sweater and no strawberries," and so on, then you know how to use The Scientific Method.

The basic principle as it applies to the ACT is that if you want to test something, you need to keep everything else constant and make sure nothing is skewing your results. We have already seen how ACT asks about the "control," which they will sometimes give a different name like "standard of comparison," but ACT will also ask about what is being tested and experimental procedures.

Here are a few examples of each:

Experiment 3

The procedure for Experiment 1 was repeated with the wooden object, varying the temperature of the polymer ramp. Results for 5 temperatures were recorded in Table 3.

Table 3	
Temperature (°C)	θ (degrees)
0	18.5
25	22.0
50	25.4
75	29.0
100	32.5

6. The main purpose of Experiment 3 was to determine the effects of temperature on which of the following variables?

F. Coefficient of static friction between wood and wood
G. Coefficient of static friction between wood and polymer
H. Mass of the wooden object
J. Total frictional force of the polymer on all objects placed on the ramp

Here's How to Crack It

We don't have a ton of information here, but we can still answer this question by falling back on The Scientific Method. The things being tested are the things changing. Choice (H) refers to mass, which does not appear on the chart, and (J) refers to force, which does not appear on the chart, so both can be eliminated. Then, the blurb mentions a *polymer ramp*, suggesting that polymer is a relevant variable, thus making (G) the correct answer.

7. Which of the following statements is most likely the reason that the students used identical springs in Trials 1–3 ?

    A. To ensure that the springs stretched similarly when a weight was attached

    B. To ensure that the springs did not share the weight evenly

    C. To compensate for the effects of oscillation on the results of the experiment

    D. To compensate for the weight of the board exerted on each of the springs

Here's How to Crack It

If a science experiment uses three identical things, the scientists must be trying to prevent some particular effect from influencing the results. In this case, there are three "identical springs," so we can assume the scientists are trying to make it so the springs act identically on all the trials. Using this logic, (B) is fairly preposterous, and (C) and (D) aren't about the springs at all. Choice (A) is the only one that could work.

As for other outside knowledge, ACT is unfortunately very inconsistent. Questions that require outside knowledge are not typically repeated, and there can be questions from biology, chemistry, and physics. But if you're unsure how to answer an outside-knowledge question, you can still use POE aggressively and get close.

Here are a few basic ideas it may help to understand.

There are three phases of matter: gas, liquid, and solid.
    -When a *solid* gets too hot, it becomes a *liquid*.
    -When a *liquid* gets too hot, it becomes a *gas*.

These operations also work in reverse, which means that the moments of transition are the same. Think about water.
    -At 0°C, *ice* becomes *water*, and *water* becomes *ice*.
        -In other words, this temperature represents both the *freezing* and the *melting* point of water.
    -At 100°C, *water* becomes *vapor*, and *vapor* becomes *water*.
        -In other words, this temperature is both the *boiling* and the *condensation* point of water.

Because ACT is so fond of relationships, remember that when…

Heat increases
>…there is no change in *mass*
>…the *volume* is increased
>>…because the *space between the molecules* increases
>>…and the *density* decreases
>…the *speed of the molecules' movement* is increased

The *speed* of an object increases
>…the *momentum* of that object increases
>…the *kinetic energy* of that object increases
>…at a set time, the *distance* increases
>…at a set distance, the *time* decreases

And some odds and ends:

pH is the measure of the *acidity* of a solution. The magic number with pH is 7.
>-At 7, a substance has neutral acidity.
>-Below 7, a substance is called "acidic."
>-Above 7, a substance is called "alkaline."

Chromosomes
>-Most humans have 46 chromosomes, or 23 pairs.
>-A male has both an X and a Y chromosome.
>-A female has two X chromosomes.
>-On the reproductive level, the male sperm and female egg are called *gametes*.
>>-They combine to form the *zygote*, the basic cell from which all the other cells in a unique organism are generated.

The Order of the Planets
>-Remember: *My Very Excellent Mother Just Sent Us Nachos*
>-Mercury, Venus, Earth, Mars, Jupiter, Saturn, Uranus, and Neptune

Here are a few outside-knowledge questions with relevant details.

Table 1	
Group	Conditions
1	These areas had significantly decreased populations of marine mammals consumed by polar bears.
2	These areas had significantly increased populations of seaweed commonly consumed by marine mammals.
3	These areas had been subject to excess thawing of Arctic sea ice.

8. Which of the following is most likely an organism that the researchers identified as exhibiting a significantly decreased population when defining Group 1 ?

   F. Snowy owl
   G. Seal
   H. Salmon
   J. Polar bear

Here's How to Crack It

The answer must be (G) because *snowy owls* and *salmon* are not marine mammals, and *polar bears* are not (we hope!) *consumed by polar bears.*

Question 9 comes from a passage that begins with the following:

Bats of the family *Vespertilionidae* (Vesper bats) are commonly found in North America.

9. Which of the following best describes the family *Vespertilionidae*?

   A. Mammals
   B. Protists
   C. Lampreys
   D. Birds

Here's How to Crack It

Not sure what "protists" or "lampreys" are? You're not alone, but you probably know that bats are *mammals*, making (A) the correct answer. Don't sweat the others!

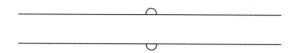

10. As the object is dropped from the rooftop, a transformation of energy takes place involving the object's heat (Q), its potential energy due to Earth's gravity (GPE_o), and its kinetic energy (KE_o). Which of the following best describes the relationship between these three variables?

    F. Energy is conserved as GPE_o and Q are converted into KE_o.
    G. Energy is lost as KE_o and Q are converted into GPE_o.
    H. Energy is conserved as GPE_o is converted to KE_o and Q.
    J. Energy is lost as Q is converted to GPE_o and KE_o.

Here's How to Crack It

We haven't provided any part of the passage for this question because no part of the passage can help us. This one is purely based on outside knowledge. The correct answer is (H). Energy is always conserved: even energy that is "lost" technically becomes something else, so no energy is ever lost, which eliminates (G) and (J). Then, *kinetic energy* is the energy of movement, so that must be on the other side of the conversion. The same is true for *heat*, because an object will not heat up when it's sitting at rest.

NO SCIENCE DRILL

In this passage, we have removed all the "science" from the passage. All the variables have been renamed with silly names, and all the text has been removed. You only have the charts and six questions. Good luck!

Passage I

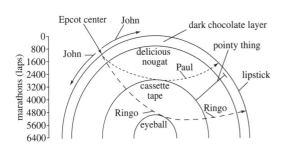

Figure 1

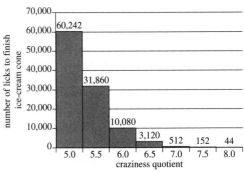

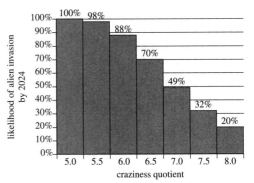

Figure 2

Table 1		
Beatle	Marathon lap range (laps)	Lipstick brightness (omg)
John	0–10	2.0–4.5
Paul	0–2921	3.0–4.0
Ringo	0–5180	5.0–7.0

1. Figure 1 defines the pointy thing as a region of the Smiley Face that overlaps with which of the following savory appetizers?

   I. Cassette tape
   II. Delicious nougat
   III. Dark chocolate layer

   A. II only
   B. I and II only
   C. II and III only
   D. I, II, and III

2. A Beatle was fawned over in a green room. The average lipstick brightness of this Beatle was 3 omgs, and his maximum marathon laps occurred in the delicious nougat. Based on Figure 1 and Table 1, the Beatle observed was most likely:

   F. John.
   G. Paul.
   H. George.
   J. Ringo.

3. Given the data in Figure 2, the likelihood of an alien invasion by 2024 decreases by more than half when comparing which of the following two craziness quotients?

   A. 5.0 and 6.0
   B. 6.0 and 6.5
   C. 6.5 and 7.5
   D. 7.5 and 8.0

4. According to Figure 2, the likelihood of an alien invasion by 2024 is lowest for which of the following ranges of craziness quotient?

   F. 5.5 to 6.0
   G. 6.0 to 6.5
   H. 6.5 to 7.0
   J. 7.0 to 7.5

5. Based on Figure 2, the ratio of craziness quotient 5.5 ice-cream-cone licks to craziness quotient 5.0 ice-cream-cone licks can be expressed approximately by which of the following fractions?

   A. $\dfrac{1}{3}$
   B. $\dfrac{1}{2}$
   C. $\dfrac{2}{3}$
   D. $\dfrac{3}{2}$

6. Suppose a fourth Beatle, George, reaches the eyeball layer. Based on Figure 1 and Table 1, the minimum lipstick brightness for George is most likely:

   F. less than 2.0 omg.
   G. between 2.0 and 3.5 omg.
   H. between 3.5 and 5.0 omg.
   J. greater than 5.0 omg.

NO SCIENCE DRILL ANSWERS AND EXPLANATIONS

1. **C** The question asks for the *savory appetizers* that *overlap* with *the pointy thing*, according to Figure 1. Look at Figure 1 for the line representing the pointy thing. The solid line representing the pointy thing covers the delicious nougat and the dark chocolate layer. Eliminate (A) and (B) because they do not include the dark chocolate layer. The line representing the pointy thing does not cover cassette tape, so eliminate (D). The correct answer is (C).

2. **G** The question asks for the *Beatle most likely observed*, based on Figures 1 and 2, given that *the average lipstick brightness of this Beatle was 3 omgs, and his maximum marathon laps occurred in the delicious nougat*. Lipstick brightness is shown in Table 1, so start by looking at Table 1. In Table 1, John has a lipstick brightness of 2.0–4.5 omgs, Paul has a lipstick brightness of 3.0–4.0 omgs, and Ringo has a lipstick brightness of 5.0–7.0 omgs. Eliminate (J) because Ringo's lipstick brightness range does not include 3.0. Eliminate (H) because George does not appear in Table 1. Next, look at the lines for John and Paul in Figure 1. John does not move past the lipstick, whereas Paul's line goes into the delicious nougat. The correct answer is (G).

3. **C** The question asks for *two craziness quotients* that, when compared, show a *decrease greater than half* in *the likelihood of an alien invasion by 2024*, according to Figure 2. Look at Figure 2 and start with (A). Choice (A) shows a decrease from 100% to 88%, which is less than half, so eliminate (A). Choice (B) shows a decrease from 88% to 70%, which is also less than half, so eliminate (B). Choice (C) shows a decrease from 70% to 32%, which is just over half. Keep (C). Choice (D) shows a decrease from 32% to 20%, which is less than half. Eliminate (D). Only (C) shows a decrease greater than half. The correct answer is (C).

4. **J** The question asks for the *craziness quotient* that results in the *lowest likelihood of an alien invasion by 2024*, according to Figure 2. Look at Figure 2 and determine the relationship between craziness quotient and the likelihood of an alien invasion by 2024. Figure 2 shows an inverse relationship—as the craziness quotient increases, the likelihood of an alien invasion by 2024

decreases. Therefore, the lowest likelihood of an alien invasion must occur at the highest craziness quotient. Choice (J) shows the highest range of craziness quotient. The correct answer is (J).

5. **B** The question asks for *the ratio of craziness quotient 5.5 ice-cream-cone licks to craziness quotient 5.0 ice-cream-cone licks*, based on Figure 2. The first graph in Figure 2 shows the relationship between craziness quotient and the number of licks to finish ice-cream cone. So, look at the first graph in Figure 2 and determine the number of ice-cream-cone licks at craziness quotient 5.5 and at craziness quotient 5.0. According to this graph, the number of ice-cream-cone licks at craziness quotient 5.5 is 31,860, and the number of ice-cream-cone licks at craziness quotient 5.0 is 60,242. The ratio 31,860:60,242 is approximately 30,000:60,000, which can be reduced to 1/2. The correct answer is (B).

6. **J** The question asks for *the minimum lipstick brightness for George*, based on Figure 1 and Table 1, given that *George reaches the eyeball layer*. Figure 1 shows the number of marathons in laps and the layers each Beatle reaches, and Table 1 shows the marathon lap range and lipstick brightness for each Beatle. Start by looking at Table 1 to determine the relationship between the number of marathon laps and lipstick brightness. Marathon lap range and lipstick brightness show a direct relationship—as the marathon lap range increases, the lipstick brightness also increases. Next, look at Figure 1 to determine the relationship between the number of marathons in laps and the layers each Beatle reaches. As the number of marathons increases, each Beatle is able to go to deeper layers. Since the eyeball layer is the deepest layer, and no other Beatle has been able to reach the eyeball layer, George will need a minimum lipstick brightness greater than any other Beatle. The lowest minimum lipstick brightness is 5.0 omgs for the other Beatles, so George needs a minimum lipstick brightness greater than 5.0. The correct answer is (J).

Chapter 21
Basic Approach

You don't need to know science facts for the ACT. For the most part, the Science test is an open book test, with the passages offering the content you need to answer nearly all the questions. According to ACT, you do need scientific reasoning skills. To earn your highest possible score on the Science test, you also need an efficient and strategic approach to working the passages. In this chapter, we'll teach you how to apply your scientific reasoning skills to quickly assess the content of the passage and figures and make your way methodically through the questions.

THE BASIC APPROACH AND "NOW" PASSAGES

The introduction to this Science section sought to make a very simple point. By the end of the previous chapter, you should have been able to work a passage from which the real science had been removed entirely. This is all part of our big strategy for the Science Test—from which everyone, from low scorers to high scorers, can benefit:

Don't try to understand the science. Just get the points.

We will continue to deepen this point as we go along, and you've already seen how Process of Elimination (POE) and The Scientific Method can help with passages that might otherwise seem hopelessly arcane.

In this chapter, we're going to talk about the basics of how to take the Science Test. We will particularly focus on POOD, or Personal Order of Difficulty, as a means to guide us through the Science Test in the most efficient way possible.

THE NUTS AND BOLTS OF ACT SCIENCE

The Science Test will always be the last of the multiple-choice sections on the ACT. Like the other three tests, the Science Test is scored from 1 to 36 and is factored into the composite score. Like the Reading Test, the Science Test takes 35 minutes and is made up of 40 questions.

The Science Test consists of six passages. ACT breaks them down into three categories: Data Representations, Research Summaries, and Conflicting Viewpoints. The last one, which we've renamed "Dual Science," is the only one you really need to be on the lookout for. See Chapter 23 for more on the strange animal known as "Dual Science."

We break sections down in a more useful way. As this chapter will discuss in detail, we break the passages down according to their difficulty rather than to the fairly arbitrary category names that ACT gives them. Who cares if we're dealing with a "Data Representations" passage or a "Research Summaries" passage if we're going to approach them both the same way?

Pacing

We have discussed pacing in previous chapters, and pacing is no less important on the Science Test than it is elsewhere on the ACT.

That said, there are 40 questions on the Science Test and 36 scaled points. That practically amounts to a one-to-one ratio, so if you're looking for a score in the 30s, you will have to do most or all of the questions.

Look back at the Scaled Score chart on page 24 of this book. On that scale, you can see that each question is essentially worth one scaled point, and if you want anything greater than a 28, you'll need to complete all of the passages.

Because there is so much weight on each passage, you must work as efficiently as possible. As such, the emphasis on the Science Test is much more on your POOD than on pacing. Even though you will need to attempt all the questions, that's not the end of the story by a long shot.

POOD

When we break down a Science Test, we're not overly concerned with the "type" of passage we're dealing with. We've got our own rubric: Now, Later, and Last passages. ACT will give you the six passages in a random order of difficulty. It's up to you to put the passages in an order than makes sense.

The order you select will ultimately be about what *you* find easiest, but here are a few guidelines as to which ACT passages we've found our students have the easiest time with.

Note: You may be asking, "If I have to do all the passages anyway, what difference does it make what order I do them in?"

- The answer is simple: even if you have to do all the passages, the Now passages still provide your best chance to maximize your score. It makes sense to focus the most attention on the passages that will generate the most points. The question that takes five seconds is worth the same amount as the question that takes five minutes!
- There is also value in warming up on the Science Test. It really is a unique section on the ACT (and there's nothing like it on the SAT or PSAT), so if you can warm up on some easy stuff, your brain will be primed for the harder stuff.

Let's think about what makes easy and hard passages. Because we're talking about POOD here, remember that this is all about what *you* find easiest, but even for the most idiosyncratic test-taker, we've got one big piece of advice about reordering the passages:

Go with your gut. If a passage or question looks easy, it probably is.

As we've said above, we like to divide passages into Now, Later, and Last. This is an inexact science (surprise on the ACT!), but here are a few basic guidelines:

Now Passages

Now passages are the ones on which you can usually get the most points in the least time. Here's what you want to look for in Now passages:

- **Easy-to-read tables and graphs**
- **Numbers in the figures**
  You'll see some figures that have words or symbols—those are much more challenging to evaluate. It's a lot easier to spot trends and patterns when you have numbers in the figures.
- **Easy-to-spot, consistent trends**
- **Numbers and number words in the questions**
  Just as figures with numbers are easy to read, questions with numbers are typically easier to answer. Also be on the lookout for what we call "number words": words like "greater," "less," "increase," and "decrease."
- **Shortness and white space**
  Short passages and short questions are typically easier for the simple reason that they contain less information. The passages with the most blank space are typically the easier ones.

Let's look at an example. Below are six figures from six different passages within a single test. Which would be the Now figures among them?

I.

Table 2			
Coin sample	Time (min)	Silver coating concentration (ppb)	Zinc nitrate concentration (ppb)
V	5	75	30
VI	15	125	55
VII	30	200	75
VIII	60	500	85

Figure I

II.

Table 1

Carbons in the chain	Name prefix	Structure		
		alkane (suffix -ane)	alcohol (suffix -anol)	aldehyde (suffix -analdehyde)
4	but-	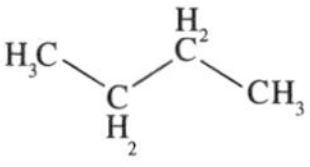	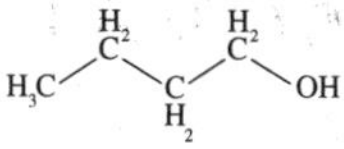	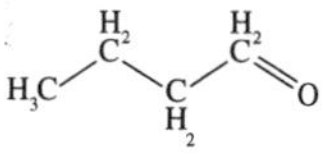
5	pent-	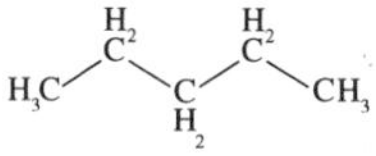	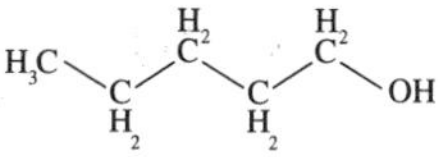	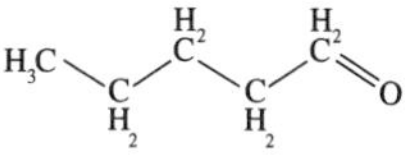
6	hex-	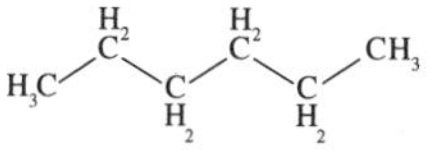	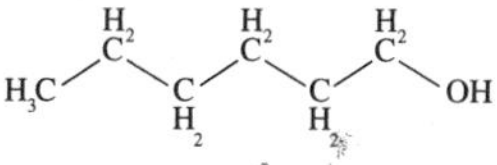	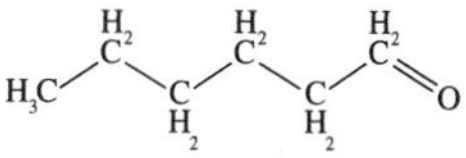
7	hept-	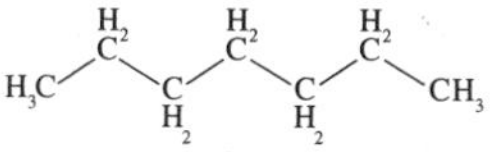	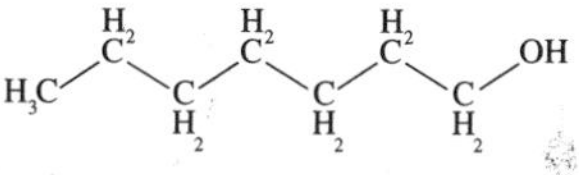	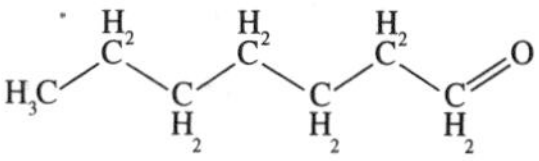
8	oct-	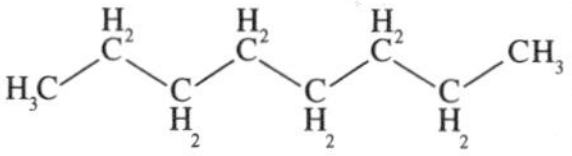	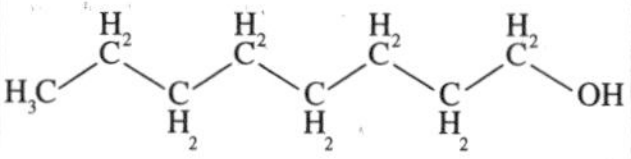	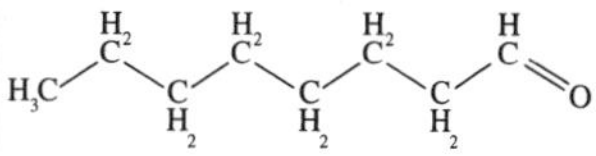

Figure II

III.

Table 1

Trial	Measured period (sec)	
	lead cube	tin cube
1	1.48	1.51
2	1.45	1.47
3	1.46	1.42
4	1.49	1.45
5	1.39	1.53

Figure III

IV.

ancestral self-replicating RNA

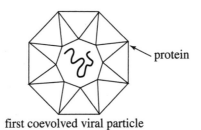

first coevolved viral particle

Figure IV

V.

Table 1				
Soil	Topsoil deflation (kg/ha) by percentage of organic cover			
	0%	25%	50%	75%
X	105,000	68,000	46,000	20,000
Y	65,000	42,000	28,500	12,000

Figure V

VI.

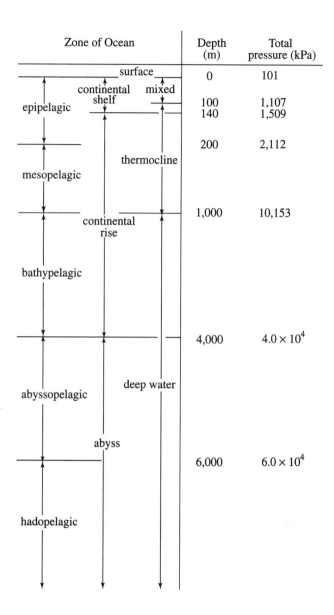

Figure VI

With no context at all, and with only one figure from each passage, you can likely already see an order of difficulty taking shape. The Now figures are those with the most obvious relationships:

Figure I is about as simple as they come: an easy-to-read chart in which all the variables increase from top to bottom.

Figure II looks like a more complicated chemistry passage. Whichever passage this belongs to will be a Later passage.

Figure III contains an easy-to-read table with two variables and multiple trials, but the relationships are not consistent, so we would certainly save this one for after Figure I.

Figure IV shows a diagram of RNA and a viral particle. There are no relationships or trends shown, so this is probably a reading heavy passage that is likely more time-consuming than the previous passages.

Figure V is a short table with consistent trends showing decreases from left to right and top to bottom. This figure should be fairly easy to work with.

Figure VI is a little complicated looking with all the overlapping ocean zones, but it does show a consistent trend between Depth and Total pressure. This figure is likely harder than Figure I or Figure V but easier than Figure II and Figure IV.

Therefore, if we were to pick out our Now passages, they would probably be the ones containing Figures I and V. The passages containing Figures III and VI would likely be Later. We'll save the passage containing Figures II and IV for Last.

THE BASIC APPROACH

Now that we've reviewed the overall layout of the Science Test and how to spot the easier passages within it, let's dive into the Basic Approach.

Our Basic Approach is informed by the three main tenets we established in Chapter 20:

- Don't try to understand the science.
- Use POE.
- Let the questions teach you what you need to know about the passage.

Our Basic Approach is just that: basic. It consists of three steps:

1. **Work the Figures**
   Look for variables and trends.

2. **Work the Questions**
   Work from easy to hard, from short to long.

3. **Work the Answers**
   Use POE.

You may note that there's nothing in this approach that says "Read the Passage." That's intentional. You will rarely need to refer to the text in an ACT Science passage. Most of the information you need will be contained within the figures. Don't read unless something in the question requires you to do so.

With all of this in mind, let's work the Now passage we selected as one of our Now passages in our analysis on page 346.

Passage V

Wind causes *topsoil deflation*, a type of erosion that is affected by plant and organic cover as well as water content of the soil. Scientists performed 2 experiments using equal-sized fields containing the same volume of soil. The soil samples were primarily a mixture of sand and silt, but differed in the percentage of clay they contained. Soil X was composed of 5% clay and Soil Y was composed of 40% clay. Large fans were used to simulate wind. Topsoil deflation was measured in kilograms per hectare (kg/ha) following 10 hours of wind.

Experiment 1

A mixture of compost and straw was used to represent plant and organic cover. The percentage of soil covered with the mixture was considered to approximate an equivalent percentage of natural vegetative cover. One field remained uncovered, and the other fields were covered with different percentages of compost and straw. The topsoil deflation from each field was recorded in Table 1.

Table 1				
Soil	Topsoil deflation (kg/ha) by percentage of organic cover			
	0%	25%	50%	75%
X	105,000	68,000	46,000	20,000
Y	65,000	42,000	28,500	12,000

Experiment 2

Rainfall was simulated using a sprinkler system. Sprinklers were turned on for either 4 hours or 8 hours for fields of each kind of soil. Two additional fields composed of each type of soil were left unwatered. Afterward, soil samples were taken from all of the fields to determine their water content percentage, which was recorded in Table 2. Wind was applied as in Experiment 1 and topsoil deflation for all fields was recorded in Table 3.

Table 2			
Soil	Water content of soil following various sprinkler times		
	0 hours	4 hours	8 hours
X	10%	13%	16%
Y	10%	14%	22%

Table 3			
Soil	Topsoil deflation (kg/ha) following various sprinkler times		
	0 hours	4 hours	8 hours
X	89,250	66,000	14,000
Y	53,400	40,100	10,300

Let's start by Working the Figures. On your practice passages and the actual test, make sure to mark these figures with arrows. Ignore the text until you need it!

Table 1

The variables are soil samples (X and Y) and topsoil deflation (kg/ha) by percentage of organic cover.

The relationships are inverse:

- For both soil samples, as the percentage of organic cover increases, topsoil deflation decreases.
- Soil X always has higher topsoil deflation values than Soil Y.

Table 2

The variables are soil samples (X and Y) and water content of soil following various sprinkler times.

The relationships are direct:

- For both soil samples, as sprinkler time increases, water content of soil also increases.
- Soil X and Soil Y have the same water content initially, but Soil X has lower water content values than Soil Y after 4 hours and after 8 hours.

Table 3

The variables are soil samples (X and Y) and topsoil deflation (kg/ha) following various sprinkler times.

The relationships are inverse:

- For both soil samples, as sprinkler time increases, topsoil deflation decreases.
- Soil X always has higher topsoil deflation values than Soil Y.

That's it! Let's move on to the questions. Here is the full set of questions for this passage, so mark these pages to come back to as we work through the questions in an order that makes sense.

28. A third soil, Soil Z, contains 45% clay. One field with Soil Z is covered with a mixture of compost and straw and subjected to 10 hours of simulated wind in the same procedure used in Experiment 1. At the conclusion of the trial, the topsoil deflation in the field was determined to be 26,000 kg/ha. The percentage of organic cover used on the field was most likely closest to:

   F.   0%.
   G.   25%.
   H.   50%.
   J.   75%.

29. According to the results of Experiments 1 and 2, topsoil deflation will be minimized by:

   A.   decreased organic cover, increased amount of rainfall, and the use of either Soil X or Y as topsoil.
   B.   decreased organic cover, decreased amount of rainfall, and the use of Soil Y as topsoil.
   C.   increased organic cover, increased amount of rainfall, and the use of Soil Y as topsoil.
   D.   increased organic cover, increased amount of rainfall, and the use of Soil X as topsoil.

30. If Experiment 1 were repeated using a soil containing 10% clay with 0% organic cover, which of the following would be the most likely topsoil deflation amount?

   F.   60,200 kg/ha
   G.   70,700 kg/ha
   H.   99,800 kg/ha
   J.   110,200 kg/ha

31. To further investigate the effect of water content on erosion from topsoil deflation, the scientists should repeat Experiment:

   A.   1, using a different type of topsoil.
   B.   1, using plastic covers over the fields.
   C.   2, using no sprinklers.
   D.   2, using fields exposed to various amounts of rainfall.

32. Which of the following assumptions was made in the design of Experiment 1 ?

    F. The quantity of topsoil deflation is independent of the percentage of clay present in the soil.

    G. The presence of straw on the soil does not accurately simulate vegetation and organic cover.

    H. Air movement from fans provides an accurate simulation of the wind responsible for topsoil deflation.

    J. Compost is more effective than water content in the prevention of topsoil erosion.

33. In Experiment 2, the water content in the two soil types was similar after 4 hours of sprinkling, yet the topsoil deflation was significantly different. Which of the following statements provides the best explanation for these findings?

    A. Topsoil erosion is independent of the water content found in the soil.

    B. Fields are susceptible to topsoil deflation only when water completely evaporates from the topsoil.

    C. Soil with a lower percentage of clay is more prone to erosion from topsoil deflation than one with a higher percentage of clay.

    D. Water is trapped in the topsoil by wind and this increases the rate of topsoil deflation.

34. If Experiment 2 were repeated with soil containing 10% clay, which of the following values would be expected for water content and topsoil deflation in a field following 8 hours of water sprinkling?

    F. Water content of 21%; topsoil deflation of 9,700 kg/ha
    G. Water content of 17%; topsoil deflation of 13,400 kg/ha
    H. Water content of 15%; topsoil deflation of 10,900 kg/ha
    J. Water content of 14%; topsoil deflation of 101,000 kg/ha

Working the Questions is largely a matter of selection. The first step is to choose the easiest available question. Use the same criteria here that you used in selecting a passage: look for numbers, number words, shortness, and simplicity.

Of the full set of questions on pages 350–351, Question 29 looks like a simple one: it is a short question with short answers based on relationships. Reread Question 29 carefully and then answer it.

Here's How to Crack #29

This question will draw upon the relationships we established as we Worked the Figures. We already know, for example, that the relationships were all consistent in that they were pure increases or decreases, with no fluctuation.

Work from the data given in the question. We want to minimize *topsoil deflation*. When we Worked the Figures in Table 1, we saw that as the percentage of organic cover increases, topsoil deflation decreases. Therefore, the smallest topsoil deflation value will occur with the highest percentage of organic cover. Eliminate (A) and (B). Both (C) and (D) include *increased amount of rainfall,* so skip to the third variable. When Working the Figures, we found that Soil X always has higher topsoil deflation values than Soil Y. So, to minimize the topsoil deflation, use Soil Y, as indicated in (C).

Question 31 looks like an easy one too: it's short and relies on the variables we identified while Working the Figures.

Here's How to Crack #31

These answer choices have two parts, so let's take them one at a time. Check the tables for water content. Only Table 2 mentions water content, which was a part of Experiment 2, so eliminate (A) and (B). From here, use common sense. If we want to study water content, the experiment must utilize different amounts of water. Only (D) mentions different amounts of water in the form of rainfall.

Question 33 requires us to use some of the introduction to find the difference between Soil X and Soil Y. Question 33 is therefore a good question to save for later.

Here's How to Crack #33

Work from the data given in the question. Skim the introduction for information about the difference between Soil X and Soil Y. The introduction says *Soil X was composed of 5% clay and Soil Y was composed of 40% clay.* Only (C) mentions clay content.

Question 30 also requires us to use some of the introduction. It mentions *clay,* which we didn't identify when Working the Figures, but we did read about to answer the previous question. Let's do that one next.

Here's How to Crack #30

Work from the data given in the question. We already know the clay content of Soils X and Y are 5% and 40%, respectively. A soil with 10% clay content should have values that fall between the values for Soil X and Soil Y at 0% organic cover. Identify 0% organic cover in Table 1; the relevant values will be in this column. The value should fall between 105,000 kg/ha and 65,000 kg/ha, so eliminate (F) and (J). From here, common sense will help: 10% clay content is much closer to 5% than 40%, so the value should be closer to the value for Soil X than Soil Y. Therefore, a value of 99,800 kg/ha is the best estimate, so choose (H).

Question 32 also uses information from the introduction, so let's do that one next.

Here's How to Crack #32

Table 1 in Experiment 1 compares topsoil deflation (kg/ha) by percentage of organic cover for two different soil samples. Because it's hard to know exactly what assumption was made in the design of Experiment 1, let's use the answer choices and POE. When Working the Figures, we determined that Soil X, which was composed of 5% clay, always has higher topsoil deflation values than Soil Y, which was composed of 40% clay. This contradicts (F), so eliminate (F). The description for Experiment 1 mentions that straw is used as the organic cover. The scientists wouldn't use straw as organic cover if it was not an accurate simulation, so we can eliminate (G). There's nothing in Table 1 that contradicts (H), so keep (H) for now. Experiment 1 does not compare the effects of compost and water content, so eliminate (J). By Process of Elimination, (H) must be correct.

Notice on this question that we avoided finding anything about fans. That information is in the introduction, but if we work the questions and answers in a smart, efficient way, we can continue to avoid that introduction.

On Question 34, we will use the same information about *clay content* in the introduction and analyze a soil with 10% clay content, so this is a good one to do next.

Here's How to Crack #34

These answer choices have two parts, so let's take them one at a time. We already know the clay contents of Soils X and Y are 5% and 40%, respectively. A soil with 10% clay content should have values that fall between the values for Soil X and Soil Y after 8 hours of sprinkler time. Identify 8 hours in Table 2; the relevant values for water content will be in this column. The value should fall between 16% and 22% water content, so eliminate (H) and (J). Identify 8 hours in Table 3; the relevant values for topsoil deflation will be in this column. The value should fall between 10,300 kg/ha and 14,000 kg/ha, so choose (G).

Question 28 also uses the *clay content* information in the introduction, but it is very long and should therefore be saved for last.

———————◯———————

Here's How to Crack #28

Work from the data given in the question. We already know that Soil X has a lower clay content than Soil Y. When Working the Figures, we determined that Soil X always has higher topsoil deflation values than Soil Y. Therefore, increasing the clay content of the soil decreases the topsoil deflation. Since the clay content for Soil Z is only slightly higher than the clay content for Soil Y, the topsoil deflation should be only slightly lower than that of Soil Y. Identify Soil Y in Table 1; the relevant values will be in this row. The value should be a little higher than 26,000 kg/ha. A topsoil deflation of 26,000 kg/ha is slightly less than the value of 28,500 kg/ha for Soil Y at 50% organic cover, as identified in (H).

———————◯———————

Passage V offers a simple application of the steps that we will use in most of the Science passages. The questions here are fairly simple, but the steps we used to answer them are the same steps that will help us to answer the most difficult questions.

Now let's look at something a bit more difficult.

For this passage, as we delve into each question, we'll also provide you with tips on how to handle some of the more complex things ACT can throw at you. Glance over this passage but then head straight to the instructional content after the questions associated with the passage.

> **Remember the Basic Approach.**
> 1. **Work the Figures**
>   Look for variables and trends.
> 2. **Work the Questions**
>   Work from easy to hard, from short to long.
> 3. **Work the Answers**
>   Use POE.

Passage II

Organic compounds are molecules that frequently contain carbon (C), hydrogen (H), and oxygen (O) joined together by covalent bonds (symbolized by straight lines in chemical notation). As the number of bonds to oxygen atoms increases in a carbon chain, the overall molecule is increasingly oxidized. For example, aldehydes are more oxidized than alcohols, which are more oxidized than alkanes, as shown in Table 1. The melting points of these compounds are listed in Table 2, and their *viscosities*, resistance to flow, are listed in Table 3.

Table 1			
Carbons in the chain	Name prefix	Structure		
		alkane (suffix -ane)	alcohol (suffix -anol)	aldehyde (suffix -analdehyde)
4	but-			
5	pent-			
6	hex-			
7	hept-			
8	oct-			

Table 2			
Carbons in the chain	Melting point (K)		
	alkane	alcohol	aldehyde
4	135	183	174
5	143	194	213
6	178	221	217
7	182	239	231
8	216	257	285

Table 3			
Carbons in the chain	Viscosity (cP) at 293 K		
	alkane	alcohol	aldehyde
4	0.01	3.0	0.4
5	0.24	5.1	0.5
6	0.29	5.4	0.8
7	0.39	5.8	1.0
8	0.54	8.4	1.2

8. Acetaldehyde is an aldehyde with a viscosity of less than 0.3 cP. Based on Tables 1 and 3, which of the following chemical structures most likely represents acetaldehyde?

F.

G.

H.

J.

9. Which organic compounds in Table 2 are solids at 215 K ?

A. All alkanes, alcohols, and aldehydes with 5 carbons or fewer

B. Alcohols and aldehydes with 6 or more carbons and octane

C. The 4- and 5-carbon alcohols and aldehydes, and all alkanes with 7 or fewer carbons

D. The 5-carbon pentane and pentanol compounds and the 4-carbon butane, butanol, and butanaldehyde

10. A scientist is emptying identical vials of several organic compounds, all in liquid form at 293 K, by tilting them downward at a consistent angle. Based on Tables 1 and 3, the vial containing which organic compound would take the greatest amount of time to empty?

    F. Octanol
    G. Octanaldehyde
    H. Hexanol
    J. Butane

11. According to Table 3, how do the different types of 5-carbon molecules differ with respect to their viscosity?

    A. The alkane has a higher viscosity than the aldehyde, and the aldehyde has a higher viscosity than the alcohol.
    B. The alkane has a higher viscosity than the alcohol, and the alcohol has a higher viscosity than the aldehyde.
    C. The alcohol has a higher viscosity than the alkane, and the alkane has a higher viscosity than the aldehyde.
    D. The alcohol has a higher viscosity than the aldehyde, and the aldehyde has a higher viscosity than the alkane.

12. For each type of organic compound, what is the relationship between the length of the carbon chain to the melting point and viscosity? As the number of carbons in the chain increases, the melting point:

    F. decreases, and the viscosity decreases.
    G. increases, and the viscosity increases.
    H. increases, but the viscosity decreases.
    J. decreases, but the viscosity increases.

13. According to Table 2, the difference in melting point between an alkane and an alcohol with the same number of carbons is approximately how much?

    A. 25 K
    B. 35 K
    C. 50 K
    D. 65 K

Let's ignore the text until we have a reason to look at it. Instead, let's focus on the tables.

Table 1

There aren't any numerical trends to note in this table, so let's just get a general idea of what it shows: the structure of various compounds and based on the number of "carbons in the chain" and whether the compound is an alkane, alcohol, or aldehyde. The name prefixes and suffixes are shown for each compound as well.

Table 2

The variables are "carbons in the chain" and "melting point (K)."

There is a consistent direct relationship:

- Within each type of compound (alkane, alcohol, or aldehyde), the melting point increases as the number of carbons in the chain increases.

Table 3

The variables are "carbons in the chain" and "viscosity (cP) at 293 K."

There is a consistent direct relationship:

- Within each type of compound, the viscosity increases as the number of carbons increases.

Now look back at the complete set of questions to determine a good order in which to work them. Make your plan; then see if it matches the order we follow below. Don't read the explanation until after you've tried each question. Remember when choosing your Now questions to look for numerical values and the number words such as *increases*, *decreases*, *higher*, and *lower* in the answer choices. Questions 12 and 13 are good questions to do first.

Here's How to Crack #12

We already noted that in Table 2, as the number of carbons in the chain increases, the melting point (K) increases. Eliminate (F) and (J). We also noted that in Table 3, as the carbons in the chain increase, the viscosity increases. Eliminate (H). The correct answer is (G).

___

Here's How to Crack #13

This question mentions Table 2, so refer to Table 2. Pick any number of carbons to start. For a four-carbon chain, the melting point of the alkane is 135 K and the melting point of the alcohol is 183 K. The difference is therefore 183 K – 135 K = 48. Eliminate (A) and (B) because they are too low. Eliminate (D) because 65 K is too big. Since 48 K is very close to 50 K, the correct answer is (C).

___

Of the remaining questions, Question 11 looks easiest because it just involves one table, is a short question, and the answer choices all include "higher viscosity," which refers to a numerical relationship.

___

Here's How to Crack #11

The question mentions Table 3, so refer to Table 3. In the 5-carbon chain, the alkane has a viscosity of 0.24 cP, the alcohol has a viscosity of 5.1 cP, and the aldehyde has a viscosity of 0.5 cP. Since the alkane has the lowest viscosity, eliminate (A), (B), and (C) because each one claims that the alkane has a higher viscosity than one of the other two types. The correct answer is (D).

___

Both Questions 8 and 10 ask about two tables, so let's try Question 9 next.

___

Here's How to Crack #9

The question mentions Table 2, so refer to Table 2. The variables in this table are carbons in the chain and melting point, but the question asks which compounds are solids at 215 K.

This question appears to be asking about a variable that is not shown in the table. A good rule of thumb is this:

If a question asks about a variable that is not labeled on a table or graph, there's a good chance that the variable is actually represented under another name. Use the relationships you know.

The melting point of a substance is the temperature at which a solid melts into a liquid. Therefore, at every temperature below the melting point, the substance is a solid; at every temperature above a melting point, the substance is a liquid (or a gas if it's above the boiling point as well). Let's do some POE. All of the alkanes except the 8-carbon alkane melt at a temperature below 215 K, so they would all be liquids at 215 K instead of solids. Eliminate (A) and (C), which both state that alkanes with fewer than 8 carbons are solids. For both the alcohols and the aldehydes, only those with 6 carbons or more have a melting point above 215 K. Eliminate (D) since there are no 4-carbon or 5-carbon compounds of any type with a melting point above 215 K. The only remaining answer is (B), so this must be correct. However, if you were confused by the octane, it can be helpful to ask yourself:

What's the link between the different figures and tables within the passage?

The number of carbons in the chain is in all of the tables. While Table 2 does not give any compound names, Table 1 does list the name prefix and suffix for each compound depending on the number of carbons in the chain and the compound type. The 8-carbon alkane has a prefix of oct- and a suffix of -ane, so octane is the 8-carbon alkane that we already noted has a melting point above 215 K. The correct answer is (B).

———————————○———————————

Since we just discussed the naming scheme of the compounds, let's do Question 10 next, which uses this concept in the answer choices.

———————————○———————————

Here's How to Crack #10

At first glance, it may not be obvious what variable we are looking for since time is not a variable in any of the tables, but there are a few clues in the question that we can use to get us started. For one, the question mentions Tables 1 and 3, so we do not need to refer to Table 2. Since Table 1 does not contain any numerical data, Table 3 is probably the best place to start. It's also helpful to know that, in general, when ACT is asking for a "least" or a "greatest," the answer will need to be one of the extremes. In this case, the answer is likely either the highest viscosity, which is the 8-carbon alcohol, or the lowest viscosity, which is the 4-carbon alkane. If we refer back to Table 1, we can see that the 8-carbon alcohol has the prefix oct- and the suffix -anol, while the 4-carbon alkane has the prefix but- and the suffix -ane. Therefore, the answer is likely to be either octanol or butane. Eliminate (G) and (H).

Pay close attention to extremes on ACT Science. ACT loves consistency!

Now, to choose between the two remaining answers, we are going to have to look for a relationship between viscosity and time. We will have to skim the passage a little to see if there is anything that relates to time. The first paragraph never mentions time, but it does define viscosity as *resistance to flow*.

Here, we're going to have to draw on one of the skills we all bring to the Science Test: common sense. If things make a kind of logical sense to you, go with the logical choice. In short:

When in doubt, use common sense. Take a leap of faith, pick an answer, and move on.

If something is resistant to flow, it makes logical sense that it would take a longer time to flow out of a vial. Therefore, the compound with the highest viscosity will likely take the greatest amount of time. The correct answer is (F).

———————————————○———————————————

Finally, let's try Question 8.

———————————————○———————————————

Here's How to Crack #8

Since this question has figures in the answers, it's good to keep in mind another basic strategy:

Shapes matter. Match the pictures to one another.

Let's look at the structures shown in Table 1. Notice that all of the alkanes end with a single line to CH_3 on the right-hand side, while all of the alcohols end in a single line to OH and all of the aldehydes end in a double line to O. Since the question states that acetaldehyde is an aldehyde, the right-hand side should be a double line to O. Eliminate (F) and (G). If you've taken chemistry, you may know that the double line indicates a double bond, but notice that this actual science knowledge wasn't necessary.

Now, to choose between (H) and (J), let's focus on the other piece of information the question stem provided: the viscosity of acetaldehyde is less than 0.3 cP. According to Table 3, this is less than the viscosity of any of the aldehydes shown. Remember that in Question 12 we already determined that the viscosity increases as the number of carbons in the chain increases. It may seem obvious, but always keep the following in mind when you are working a science passage:

Correct answers must agree with each other. Use answers from questions you've already completed to help with those you haven't.

Since the viscosity of acetaldehyde is lower than all of those shown in Table 3, it must have fewer than 4 carbons in the chain. Eliminate (H), which has 9 carbons. The correct answer must be (J).

CONCLUSION

In these two passages, we've shown you all the basic skills you'll need on the Science Test. Our strategy is driven by three main ideas:

- Don't try to understand the science.
- Use POE.
- Let the questions teach you what you need to know about the passage.

We'll talk more about the third idea in the next chapter, but we've already applied all of these ideas in the above passages. Notice how much easier the Science Test becomes when we remove all that distracting "science" from it!

These three main ideas have encouraged us to keep our Basic Approach simple and applicable to all Science Test passages. The Basic Approach consists of three steps:

1. **Work the Figures**
   Look for variables and trends.

2. **Work the Questions**
   Work from easy to hard, from short to long.

3. **Work the Answers**
   Use POE.

This approach will work on any Science passage, though some steps will be easier or harder depending on the type of passage. As we saw in this chapter as we worked through Passage II, there are a few basic trends and tricks for attacking ACT Science questions. Bear these in mind if you get stuck on a particular question:

1. **Pretty pictures**

   Shapes matter. Match the pictures to one another.

2. **Extreme consistency**

   Pay close attention to extremes on ACT Science. ACT loves consistency!

3. **Hidden in plain sight**

   If a question asks about a variable that is not labeled on a table or graph, there's a good chance that the variable is actually represented under another name. Use the relationships you know.

4. **Right now, right again**

   Correct answers must agree with each other. Use answers from questions you've already completed to help with those you haven't.

5. **Common sense**

   When in doubt, use common sense. Take a leap of faith, pick an answer, and move on.

> Now try these strategies on your own. Go online to your Student Tools and answer the Chapter 21 Drill.

Chapter 22
Trends and Patterns

The Science Test on the ACT is fundamentally assessing your ability to work with data. This can almost always be done with no reference to the text. Be trendy! The bulk of the questions require you to spot, evaluate, and synthesize trends and relationships in figures and viewpoints, so look for trends within a figure or viewpoint. Most charts and graphs on the ACT Science contain basic trends. You can use these trends to predict values that are not explicitly shown on the figures. Sometimes you will have to read two sets of data at once, and these figures can seem unrelated to one another. The key to decoding passages with such figures is to find the link between the figures—there will always be one. Look for relationships between figures or viewpoints to find the points of intersection and consistency. If you are unable to decode the figures or identify any trends, move on to the questions. Use the keywords or key data points from the questions and answers to get you started. Let these teach you what the passage means.

"LATER" AND "LAST" PASSAGES: THE QUESTIONS HOLD THE ANSWERS

In this chapter, we will look at some more difficult Science passages and some of the ways that the answer choices can teach us what we need to know about challenging passages. Our Basic Approach remains the same:

1. **Work the Figures**
   Look for variables and trends.

2. **Work the Questions**
   Work from easy to hard, from short to long.

3. **Work the Answers**
   Use POE.

Believe it or not, as the passages become more complex, it is equally important to remember: *Don't try to understand the science.* In this chapter, we will particularly focus on effective ways to use POE and to let the questions teach us about the passage.

Passage V is a bit of a monster, but if we use the questions, we can find everything we need to know and select answer choices confidently.

Passage V

The term "evolution" is often used in the context of biological changes in organism populations over time, but it can also be applied to the change in the chemical composition of the Earth's atmosphere. The hypotheses of two studies claim that this *chemical evolution* has altered the types of chemicals found in the atmosphere between the early stages of Earth's existence and the present day.

Study 1

Based on the hypothesis that volcanic eruptions were the source of gases in the early Earth's atmosphere, scientists recreated four model volcanic eruptions in closed chambers, each containing different percentages of the same volcanic particulate matter. They then observed the gases in the air above this model over time. The percent composition of this air after 1 day, when the air achieved a *steady state* of constant gas concentrations, is represented in Table 1.

Since the experiment provided only a suggestion of the gas levels in the early Earth's atmosphere, the scientists then analyzed the amount of trapped gases in sediment layers, which indicate the changing atmospheric levels of gases over billions of years. The data collected on O_2 and H_2O vapor are presented in Figure 1.

Study 2

A separate study used the same volcanic models as in Study 1, but hypothesized that the scientists in Study 1 underestimated the amount of H_2 in the early Earth atmosphere. They proposed a different composition of gases, highlighting an increased H_2 level in the atmosphere, also represented in Table 1. Based on this new data, the scientists proposed an alternative graph for the changing atmospheric levels of O_2 and H_2O vapor, also shown in Figure 1.

Table 1					
		Percent composition of gas			
Volcanic eruption models		1	2	3	4
Study 1 (low H_2 atmosphere)	H_2	3	2	1	0
	H_2O vapor	85	80	75	70
	CO_2	10	10	10	15
	H_2S	2	5	7	8
	N_2	0.5	1	2	2
	CH_4	0.3	0.3	0.3	0.3
	CO	0.05	0.05	0.05	0.05
Study 2 (high H_2 atmosphere)	H_2	45	40	35	30
	H_2O vapor	40	40	35	35
	CO_2	10	10	10	15
	H_2S	2	5	7	8
	N_2	0.5	1	2	2
	CH_4	0.3	0.3	0.3	0.3
	CO	0.05	0.05	0.05	0.05

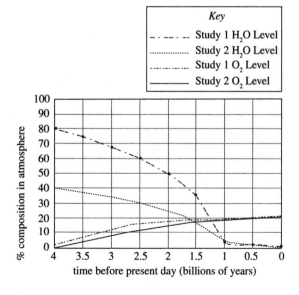

Key
– . –– . –– Study 1 H_2O Level
.... Study 2 H_2O Level
–– . –– . –– Study 1 O_2 Level
———— Study 2 O_2 Level

Figure 1

When we Work the Figures in this passage, we come up with almost nothing. Table 1 has no consistent trends, and Figure 1 has two contrary trends. The one thing we can see from Figure 1 is that the H_2O levels go down as the O_2 levels go up. Since there's not much we can do with the figures, let's see if the questions can help to elucidate the passage. Glance through the complete set, then we will work through them together.

29. According to the results of Study 2, between 4 and 3 billion years before the present day, the percent composition of O_2 in the atmosphere:

    A. increased only.
    B. increased, then decreased.
    C. decreased only.
    D. decreased, then increased.

30. According to the results of Study 1, the percent composition of H_2O vapor in the atmosphere decreased most rapidly over what period of time?

    F. Between 2.5 and 2 billion years ago
    G. Between 2 and 1.5 billion years ago
    H. Between 1.5 and 1 billion years ago
    J. Between 1 and 0.5 billion years ago

31. Suppose that the actual early Earth atmosphere had a high H_2 composition of 42%. Based on Study 2, is it likely that the corresponding H_2S and N_2 compositions of this atmosphere were each 3% ?

	3% H_2S	3% N_2
A.	Yes	Yes
B.	Yes	No
C.	No	Yes
D.	No	No

32. Suppose that in a new trial in Study 2, the percent composition of H_2 in the atmosphere was set at 33% and the percent composition of N_2 was found to be 2%. The percent composition of H_2O vapor in this trial would most likely be:

    F. greater than 30% and less than 35%.
    G. exactly 35%.
    H. greater than 35% and less than 40%.
    J. greater than 40%.

33. Consider an early Earth environment that featured microorganisms. Based on the results of Study 2, is it more likely that *aerobic organisms* (those that require O_2 to survive) or *anaerobic organisms* (those that do not require O_2 to survive) would have existed on Earth 4 billion years ago?

    A. Aerobic organisms, because of the high H_2O level 4 billion years ago

    B. Aerobic organisms, because of the low O_2 level 4 billion years ago

    C. Anaerobic organisms, because of the high H_2O level 4 billion years ago

    D. Anaerobic organisms, because of the low O_2 level 4 billion years ago

34. According to Study 2, how long did it take the H_2O vapor level to decrease to 75% of its composition 4 billion years before the present day?

    F. 0.5 billion years

    G. 1 billion years

    H. 1.5 billion years

    J. 2 billion years

Looking at this set of questions, you can see that Question 29 is clearly the place to start because it is short and has number words in the answer choices.

Here's How to Crack #29

This question is about as easy as they come. Let's go back to Figure 1 and look between 4 and 3 billion years before the present day. The question asks about the O_2 level, which increases during this period. The best answer is (A).

Let's move on to Question 30, which deals with the same figure and is similarly short.

Here's How to Crack #30

Again, let's use Figure 1, though this time we will look at H_2O rather than O_2. Because it's hard to know exactly which range showed the most rapid decrease, let's use the answer choices and POE.

Between 2.5 and 2 billion years ago, the percent composition decreased by about 10. Between 2 and 1.5 billion years ago, it decreased by about 15. Between 1.5 and 1 billion years ago, it decreased by about 30. Between 1 and 0.5 billion years ago, it decreased very little. The greatest decrease occurred between 1.5 and 1 billion years ago, as (H) suggests.

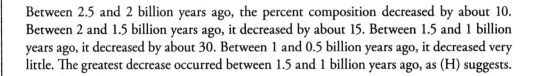

Question 31 asks about Table 1, which we have not yet used because we found no consistent trends. This question will help us to see how the table works.

Here's How to Crack #31

This question asks us to determine a relationship where we could not find one before. Let's look back at the chart now that we know what we're looking for: an H_2 composition of 42%.

In Study 2 on Table 1, H_2 values decrease from left to right. The other relevant values for this question, H_2S and N_2, increase as H_2 values decrease. With this pattern in place, we can begin to make some predictions. An H_2 composition of 42% would fall between volcanic eruption models 1 and 2. As a result, the H_2S and N_2 will need to be between the model 1 and 2 values as well. That puts H_2S between 2% and 5% and N_2 between 0.5% and 1%. With these ranges, we can answer the question: H_2S could be 3%, but N_2 could not, as (B) indicates.

Question 32 asks a very similar question, one that begins with the word *Suppose.*

Here's How to Crack #32

We saw in the last question that there are more relationships in Table 1 than initially meets the eye. H_2, for example, decreases, making predictions about H_2 levels possible.

If the H_2 level in this question is 33%, that would put the value right between volcanic eruption models 3 and 4. Further, the N_2 value in both models 3 and 4 is 2%, which matches what is given in our question. Finally, we look at H_2O vapor, which is 35% in both trials, at H_2 compositions of both 30% and 35%. We have no good reason to think that the H_2O vapor levels will change, so we can infer that the value will be exactly 35%, as it was in the other two models. Choice (G) is the only answer that can work.

———————○———————

Question 33 is much wordier than the others we've seen, but hopefully by this point, you're able to see all the POE opportunities in the answer choices before you've even read the question.

———————○———————

Here's How to Crack #33
Right off the bat, we can eliminate (A) and (C), which address the H_2O levels in a question that is exclusively concerned with O_2 levels. Then, because all that remains are options that refer to "the low O_2 level 4 billion years ago," the organisms *must* be anaerobic, given that anaerobic organisms "do not require O_2 to survive." Only (D) can work, and we didn't need the figures at all! All you need is POE.

———————○———————

Question 34 seems to ask for a synthesis of all the information in the passage, but let's see.

———————○———————

Here's How to Crack #34
We're back to the graph. Don't overthink this one! In Study 2, 4 billion years ago, the H_2O vapor level was 40%, and 75% of that would be an H_2O vapor level of 30%. In Study 2, the H_2O vapor level is 30% approximately 2.5 billion years ago. From 4 billion to 2.5 billion is 1.5 billion, or (H).

———————○———————

In conclusion, we entrusted our knowledge of this passage to the questions, and as we've now seen, we need to know *very* little about the passage itself beyond the figures. The questions helped us to see the relationships in the figure that we would not have otherwise seen, and they guided us through a series of figures we had an almost impossible time trying to "work" in the first step.

CONFUSING FIGURES AND THE QUESTIONS WHO LOVE THEM

In this exercise, you will be given a confusing figure and a question associated with it. Note how the question tells you what you need to know about the figure. Answers and explanations will be at the end of the exercise.

Table 1		
% shells with the following scute pattern:		
Age of shells (years)	M-m-M-M-m	M-M-m-m-M	M-m-M-m-M
120,000	46	44	10
90,000	42	54	4
87,000	30	67	3
85,000	21	72	7
80,000	20	66	14
50,000	76	21	3
27,000	100	0	0
15,000	100	0	0
8,000	100	0	0
4,000	100	0	0
1,000	68	28	4
300	74	20	6
0	86	2	12

1. Suppose, in Study 1, the scientists had found another seabed layer with fossilized shells that were radiocarbon dated and found to be 86,000 years old. Based on the results of Study 1, the scute pattern percents for the group of shells would most likely have been closest to which of the following?

	M-m-M-M-m	M-M-m-m-M	M-m-M-m-M
A.	100%	0%	0%
B.	50%	25%	25%
C.	36%	61%	4%
D.	26%	69%	5%

Table 1						
	Relative abundance (%)			Altitude above cloud tops where most abundant (km)		
Gas	Jupiter	Neptune	Saturn	Jupiter	Neptune	Saturn
H	86.1	79.0	96.1	−1,000 to −70,000	−10,000 to −23,000	−1,000 to −60,000
He	13.6	18.0	3.3	−500 to −1,000	−500 to −10,000	−500 to −900
CH_3	0.2	3.0	0.4	0 to 300	−100 to 0	0 to 200
NH_3	0.0045	0	0.0035	0 to −100	–	−50 to −200
H_2O vapor	0.0055	0	0.0065	−50 to −100	–	−200 to −300

2. Considering only the gases listed in Table 1, which gas is more abundant in the atmosphere of Jupiter than in the atmosphere of either Neptune or Saturn?

   F. H
   G. CH_3
   H. NH_3
   J. He

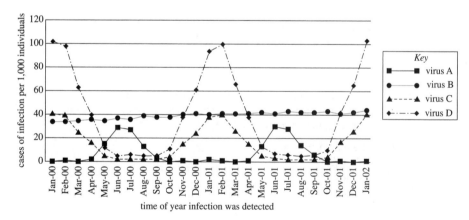

Figure 1

3. According to Figure 1, the incidence of *at least 3* of the viruses is most alike during which of the following months?

   A. April 2000
   B. September 2000
   C. November 2001
   D. January 2002

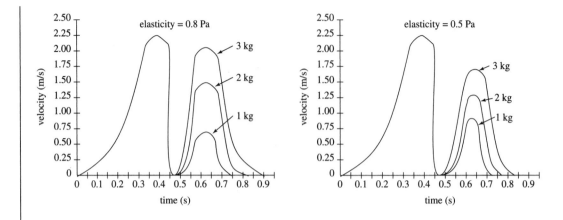

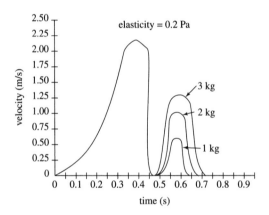

Figure 2

4. Based on the information in Figure 2, a ball being dropped from a 1 meter height with an elasticity of 0.2 Pa and a weight of 0.5 kg would have a maximum post-impact velocity of:

   F. less than 0.50 m/s.
   G. 0.75 m/s.
   H. 1.0 m/s.
   J. greater than 1.25 m/s.

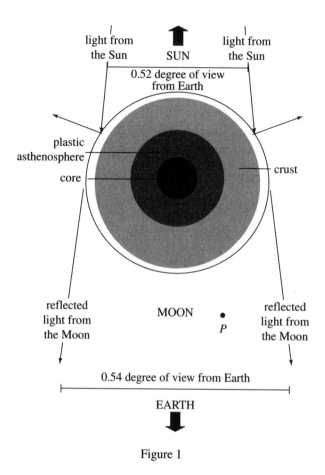

light from
the Sun

SUN

light from
the Sun

0.52 degree of view
from Earth

plastic
asthenosphere

core

crust

reflected
light from
the Moon

MOON

• P

reflected
light from
the Moon

0.54 degree of view from Earth

EARTH

Figure 1

5. Figure 1 shows that a lunar orbiter at point *P* would be able to view which of the following?

A. The Moon only
B. The Sun only
C. The Moon and the Earth only
D. The Moon, the Sun, and the Earth

CONFUSING FIGURES DRILL ANSWERS AND EXPLANATIONS

1. **D** The question asks for the *scute pattern percents* for *fossilized shells that were radiocarbon dated and found to be 86,000 years old*, based on the results of Study 1. The results of Study 1 are shown in Table 1, so look for 86,000 years in Table 1. 86,000 years is not shown in Table 1, but 87,000 years and 85,000 years are both shown in Table 1. The scute pattern percents for shells 86,000 years old should fall between the percents for shells 85,000 years old and 87,000 years old. 21% of shells 85,000 years old have the M-m-M-M-m scute pattern. 30% of shells 87,000 years old have the M-m-M-M-m scute pattern. Thus, between 21% and 30% of shells 86,000 years old should have the M-m-M-M-m scute pattern. The only value between 21% and 30% for M-m-M-M-m is 26% in (D). The correct answer is (D).

2. **H** The question asks for the gas that is *more abundant in the atmosphere of Jupiter than in the atmosphere of either Neptune or Saturn*, according to Table 1. Look at Table 1 and determine which gas has a higher relative abundance for Jupiter than for Neptune or Saturn. The relative abundance of NH_3 is 0.0045% for Jupiter, 0% for Neptune, and 0.0035% for Saturn. The correct answer is (H).

3. **B** The question asks for the month when *the incidence of at least 3 of the viruses is most alike*, according to Figure 1. Refer to Figure 1 for each month given in the answer choices. Find the month in which at least 3 of the viruses have a similar number of cases of infection. Choices (A), (C), and (D) all refer to months in which the number of cases of infection for the viruses is fairly spread out. Only (B) gives a month, September 2000, in which 3 viruses, viruses A, C, and D, have similar numbers of cases. The correct answer is (B).

4. **F** The question asks for the *maximum post-impact* velocity of *a ball* dropped from a *1 meter height with an elasticity of 0.2 Pa and a weight of 0.5 kg*, based on Figure 2. The third graph in Figure 2 shows 0.2 Pa, so look at the third graph to determine the relationship between mass and velocity. The figure shows that as the mass decreases from 3 kg to 2 kg to 1 kg, the velocity at any given time also decreases. Since there is a direct relationship between mass and velocity, and 0.5 kg is less than 1 kg, the maximum post-impact velocity

of a ball weighing 0.5 kg will be less than the maximum post-impact velocity of a ball weighing 1.0 kg. The maximum post-impact velocity of the 1.0 kg ball is approximately 0.50 m/s, so the maximum post-impact velocity of a 0.5 kg ball will be less than 0.50 m/s, as (F) indicates. The correct answer is (F).

5. **C** The question asks what *a lunar orbiter at point P would be able to view*, according to Figure 1. Find Point *P* in Figure 1. Point *P* is between the Moon and the Earth, so someone standing at point *P* would be able to see both the Moon and the Earth. Eliminate (A), which does not contain the Earth, and eliminate (B), which does not contain the Moon. Since the Moon is between Point *P* and the Sun, thus blocking the light from the Sun, an orbiter at Point *P* would not be able to see the Sun. Eliminate (D). Only (C) contains both the Moon and the Earth, but not the Sun. The correct answer is (C).

Now try these strategies on your own. Go online to your Student Tools and answer the Chapter 22 Drill.

Chapter 23
Dual Science
Passages

There is one more type of passage on the Science test, one which is based on more than one theory or viewpoint. Two, three, or possibly more conflicting views on a scientific phenomenon will be presented. The biggest difference from other Science passages is that they rarely depict much information in figures, which means that you have to read. While that probably puts them close to the end of your POOD on the Science Test, it does not mean you have to panic when you get there: treat these passages as the reading passages they really are. Plan out the order in which you will read the scientists' theories, and work one theory at a time before tackling the questions that require comparing and contrasting all of the theories.

DUAL SCIENCE PASSAGES

The previous two chapters have discussed how to work just about any science passage on the ACT, particularly giving some tips and tricks for how to deal with even the most difficult questions. In particular, we've shown how to work with any type of figure—whether working that figure early on or using the questions to understand the figures.

But there's one type of ACT Science passage that sometimes has no figures at all. In fact, this kind of passage is frequently all words, and the questions are long with no numbers or number words. If you come across one of these passages, don't worry. You're probably looking at ACT Science's anomaly: "Conflicting Viewpoints," or as we like to call it, "Dual Science."

We've given these passages their own chapter because they require a different approach. Whereas the other passages are built around working with figures, Dual Science passages don't give us that luxury. Sometimes they'll have figures; sometimes they won't. Sometimes the paragraphs are short; sometimes they're really long. Sometimes there will be two scientists or students duking it out; sometimes there will be more.

We do know a few things for sure, though:

- There will always be one Dual Science passage on the Science Test.
- That passage will have 7 questions.
- That passage will have more text than many of the others in the section.

This isn't much info, but from this alone, we can see also that Dual Science is last in many people's POODs. Think about all the things that are made for "Now" passages (numbers, number words, trends, charts, graphs, shortness). None of that is necessarily in the Dual Science passage.

If you love to read, however, or if you're scoring 32 or above on the Reading Test, then Dual Science might draw on some of your most refined skills. For you, the Dual Science might be the first passage you attempt because it will give you the natural transition in from the Reading Test.

Whatever your skill set may be, we've got a Basic Approach for Dual Science that will help you on this part of the test whether you're doing it first or last.

Dual Science Basic Approach

- **Read the Introduction**
  - Look in particular for what the substance of the disagreement is. In other words, try to answer the question: *What are these scientists debating?*
  - Note: The longer the introduction, the more the questions will ask about it.

- **Preview the Questions**
  - As we saw in the previous chapter, the questions can often help to elucidate difficult passages.
  - In Dual Science, preview the questions to see where most of them focus—the Introduction? Scientist 1? Scientist 2?

- **Do One Hypothesis at a Time**
  - Dual Science is long: don't take it all in one gulp!
  - Pick the most popular Scientist from the previous step, and read his or her theory first.

- **Use your POOD**
  - Answer the questions in an order that makes sense. If you haven't read Scientist 2 yet, don't try a question that asks about him!
  - If the Dual Science passage itself is too hard, cut your losses and move on to something that will get you more points.

Let's apply this Basic Approach to an actual passage.

Passage V

Comets originate from regions of our solar system that are very far from the Sun. The comets are formed from debris thrown from objects in the solar system: they have a nucleus of ice surrounded by dust and frozen gases. When comets are pulled into the Earth's atmosphere by gravitational forces and become visible, they are called *meteors*. Meteors become visible about 50 to 85 km above the surface of Earth as air friction causes them to glow. Most meteors vaporize completely before they come within 50 km of the surface of Earth.

Recently, images taken by two instruments, UVA and VIS, revealed dark spots and streaks in the Earth's atmosphere. The significance of these dark spots and streaks is not fully understood. The Small Comet Theory asserts that these spots and streaks are due to a constant rain of small ice comets, but some scientists argue that the spots are just random technological noise.

UVA and VIS technologies provide images of energy that cannot be seen by the human eye. Both instruments take images in the magnetosphere, in which they orbit. The layers of Earth's atmosphere are shown in Figure 1.

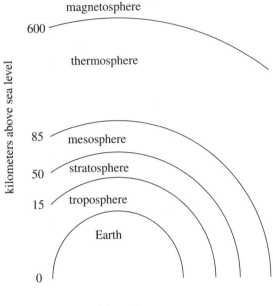

Figure 1

Two scientists debate whether there is a constant rain of comets burning up in Earth's magnetosphere.

Scientist 1

Small comets are pulled into Earth's atmosphere by gravitational effects and burn up in the magnetosphere. Small comets are about 20 to 30 feet in diameter and burn up in the magnetosphere because they are much smaller than the comets that become meteors. Comets with larger diameters will burn up in portions of the atmosphere much closer to Earth. About 30,000 small comets enter the Earth's magnetosphere every day. The dark spots and streaks on UVA and VIS images occur when the small comets begin to boil in the magnetosphere, releasing krypton and argon and creating gaseous H_2O, which interacts with hydroxyl, OH^-, radicals. Images taken by these instruments at different points in time show the same frequency of dark spots and streaks and give conclusive evidence in favor of the Small Comet Theory. If the spots and streaks were due to random technological noise, then the frequency of their appearance would fluctuate.

Scientist 2

The dark spots and streaks in the UVA and VIS images are due to technological noise, not small comets. If the Small Comet Theory were true, and 20 small comets bombarded Earth's atmosphere per minute, there would be a visible bright object at least twice every five minutes. This is because, as objects enter the Earth's mesosphere, they burn up, creating large clouds of ice particles. As the ice particles vaporize, they become approximately as bright in the sky as Venus. Because comets rarely enter Earth's atmosphere, such bright flashes are rare, occurring far less than two times every five minutes. Therefore, the Small Comet Theory cannot be correct. Further, since comets originate from regions of space beyond the orbit of the farthest planet, they contain argon and krypton. If the Small Comet Theory were true and Earth were bombarded by 30,000 comets per day, there would be 500 times as much krypton in the atmosphere as there actually is.

23. According to Scientist 2, which of the following planets in our solar system is most likely the closest to the region of space where comets originate?

    A. Jupiter
    B. Neptune
    C. Saturn
    D. Venus

24. Based on Scientist 1's viewpoint, a comet that burns up in the thermosphere would have a diameter of:

    F. 5–10 ft.
    G. 10–20 ft.
    H. 20–30 ft.
    J. greater than 30 ft.

25. Which of the following generalizations about small comets is most consistent with Scientist 1's viewpoint?

    A. No small comet ever becomes a meteor.
    B. Some small comets become meteors.
    C. Small comets become meteors twice every five minutes.
    D. All small comets become meteors.

26. During the *Perseids*, an annual meteor shower, more than 1 object visibly burns up in the atmosphere per minute. According to the information provided, Scientist 2 would classify the Perseids as:

    F. typical comet frequency in the magnetosphere.
    G. unusual comet frequency in the magnetosphere.
    H. typical meteor frequency in the mesosphere.
    J. unusual meteor frequency in the mesosphere.

27. Given the information about Earth's atmosphere and Scientist 1's viewpoint, which of the following altitudes would most likely NOT be an altitude at which small comets burn up?

    A. 550 km
    B. 650 km
    C. 700 km
    D. 750 km

28. Suppose that a study of meteors of various sizes revealed that a large meteor observed during the study period was visible in the stratosphere before it vaporized completely. How would the findings of this study most likely affect the scientists' viewpoints, if at all?

    F. It would not affect either scientist's viewpoint.
    G. It would strengthen Scientist 1's viewpoint only.
    H. It would strengthen Scientist 2's viewpoint only.
    J. It would weaken both scientists' viewpoints.

29. Scientist 1 would most likely suggest that astronomers attempting to take pictures of small comets in the atmosphere should use enhanced imaging technology to look in which region?

    A. The region between 15 km above sea level and 50 km above sea level
    B. The region between 50 km above sea level and 85 km above sea level
    C. The region between 85 km above sea level and 600 km above sea level
    D. The region above 600 km above sea level

Read the Introduction

The core of the disagreement comes in the second paragraph: *The Small Comet debate centers on whether dark spots and streaks seen in images of the Earth's atmosphere are due to random technological noise or a constant rain of comets composed of ice.*

We may not quite know what any of this means, and it's actually not that important. We could sum the disagreement up like this: *What's with these dark spots? Where do they come from?*

Preview the Questions

Let's see who is more popular.

Question 23—Scientist 2
Question 24—Scientist 1
Question 25—Scientist 1
Question 26—Scientist 2
Question 27—Scientist 1
Question 28—Scientists 1 and 2
Question 29—Scientist 1

Scientist 1 is the favorite by a few questions, so let's read Scientist 1 first.

Do One Hypothesis at a Time

When reading Scientist 1, look in particular for his answer to the central question of the fight (*What's with these dark spots? Where do they come from?*).

Scientist 1's answer to this conundrum comes in the middle of the paragraph: *The dark spots and streaks on UVA and VIS images occur when the small comets begin to boil in the magnetosphere, releasing krypton and argon and creating gaseous H_2O, which interacts with hydroxyl, OH^-, radicals.*

Although Scientist 1 doesn't believe the theory of "technological noise" producing the dark spots, he's certainly given us a lot of noise here! The important thing to draw from this statement is that the dark spots occur *when the small comets begin to boil in the magnetosphere.*

Once we've answered this central question, we can move on to the questions themselves. These questions will help us to know what else in the passage is important.

Use Your POOD

Let's reorder the questions as we've always done (easiest to hardest), but let's also be mindful of the fact that we want to use our time and knowledge efficiently. We've read only Scientist 1, and his ideas are relatively fresh in our minds, so let's do ONLY the questions that deal with Scientist 1 first.

Question 24 has numbers! Let's start there.

Here's How to Crack #24

Let's use the information from the question to find the relevant part of the passage. It comes in the first to third lines: *Small comets are pulled into Earth's atmosphere by gravitational effects and burn up in the magnetosphere. They are about 20 to 30 feet in diameter and burn up in the magnetosphere because they are much smaller than the comets that become meteors. Comets with larger radii will burn up in portions of the atmosphere much closer to Earth.*

Use the figure. The magnetosphere is the region furthest from Earth, so any region closer to Earth will need comets that are larger than the comets that burn up in the magnetosphere. In other words, comets of 20 to 30 feet burn up in the magnetosphere, and comets in any other region shown on the figure will have radii of greater than 30 feet, as (J) indicates.

Question 27 has numbers in it also. Let's go there next.

Here's How to Crack #27

As we saw in the previous question, small comets burn up in the magnetosphere. According to the figure, this is any region with an altitude greater than 600 km. Therefore, if we are looking for a place where small comets will NOT burn up, it must be outside the magnetosphere, or less than 600 km, which only (A) is.

Question 29 seems to draw on these altitude values as well. Let's try that one next.

Here's How to Crack #29

From the previous two questions, we have already seen that Scientist 1 is primarily concerned with the *magnetosphere* and that that region is 600 km above sea level. This conclusion is echoed in this statement: *The dark spots and streaks on UVA and VIS images occur when the small comets begin to boil in the magnetosphere.* In fact, Scientist 1 does not mention any spheres other than the magnetosphere, so he is most likely concerned with the region above 600 km above sea level, or (D).

Question 25 is the last remaining question that deals only with Scientist 1.

Here's How to Crack #25

Each answer choice seems to draw on Scientist 1's view of the relationship between comets and meteors. The parts of the passage that we've looked at so far contain the answer: *[Small comets] are about 20 to 30 feet in diameter and burn up in the magnetosphere because they are much smaller than the comets that become meteors.*

In other words, small comets are simply not large enough to become meteors, and this is why small comets never become meteors, as (A) suggests.

Rinse and Repeat

Let's take the same approach with Scientist 2 that we took with Scientist 1.

When reading Scientist 2, look in particular for his answer to the central question of the fight (*What's with these dark spots? Where do they come from?*).

Scientist 2's answer to this conundrum comes in the first sentence: *The dark spots and streaks in the UVA and VIS images are due to technological noise, not small comets.*

Scientist 1 is the small-comet guy, and Scientist 2 is the technological-noise guy. Once we've answered this central question, we can move on to the questions themselves. These questions will help us to know what else in the passage is important.

Question 23 is short, so let's start there.

––––––––––––––––––––⌣––––––––––––––––––––

Here's How to Crack #23

This question requires a bit of outside knowledge because not all these planets are mentioned in the passage. The passage says, *comets originate from regions of space beyond the orbit of the farthest planet.*

The outside knowledge you will need to summon here is this: of the four planets listed, which is the furthest from the Sun? Now that Pluto is no longer considered a planet, Neptune is the outermost planet in our solar system. If you have trouble remembering the order of the planets, remember this: My Very Excellent Mother Just Sent Us Nachos (Mercury, Venus, Earth, Mars, Jupiter, Saturn, Uranus, Neptune).

––––––––––––––––––––⌣––––––––––––––––––––

Question 26 looks difficult, but it's the only one left that deals only with Scientist 2.

––––––––––––––––––––⌣––––––––––––––––––––

Here's How to Crack #26

We will need to draw upon a few parts of the passage to answer this question. First, we should determine in which *-sphere* Scientist 2 is particularly interested. We know that Scientist 1 is interested in the magnetosphere, and Scientist 2 is interested in the *mesosphere*, where objects *burn up, creating large clouds of ice particles.* Given Scientist 2's interest in the *mesosphere*, we can eliminate (F) and (G).

Scientist 2 continues, *Because comets rarely enter Earth's atmosphere, such bright flashes are rare occurrences, far less than two times every five minutes.* The question mentions a time in which "more than 1 object burning up in the atmosphere is visible per minute." According to the quotation from Scientist 2, this rate of visibility is exceptionally high, or *unusual,* as (J) suggests.

––––––––––––––––––––⌣––––––––––––––––––––

Question 28 deals with both scientists, so we've saved it for last.

Here's How to Crack #28

This is not a subject we have seen so far, but let's use our time efficiently. The question seems to be largely about *krypton*, so here's what each scientist says about it:

Scientist 1: *The dark spots and streaks on UVA and VIS images occur when the small comets begin to boil in the magnetosphere, releasing krypton and argon and creating gaseous H_2O, which interacts with hydroxyl, OH^-, radicals.*

Scientist 2: *Further, since comets originate from regions of space beyond the orbit of the farthest planet, they contain argon and krypton.*

In other words, for Scientist 1, there's extra krypton when comets boil in the magnetosphere, but for Scientist 2, krypton is just always there. The situation posed in the question would therefore support Scientist 1, who says krypton goes to abnormal levels, and only (G) can work.

DUAL SCIENCE 2.0

We've seen ACT change things up a bit on some recent tests, and one of the big changes has been to the occasional Dual Science passage. While the majority of Dual Science passages used to have only two scientists, it's now just as common to have 3 or 4 scientists or students. Occasionally there have been as many as five scientists engaged in theoretical fisticuffs!

Our Dual Science approach applies just as much to these weird passages as it does to the more traditional ones. Let's recall that Basic Approach.

Read the Introduction

When working on Dual Science passages, it is important to read the introduction so that you know what the scientists are fighting over. In fact, that is our central task in reading this introduction: *What are these scientists fighting about?*

As a general rule of thumb, the longer the introduction, the more important it will be to answering the questions. Also, if the intro contains figures, check them out to see if they are helpful (they aren't always helpful!).

Preview the Questions

When there are more than two scientists or students, there will be fewer questions devoted to each individual theory. More of the questions will compare and contrast the theories.

Do One Experiment at a Time

With three or more scientists, the only difference to the approach is that you will continue to repeat this step until you have finished with all of the hypotheses. Say your preview of a Dual Science passage shows 1 question about each of 4 different passages and then 3 questions about more than one theory. In this case, there is no "popular" theory, so you can start with any one you want. Perhaps one theory has a very short associated question compared to the others. If so, start there.

Use Your POOD

For all Dual Science passages, save the questions about more than one theory for the end. Do the same for questions that are not clearly about any one theory. And then you're done!

Conclusion

Dual Science passages can be very difficult, but if you rely on the basic principles of ACT Science along with the Basic Approach we've outlined in this chapter, you will be able to handle any pugnacious scientist that comes your way.

Let's recall the basic principles of ACT Science:

- Don't understand the science.
- Use POE.
- Let the questions teach you what you need to know about the passage.

> Now try these strategies on your own. Go online to your
> Student Tools and answer the Chapter 23 Drill.

Chapter 24
Science Drills

Apply your new ACT Science skills to the following passages. We've picked three that are somewhat difficult. Drill 1 is a Dual Science passage, so make sure to tackle the theories one at a time before moving on to the questions about more than one theory. Drill 2 has several experiments and figures for you to work with, as well as a lot of text, and Drill 3 has big blocks of text and several figures. Make sure you are using the figures and the questions to determine what is important in the passage. Only read when you can't find the answers on the figures.

DRILL 1

Passage II

A scientist mixed three drops each of Red #3 and Blue #1, dyes commonly used to color food, together to form a purple spot at the base of a square of filter paper and placed the filter paper in a beaker. Next, 15 mL of *acetone* (AC), a slightly polar solvent, was added to the beaker, and the solvent was allowed to migrate up the filter paper for ten minutes. Next, the filter paper was rotated 90 degrees and placed in a new beaker. A second solvent was made by dissolving 19 grams of *magnesium chlorate* (MC) in 100 mL of water, and 30 mL of this solution was added to the beaker. The solvent was allowed to migrate up the filter paper for another ten minutes, resulting in the filter paper having a total of 20 minutes of soaking in solvents. The dyes on the filter paper migrated to the pattern shown in the figure below.

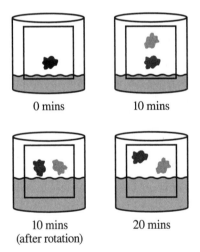

| 0 mins | 10 mins |
| 10 mins (after rotation) | 20 mins |

Note: the darkest colored spot represents purple, the dark gray spot represents blue, and the light gray spot represents red.

The scientist asked each of 4 students to explain what occurred on the filter paper over the 20 min period.

Student 1

Over the 20 min, the mixture of food dyes separated because Red #3 is more polar than Blue #1 and was more attracted to the filter paper. Blue #1 migrated further in AC, and Red #3 migrated further in MC. Red #3 dissolved more in the MC, because MC is a covalent solid and forms a nonpolar solution when dissolved in water. Blue #1 is less polar, so it was more soluble in the slightly polar AC.

Student 2

Over the 20 min, the mixture of food dyes separated because Blue #1 is more polar than Red #3 and was more attracted to the filter paper. Red #3 migrated further in AC, and Blue #1 migrated further in MC. Blue #1 dissolved more in the MC, because MC is a covalent solid and forms a nonpolar solution when dissolved in water. Red #3 is less polar, so it was more soluble in the slightly polar AC.

Student 3

Over the 20 min, the mixture of food dyes separated because Blue #1 was more soluble in the AC, causing the blue dye to migrate further up the filter paper. Red #3 is more polar than Blue #1. Red #3 dissolved more in the MC, because MC is an ionic solid and forms a polar solution when dissolved in water. Blue #1 is less polar, so it was more soluble in the slightly polar AC.

Student 4

Over the 20 min, the mixture of food dyes separated because Blue #1 was more soluble in the MC, causing the blue dye to migrate further up the filter paper. Blue #1 is more polar than Red #3. Blue #1 dissolved more in the MC, because MC is an ionic solid and forms a polar solution when dissolved in water. Red #3 is less polar, so it was more soluble in the slightly polar AC.

7. Which of Students 1 and 2, if either, claimed that Red #3 is more polar than Blue #1 ?

   A. Student 1 only
   B. Student 2 only
   C. Both Student 1 and Student 2
   D. Neither Student 1 nor Student 2

8. Suppose that 3 drops of Red #3 and 3 drops of Blue #1 are mixed together, placed at the base of a strip of filter paper, and placed in a beaker with 15 mL of MC. Based on Student 2's explanation, the resulting filter paper would best be represented by which of the following diagrams?

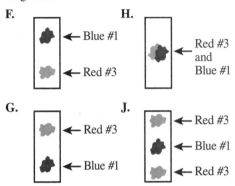

F.

← Blue #1

← Red #3

H.

← Red #3 and Blue #1

G.

← Red #3

← Blue #1

J.

← Red #3

← Blue #1

← Red #3

9. Consider the diagram below.

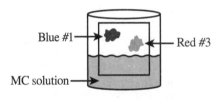

Blue #1 →

← Red #3

MC solution →

The locations of the Blue #1 dot, Red #3 dot, and MC solution shown in the diagram are consistent with the explanation(s) given by which student(s)?

A. Student 1 only
B. Student 2 only
C. Student 1 and Student 3 only
D. Student 2 and Student 4 only

10. Based on the figure, when the filter paper was first placed in the container with the AC, would the mixture of dyes spotted on the filter paper be more appropriately categorized as a homogeneous or heterogeneous mixture?

F. Homogeneous, because the distribution of the dyes differed from one part of the spot to another.
G. Homogeneous, because the dyes were evenly distributed throughout the spot.
H. Heterogeneous, because the distribution of the dyes differed from one part of the spot to another.
J. Heterogeneous, because the dyes were evenly distributed throughout the spot.

11. Which students, if any, would be likely to agree that the AC and MC solvents both interacted more strongly with the same dye?

A. Students 1 and 3 only
B. Students 2 and 4 only
C. Students 1, 3, and 4 only
D. None of the students

12. The statement "A solute will be more soluble and migrate further when mixed with a solvent of similar polarity" is consistent with the explanation(s) given by which of Students 1 and 3, if either?

F. Student 1 only
G. Student 3 only
H. Both Student 1 and Student 3
J. Neither Student 1 nor Student 3

13. The formula of MC is $Mg(ClO_3)_2$. Based on Student 4's explanation, which of the following chemical equations best represents a process that occurred in the water when the scientist made the MC solution?

A. $Mg(ClO_3)_2 \rightarrow Mg + 2ClO_3$
B. $Mg(ClO_3)_2 \rightarrow Mg^{2+} + 2ClO_3^-$
C. $Mg(ClO_3)_2 \rightarrow 2MgClO_3$
D. $Mg(ClO_3)_2 \rightarrow 2MgClO_3^{2-}$

DRILL 2

Passage III

A baseball team's general manager tested the performance of 3 brands of pitching machines under differing conditions.

Experiment 1

Each brand of pitching machine (Brand A, Brand B, and Brand C) was loaded with game-used baseballs and set to throw 30 pitches, 15 at the "fastball" setting and 15 at the "changeup" setting. During each pitch, the following procedure was followed:

1. The manager set the pitching machine to the appropriate setting and activated the machine by pressing a button.

2. A ball was placed into the machine, and a radar gun set up next to the machine recorded the *initial velocity, V*, of the pitch.

3. The point at which the ball hit the ground was recorded, and the *horizontal displacement, d*, to the pitching machine was measured. It was found that the horizontal displacement of each pitch from the pitching machine could be estimated as a function of initial velocity of the pitch by the equation

$$d = \frac{0.2\,V^2}{32 \text{ ft/sec}^2}$$

The results of each set of 15 pitches were averaged to get average values of *V* (in ft/sec) and *d* (in ft) for each pitch setting, fastball and changeup, on each brand of pitching machine. The results of the experiment are shown in Table 1.

Table 1			
Pitching machine	Pitch setting	Average *V* (ft/sec)	Average *d* (ft)
Brand A	fastball	126.6	100.3
	changeup	101.3	64.0
Brand B	fastball	120.4	90.7
	changeup	98.3	60.4
Brand C	fastball	128.8	103.9
	changeup	102.7	65.2

Experiment 2

The three pitching machines were tested with new baseballs using the procedure for Experiment 1. The results were recorded and are shown in Table 2.

Table 2			
Pitching machine	Pitch setting	Average *V* (ft/sec)	Average *d* (ft)
Brand A	fastball	123.3	95.0
	changeup	99.2	61.8
Brand B	fastball	118.5	87.1
	changeup	97.1	58.9
Brand C	fastball	125.5	98.2
	changeup	101.9	64.3

Experiment 3

The pitching machine produced by Brand A was tested with a teeball, a softball, a youth baseball, and a major league baseball that were each previously used in a game. The procedure used in Experiment 1 was repeated for each type of ball using both the fastball and changeup settings. The results are shown in Figure 1.

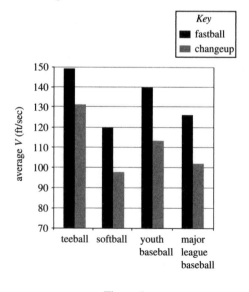

Figure 1

14. Which of the following statements about the design of the 3 experiments is consistent with their descriptions?

F. Experiment 1 was the only experiment in which more than 3 types of ball were involved.

G. Experiment 3 was the only experiment in which the pitching machines were tested with game-used balls.

H. Experiments 1 and 2 were the only experiments in which more than one brand of pitching machine was tested.

J. Experiments 2 and 3 were the only experiments in which the pitching machines were tested on more than one pitch setting.

15. Any pitching machine that produced an average d less than 60.5 ft would not be able to reach home plate and was designated as "unsatisfactory" by the general manager. Based on the results of Experiments 1 and 2, which machine(s) was(were) most likely designated as "unsatisfactory" under at least 1 setting?

A. Brand B only

B. Brands A and B only

C. Brands B and C only

D. Brands A, B, and C

16. The table below gives the mass of each of the balls used in Experiment 3.

Ball type	Mass (oz)
Teeball	4.178
Softball	6.230
Youth baseball	4.499
Major league baseball	5.125

For a given pitch setting, as mass increased, the average V:

F. increased only.

G. decreased only.

H. did not vary.

J. varied, but with no general trend.

17. Consider the 15 pitches in Experiment 2 in which the pitching machine produced by Brand B was set to throw fastballs. Which of the following statements about the 15 pitches' initial velocities is most likely correct?

A. All 15 velocities were less than 118.5 ft/sec.

B. All 15 velocities were greater than 118.5 ft/sec.

C. Some of the velocities were less than 118.5 ft/sec, and some of the velocities were greater than 118.5 ft/sec.

D. All 15 velocities were equal to 118.5 ft/sec.

18. Suppose that in Experiment 3, a fifth ball had been tested on the fastball setting, and its average d was determined to be 90.7 ft. Based on the results of Experiment 1, the average V for this ball on the fastball setting would most likely have been closest to the average V in Experiment 3 for which other type of ball on the fastball setting?

F. Teeball

G. Softball

H. Youth baseball

J. Major league baseball

19. According to the results of Experiments 1 and 2, compared to the pitches on the fastball setting, the pitches on the changeup setting resulted in:

A. greater average initial velocities and greater average distances.

B. greater average initial velocities and lesser average distances.

C. lesser average initial velocities and greater average distances.

D. lesser average initial velocities and lesser average distances.

20. In a new trial of 15 pitches using the fast-ball setting, the pitching machine produced by Brand C was tested with game-used baseballs in a high-altitude environment with lower air resistance. To estimate d, the following equation was used:

$$d = \frac{0.23\, V^2}{32 \text{ ft/sec}^2}$$

The average V for this set of trials was 128.8 ft/sec. Was the average d more likely less than 103.9 ft or more than 103.9 ft ?

F. Less; a pitch at the same initial velocity encountering less air resistance will not travel as far.

G. Less; a pitch at the same initial velocity encountering more air resistance will not travel as far.

H. Greater; a pitch at the same initial velocity encountering less air resistance will travel farther.

J. Greater; a pitch at the same initial velocity encountering more air resistance will travel farther.

DRILL 3

Passage IV

A team of volcanologists studied ash deposits in the wake of a volcanic eruption. They measured the thickness and composition of the ash at four different points along the slope of the volcano (see diagram). At each point, cores of ash were cut away at several locations 0.5 m apart in order to measure the thickness of the ash layer using a ruler.

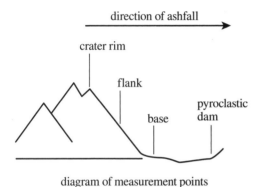

direction of ashfall

diagram of measurement points

Study

The ash layer at each of the four points was measured on the day of the eruption using a coring device to remove the ash layer and a centimeter ruler to determine its thickness. On subsequent days, the volcanologists returned to measure the ash thickness at each point. To account for the uneven distribution of the ash layer, several cores were taken at each of the four points. Each measurement was converted to a *relative ash thickness* (the average measured thickness of the ash layer at a point divided by the average value of the ash thickness at the same point on the day of the eruption). The results are shown in Figure 1.

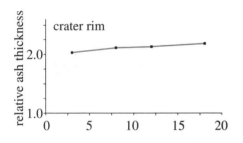

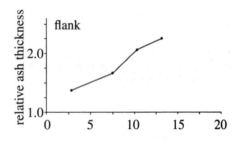

days after eruption

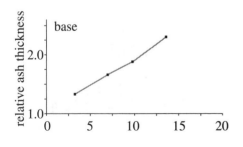

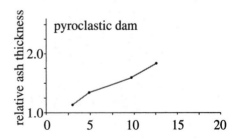

days after eruption

Figure 1

On the day of the eruption, air samples of known volume were collected at each of the 4 measurement points and a special filter was used to remove all particles smaller than 12 μm in diameter, which are known to be particularly hazardous to human health. The total mass of the particles was obtained. The particles were further passed through a series of 11 filters to sort them by size and assigned a value on the *PM scale* (a measure of the diameter of small particles), where PM1 was used to denote all particles smaller than 1 μm in diameter, PM2 all particles smaller than 2 μm but larger than 1 μm, and so on. Each of the 12 groups of particles corresponding to the 12 PM scale values was separately weighed, followed by dividing each group's total mass by the volume of the air sample to obtain the concentration of each type of particle in the air (see Figure 2).

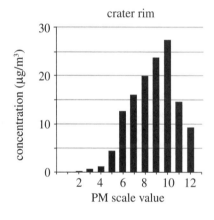

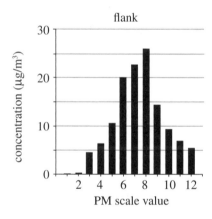

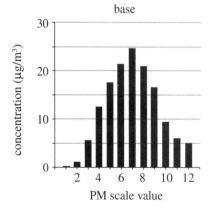

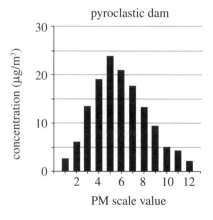

Figure 2

21. According to Figure 1, at the base site, as the number of days after eruption increased, the relative ash thickness:

   A. decreased only.
   B. increased only.
   C. decreased, then increased
   D. increased, then decreased.

22. According to Figure 2, at the crater rim, ash particles corresponding to which 2 adjacent PM scale values both had a concentration greater than 20 µg/m³ ?

   F. PM6 and PM7
   G. PM7 and PM8
   H. PM8 and PM9
   J. PM9 and PM10

23. If in the study the volcanologists had returned to the crater rim on Day 21 after the eruption, the relative ash thickness at that time would most likely have been closest to which of the following?

   A. 1.4
   B. 1.8
   C. 2.3
   D. 2.7

24. The ash particles with the highest *fall speed* in the study were the particles with the largest median in terms of diameter. Based on Figure 2, the collected ash particles from which measurement point had the highest fall speed?

   F. Crater rim
   G. Flank
   H. Base
   J. Pyroclastic dam

25. What was the average ash thickness measured on the day of the eruption at the crater rim?

   A. 1.0 cm
   B. 2.0 cm
   C. 5.0 cm
   D. Cannot be determined from the given information

26. Suppose that the air sample taken at the pyroclastic dam had a total volume of 20 m³. Based on Figure 2, the ash particles making up the PM10 category would have a mass closest to which of the following?

   F. 100 µg
   G. 200 µg
   H. 300 µg
   J. 400 µg

27. Ash particles in categories PM1-PM3 are classified as *fine inhalable particles*, and ash particles in categories PM10-PM12 are classified as *non-inhalable particles*. According to Figure 2, from site to site in the direction of ashflow, how did the concentration of fine inhalable particles change, and how did the concentration of non-inhalable particles change?

	fine inhalable particles	non-inhalable particles
A.	decreased	increased
B.	increased	decreased
C.	increased	increased
D.	decreased	decreased

SCIENCE DRILLS ANSWER AND EXPLANATIONS

Drill 1

7. **A** The question asks which student(s) would say that *Red #3 is more polar than Blue #1*. The question mentions only Students 1 and 2, so read those explanations and use Process of Elimination. Student 1's explanation states directly that *Red #3 is more polar than Blue #1*, so Student 1 agrees with the statement. Eliminate (B) and (D), which do not include Student 1. Student 2's explanation states that *Blue #1 is more polar than Red #3*, so Student 2 would not agree with the statement. Eliminate (C), which includes Student 2. The correct answer is (A).

8. **F** The question asks for the diagram that would best represent *filter paper* spotted with *3 drops of Red #3 and 3 drops of Blue #1…mixed together* and *placed in a beaker with… MC*, according to Student 2. All of the diagrams include spots of Blue #1 and Red #3. According to Student 2, *Blue #1 migrated further in MC* than Red #3. Eliminate (G), (H), and (J), which do not show Blue #1 above Red #3. The correct answer is (F).

9. **D** The question asks for the student(s) whose explanations are consistent with *the locations of the Blue #1 dot, Red #3 dot, and MC solution* in the given diagram. Students 1 and 2 are listed in more than one answer choice, so read those explanations first. Student 1 states that *Blue #1 migrated further in AC, and Red #3 migrated further in MC*. The diagram in the question shows Blue #1 at the top of the filter paper after soaking in MC, which is not consistent with Student 1's explanation. Eliminate (A) and (C), which include Student 1. The difference between (B) and (D) is whether or not Student 4 is included, so read Student 4's explanation next. Student 4 states that Blue #1 migrated *further up the filter paper* in MC, which is consistent with the figure in the question. Eliminate (B) because it does not include Student 4. The correct answer is (D).

10. **G** The question asks if the *mixture of dyes spotted on the filter paper* when *the filter paper was first placed in the container with the AC* would be classified as *homogeneous or heterogeneous*. Scan the passage for any mention of these words. They do not appear in the passage, so look for a reason to eliminate answer choices. The answer choices refer to the distribution of the dyes throughout the spot. Read the description of the dyes in the passage, which states that *three drops each of Red #3 and Blue #1* were mixed together *to form a purple spot*. The *purple* appearance indicates that the two

dyes mixed together uniformly, so eliminate (F) and (H), which indicate uneven distribution. To decide between (G) and (J), some outside knowledge is needed. A *homogeneous* mixture has the same composition and appearance throughout, and a *heterogeneous* mixture contains visibly different substances. Eliminate (J), as the dyes being *evenly distributed throughout the spot* is not consistent with *heterogeneous*. The correct answer is (G).

11. **D**   The question asks which students would agree that *the AC and MC solvents both interacted more strongly with the same dye*. Students 1, 3, and 4 are listed in more than one answer choice, so read one of those explanations first. Student 1 states that *Blue #1 migrated further in AC, and Red #3 migrated further in MC,* so Student 1 would not agree that both solvents interacted more strongly with the same dye. Eliminate (A) and (C), which indicate that Student 1 would agree. Choice (B) refers to Students 2 and 4, so read Student 2's explanation next. Student 2 states that *Red #3 migrated further in AC, and Blue #1 migrated further in MC,* so Student 2 would not agree that both solvents interacted more strongly with the same dye. Eliminate (B), which indicates that Student 2 would agree. The correct answer is (D).

12. **G**   The question asks which student(s) would agree with the statement that *a solute will be more soluble and migrate further when mixed with a solvent of similar polarity*. The question mentions only Students 1 and 3, so read those explanations and use Process of Elimination. Student 1's explanation states that *Red #3 is more polar* and *dissolved more in the MC* which *forms a nonpolar solution,* so Student 1 disagrees with the statement. Eliminate (F) and (H), which include Student 1. Student 3's explanation states that *Red #3 is more polar* and *dissolved more in the MC* which *forms a polar solution,* so Student 3 would agree with the statement. Eliminate (J), which does not include Student 3. The correct answer is (G).

13. **B**   The question asks for the chemical equation that represents *a process that occurred in the water when the scientist made the MC solution,* according to Student 4. Student 4's explanation states that *MC is an ionic solid and forms a polar solution when dissolved in water.* Some outside knowledge is needed. *Magnesium chlorate* is an ionic compound made up of a positive cation (Mg^{2+}) and a negative polyatomic anion (ClO_4^-). When an ionic compound is dissolved in water, the polar solvent breaks the compound down into its ions. Eliminate (A) and (C) because they do not include any charges on any of the products. Eliminate (D) because it does not show a breakdown of the compound into separate ions. The correct answer is (B).

Drill 2

14.   **H**   The question asks for the statement that is consistent with the design of the three experiments. Read each answer and use Process of Elimination based on the descriptions of the experiments. Choice (F) says that Experiment 1 was the only one to use *more than 3 types of ball*. Neither the description of the experiment nor the data in Table 1 mentions anything about different types of balls, so eliminate (F). Choice (G) says that Experiment 3 was the only one to test *game-used balls*. Scan the descriptions of the experiments for the words "game-used balls." The description of Experiment 1 uses this phrase, so Experiment 3 was not the only one to test these balls. Eliminate (G). Choice (H) says that Experiments 1 and 2 were the only ones to test *more than one brand of pitching machine*. Tables 1 and 2 show the data for these experiments, and both tables list three brands of machine. Experiment 3 did not have these different brands, instead testing only the *pitching machine produced by Brand A*, so (H) is true. Check (J) just in case. Choice (J) says that Experiments 2 and 3 were the only ones to test *more than one pitch setting*, but all three experiments had both the fastball and changeup settings. Eliminate (J). The correct answer is (H).

15.   **A**   The question asks which machines would be designated as "unsatisfactory" in Experiments 1 and 2. To receive this designation, the machine must produce an average *d* that is less than 60.5 ft. Look at Tables 1 and 2 for *d* values less than 60.5 ft. Table 1 shows a *d* value of 60.4 ft for the Brand B machine in the changeup setting. This means that the Brand B machine would be "unsatisfactory." Look at the answers to see if any can be eliminated based on this. All four answer choices indicate that Brand B is "unsatisfactory," so no choices can be eliminated. Look at the values of *d* for Brand A in both tables. The values are all above 60.5 ft, so Brand A would not be "unsatisfactory." Eliminate (B) and (D) since they include Brand A. Now check the *d* values for Brand C in both tables. These are also all above 60.5 ft, so Brand C is not "unsatisfactory." According to (C), Brand C is unsatisfactory, so eliminate (C). The correct answer is (A).

16.   **G**   The question asks for the relationship between the mass of the balls tested in Experiment 3 and the average *V* values obtained for a given pitch setting. The table in the question lists the masses of the balls, but they are not in increasing order. Reorder the balls from least mass to greatest mass: teeball, youth, major league,

softball. Now look up the values for *V* in Experiment 3, shown in Figure 1, for the balls in this same order for a given pitch setting. For the fastball setting, represented by the black bars, the average *V* for the teeball was close to 150 ft/sec, the average *V* for the youth ball was 140 ft/sec, the average *V* for the major league ball was about 126 ft/sec, and the average *V* for the softball was close to 120 ft/sec. These values of *V* decreased as the masses of the balls increased. The correct answer is (G).

17. **C** The question asks for the statement that is *most likely correct* about the initial velocities of the fastball pitches produced by the Brand B machine in Experiment 2. The results of Experiment 2 are shown in Table 2. *Velocity* is represented by *V*, and Table 2 lists the average *V* value for fastballs from the Brand B machine as 118.5 ft/sec. The answer choices all refer to this value, which is obtained by taking the sum of the velocities for each pitch and dividing by the number of pitches. Choice (A) say that all 15 velocities were *less than* 118.5 ft/sec, and (B) says that the velocities were all *greater than* this. If either were true, the average would not be 118.5 ft/sec. Eliminate (A) and (B). Choice (C) says that some velocities were higher than 118.5 ft/sec and some were lower than 118.5 ft/sec, and (D) says all velocities were equal to 118.5 ft/sec. No information is given about the velocity of any individual pitch, but both (C) and (D) could produce the given average value of *V*. However, it is very unlikely that all pitch velocities were the same exact value, and if they were, there would be no need to average them. Choice (C) is a more realistic scenario for arriving at the given average. The correct answer is (C).

18. **G** The question asks for the ball on the fastball setting that would have the value of *V* in Experiment 3 closest to the *V* value of a ball on the fastball setting with an average *d* of 90.7 ft, based on the results of Experiment 1. Look at the results of Experiment 1, shown in Table 1, for a fastball with 90.7 ft for the average *d* value. This was seen with the Brand B machine. In Experiment 3, the graph shows only velocity, not distance, so look up the velocity that corresponded with the *d* of 90.7 ft in Table 1. This was 120.4 ft/sec. Now look at Figure 1 for Experiment 3 to find the fastball pitch that had this velocity. The black bars represent the fastball pitches, and the black bar for the softball shows an average *V* value of 120 ft/sec. The correct answer is (G).

19. **D** The question asks for the results of the changeup pitches in Experiments 1 and 2 compared to the results of the fastball pitches. The results of Experiment 1 are shown in Table 1. For Brand A, the fastball pitches resulted in an average *V* value of 126.6 ft/sec, and the changeup pitches resulted in average *V* value of

101.3 ft/sec. Check the other brands to see if the changeup pitches also had smaller *V* values than the fastball pitches. This trend is shown for all three brands in both tables. Therefore, the changeup velocity was always less than the fastball velocity for Experiments 1 and 2. Eliminate (A) and (B), which indicate that the changeup pitches had *greater average initial velocities*. The difference between (C) and (D) is the relationship between changeup distances and fastball distances, so use Tables 1 and 2 to determine that relationship. All brands in both tables show smaller *d*, or average distance, values for the changeup pitches than for the fastball pitches. Eliminate (C), which indicates that the changeup pitches had *greater average distances*. The correct answer is (D).

20. **H** The question asks if the average *d* value of a fastball under certain conditions would be greater than or less than 103.9 ft. There are many variables mentioned in the question, so look to the answer choices to see which ones to focus on. All four answer choices mention air resistance. The question states that the new test was conducted at high altitude *with lower air resistance*. Eliminate (G) and (J), which indicate that this set of trials had *more air resistance*. The difference between (F) and (H) is whether the average *d* would be greater or less than 103.9 ft. An equation is given in the question, so compare that to the original equation in Experiment 1. The numerator is greater for the high-altitude equation, since it is multiplied by 0.23 rather than by 0.2 as in the original equation. This will produce greater values of *d* for a given value of *V* than the original equation would. Outside knowledge can also be used to eliminate (F), as air resistance slows down objects in flight, so an object encountering less air resistance will travel farther than it would when encountering greater air resistance when thrown at the same initial velocity. Eliminate (F). The correct answer is (H).

Drill 3

21. **B** The question asks for the change in the *relative ash thickness* at the *base site* as the number of days increased, according to Figure 1. On Figure 1, the graph for the base site is the third one, and *days after eruption* is shown on the horizontal axis. As the number of days increases, the relative ash thickness also increases. The correct answer is (B).

22. **J** The question asks for the two *adjacent PM scale values* that were both above 20 µg/m³ at the *crater rim*, according to Figure 2. On Figure 2, the data for the crater rim is shown in the upper left, with the concentration on the vertical axis and the PM scale value on the horizontal axis. Look on the vertical axis for a concentration of 20 µg/m³; then determine which bars on the graph extend above the corresponding gridline. These bars represent PM scale values of 9 and 10. Be careful with the bar for PM8, which appears to show a concentration of exactly 20 µg/m³, as the question referred to PM scale values *above* 20 µg/m³. The correct answer is (J).

23. **C** The question asks for the likely *relative ash thickness* if the volcanologist measured it at the *crater rim* on *Day 21*. Relative ash thickness is shown in Figure 1, and the crater rim data is on the first graph of Figure 1. The graph ends at Day 20, with the data stopping at about Day 18. All relative ash thickness values on the graph are above 2.0 and consistently increase over time. The value at Day 21 is likely to be greater than 2.0, so eliminate (A) and (B). To determine the value for Day 21 more precisely, extend the line of the data just past the right edge of the graph. It looks like it would hit at around 2.3 for Day 21, and it will not increase dramatically enough to reach 2.7. The correct answer is (C).

24. **F** The question asks for the *measurement point* that would have particles with the *highest fall speed*, defined as those with the *largest median in terms of diameter*, based on Figure 2. Figure 2 shows concentration based on PM scale value, so scan the passage for information about particle diameter. The passage defines the *PM scale* as *a measure of the diameter of small particles* and goes on to indicate that smaller PM values correspond to smaller diameters. Therefore, the PM value on the scale indicates the diameter, and the particles with the highest fall speed will be those with the largest median in terms of PM value. The *median* of a list of values is the value that falls in the middle. The particles at crater rim are clustered at higher PM values than any of the others, so the median will be highest here. The median at the crater rim is likely 9 or 10, while at the flank it looks to be 7 or 8, at the base it is 7, and at the pyroclastic dam it is likely 5 or 6. The correct answer is (F).

25. **D** The question asks for the *average ash thickness* at the *crater rim* on the *day of the eruption*. *Relative ash thickness* is shown in Figure 1, and the crater rim data is in the top graph of Figure 1. However, there is no information about the relationship between *relative ash thickness* and *average ash thickness*. Furthermore, the data on the

graph begins at Day 3 *after eruption*, so there is no way to determine anything about ash thickness on the day of the eruption. The correct answer is (D).

26. **F** The question asks for the *mass* closest to that of ash particles in the *PM10 category* in an air sample with a *total volume of 20 m³* taken at the *pyroclastic dam*, based on Figure 2. On Figure 2, the data for the pyroclastic dam is shown in the lower right. Find the bar that corresponds to PM10 and has a concentration of 5 µg/m³. The question refers to *mass*, not *concentration*, and the answers all show the unit µg. Set up a proportion to determine the mass in a sample with a volume of 20 m³:

$$\frac{5 \text{ µg}}{1 \text{ m}^3} = \frac{x}{20 \text{ m}^3}$$. Cross-multiply to get $x = 100$ µg. The correct answer is (F).

27. **B** The question asks for the change in concentration of both *fine inhalable particles* and *non-inhalable particles* from site to site moving in the direction of ashflow, based on Figure 2. Figure 2 shows the concentration of 4 different sites, but it does not indicate the direction of ashflow. Scan the passage to find this information. The word *ashflow* appears in the diagram of measurement points, with the arrow indicating that ashflow went from crater rim to flank to base to pyroclastic dam. The graphs in Figure 2 follow in this same order, from left to right in the top row and then left to right in the bottom row. The question states that *fine inhalable particles* are found in PM1, PM2, and PM3, so look for the trend in concentration of these PM values moving from graph to graph in order. At the crater rim, PM1, PM2, and PM3 have concentrations at or near 0. At the flank, the concentrations are slightly greater for PM1, PM2, and PM3 than at the crater rim. This trend of increasing concentrations continues at the base and the pyroclastic dam. Therefore, in the direction of the ashflow, the concentration of fine inhalable particles increases. Eliminate (A) and (D), which indicate a decrease. Now follow the same process to see the trend in concentration of PM10, PM11, and PM12 from site to site in order. The values at the crater rim range from about 27 µg/m³ to about 8 µg/m³, and these values get smaller moving in the direction of ashflow. Therefore, the concentration of non-inhalable particles decreases, and (C) can be eliminated. The correct answer is (B).

NOTES

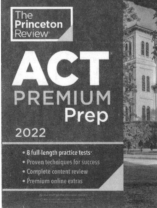

31901067884363